IN THE SHADOW OF THE

ROCKIES

AN OUTSIDER'S LOOK INSIDE
A NEW MAJOR LEAGUE BASEBALL TEAM

ALAN GOTTLIEB

ROBERTS RINEHART PUBLISHERS

For my father, Harry N. Gottlieb, who taught me to love
baseball without taking it too seriously.

Copyright © 1994 by Alan Gottlieb
International Standard Book Number 1–879373–91–2
Library of Congress Catalog Card Number 94–65084
Published by Roberts Rinehart Publishers
121 Second Avenue
Niwot, Colorado 80544

Portions of this material appeared previously and in a different form in
The Denver Post.
Printed in the United States of America
Cover and book design by Jody Chapel, Cover to Cover Design

CONTENTS

PHOTO CREDITS

Page 1
Courtesy of John Lewis, Boulder, Colorado
The first Rockie at bat, Eric Young, hits a home run on opening day in front of 80,227 fans at Mile High Stadium.

Page 9
Denver Post *file photo by Ed Gray*
Bears Stadium, now Mile High Stadium, April 25, 1968.

Page 29
Courtesy of Greg May, Lakewood, Colorado
David Nied delivers the first pitch in the Rockies first spring training game on March 6 at Tucson's Hi Corbett Field to Willie McGee of the San Francisco Giants.

Page 50
Courtesy of Bob Blank, Arvada, Colorado
The heavy artillery of the news media is focussed on the Rockies on opening day.

Page 70
Courtesy of Larry Sifford, Denver, Colorado
Rockies shortstop Vinny Castilla basks in the glow of fan adulation during the Rockies parade through downtown Denver on April 8, 1993.

Page 82
Courtesy of Dave Leasure, Littleton, Colorado
Vendor Dave Leasure, hard at work in the south stands, finds time to mug for the camera.

Page 112
Courtesy of Bob FitzPatrick, Lakewood, Colorado
Rockies coach Don Zimmer, a decades-long fixture in major league baseball, enjoys a chew.

Page 141
Courtesy of J.A. Flower, Lillian, Alabama
Jeff Parrett warms up under the watchful eyes of early-arriving fans at Chicago's Wrigley Field.

Page 173
Courtesy of Dane Carr, St. Louis, Missouri
The author (second from right) and friends Bryan Carr, Doug Jewell, and Dan Gardner endure the heat of Busch Stadium in St. Louis.

Page 192
Courtesy of Gary Goold, Durango, Colorado
Young fan Jana Goold, upper deck Mile High Stadium.

Page 215
Courtesy of Bob Blank, Arvada, Colorado
Dale Murphy trotting off the field at Mile High during his brief stint with the Rockies.

Page 230
Courtesy of L. Kolacny, Loveland, Colorado
The Mile High Stadium scoreboard touts one of the Rockies' many 1993 attendance records.

Page 243
Courtesy of Elizabeth Randall, Denver, Colorado
The author at home in Mile High Stadium.

ACKNOWLEDGMENTS

I incurred many debts of gratitude over the eight months I worked on this project. First and foremost, I thank my wonderful wife Elizabeth Randall and my daughter Marian Randall Gottlieb for their patience and understanding during so many prolonged absences, long nights at the ballpark, and endless (or so it seemed) weeks putting the book together.

Heartfelt thanks go out as well to editors and colleagues at *The Denver Post* who made this possible. Thanks to my bosses, Gil and Isabel Spencer, Neil Westergaard and Todd Engdahl for letting me do this while shirking my more important reportorial duties. Thanks to Milan Simonich for being a fine editor with a nice, light touch. Undying gratitude to Mark Stevens for reading the manuscript and offering helpful advice. I'm also indebted to Bob Sheue for computer assistance; to sports editor Mike Connelly, his editorial assistant Peggy Hoffman for advice and support, and to sportswriters Jim Armstrong, Jerry Crasnick and Irv Moss for putting up with me and all of my stupid questions. A special thanks to sports columnist Woody Paige, who went out of his way to offer advice and guidance.

Thank you to the staff of St. John's Episcopal Cathedral for allowing me to hide away in my wife's office to write.

Finally, thanks for all sorts of reasons to Jean & Harry Gottlieb, Peter Medvin, Barb Edwards, Alan Houston, Bruce Ostler and Annie Gottlieb.

PROLOGUE

FOR OPENERS

On the morning of April 9, 1993, the city of Denver, Colorado was bathed in a surreal amber glow. The spring sun had punched a hole through a thin layer of clouds on the eastern horizon at 6:15 a.m.

Two miles west of downtown, on the site of an old garbage dump, the steel facade of Mile High Stadium reflected the glow—a giant ember in a mountain campfire in the eerie dawn light. As I drove up to the golden gates, I saw the light sharpen, almost prophetically, before it was suddenly gone.

This was the day Denver had been anticipating for at least 15 years—the day a real, live major league baseball game was going to be played here for the first time. Helicopters already hovered over the stadium and even at dawn, I could sense the city humming. That morning people would shuffle to their front porches to find fat special sections in both *The Denver Post* and the *Rocky Mountain News* heralding the momentous occasion. Radio and TV newscasts talked of little else. Everyone seemed to be sniffing the breeze to gauge the likelihood of rain or—God forbid—snow.

If you lived in Colorado that day, it didn't matter a whit

whether you loved baseball, hated it, or felt utterly indifferent toward it. You weren't going to be able to ignore it. All those years of pent-up demand gave birth to a sense of longing, of need, really, to participate in the day's celebration. Even non-fans scrambled around looking for opening-day tickets, which were selling for as high as $150 outside the stadium, an hour before the first pitch.

Inside Mile High Stadium, dozens of people had been working furiously for 24 hours straight, trying to ensure that the big show would come off without a hitch. Up in the score board control room near the press box, for instance, J.D. McWilliams sat carefully tapping a keyboard, programming in the names of all the dignitaries slated to participate in pre-game festivities. Those names would be flashed on the board in huge letters, and McWilliams didn't want any glaring typographical errors.

This was to be McWilliams' eleventh year running the stadium scoreboard. For the most part, his work over the years had gone smoothly. But during the stadium's last big baseball event—a July 4th, 1992 game between the Cuban and U.S. Olympic teams— McWilliams had misspelled U.S. Senator Tim Wirth's name. "Yeah, I spelled it Worth, and man that was embarrassing," he said with a rueful grin. "I guess that was my moment of infamy."

Another key player that morning was Todd Zeo, the Rockies 25-year-old assistant stadium operations manager. Zeo had the dubious distinction of being the only Rockies employee to spend the entire night of April 8 inside the stadium. He was responsible for getting 200,000 opening-day programs safely unloaded off of eight tractor-trailers, and distributed throughout the stadium by forklift. He caught ninety minutes of shut-eye from 4-5:30 a.m. on a couch in the Rockies executive offices, but by mid-morning he was staggering around in a semi-daze. "I'm fine, I'm fine," he kept muttering to anyone who cared to listen.

Meanwhile, outside the stadium, excitement was building to an uncomfortable pitch. Hundreds of pilgrims from as far away as Helena, Montana and Bismark, North Dakota felt compelled to arrive at Mile High hours before the gates were to open at noon, just to soak up the moment. One of the first fans to arrive was Bob Arnold, a Chicago native who used to go to Comiskey Park and Wrigley Field hours before game—the only possible way, he felt, to get a well-rounded, complete baseball experience. "I'm here now because I want to enjoy the whole day as much as possible," he said at 9:00 a.m., seated on a low concrete wall outside one of the main gates, a paperback mystery in his hands.

By 12:01 p.m., when Mark Zessin, chief supervisor for Andy Frain Services bellowed, "Let 'em in!" Arnold had been joined by thousands of others who waited restively under a partly cloudy sky, with temperatures hovering in the mid-60s.

Finally, a young usher scurried up to the gate, key in hand, and tried to open the fist-sized padlock. Jammed. His head swiveled around as he desperately sought help. But no one was there, and the lock wouldn't open. Fans who had been pressed against the gate for hours grabbed the iron bars and started rattling them. All those years of waiting and now this.

After three minutes, a supervisor hurried over, and with a few deft moves unjammed the padlock. People fairly exploded through the turnstiles, letting out war whoops and rebel yells. Pete Adams, a burly guy covered with tattoos, was the first fan through. "I am ready for baseball!" he bellowed.

Who wasn't? While hundreds of people made a beeline for the Dugout Store on the concourse behind home plate to buy opening-day souvenirs at grossly inflated prices, others headed for the field level in search of autographs.

Down on the field, players had emerged from the clubhouse at 11:30 a.m., earlier than usual for batting practice for a 3:05 p.m. game. Now, just past the noon hour, they stared up at the rapidly filling stands and the hundreds of photographers and reporters already clustered around the batting cage.

Eric Young, the Rockies 25-year-old starting second baseman and leadoff hitter, stretched for a few minutes, then played catch with his 7-year-old son, "little E.Y." on the grass behind the batting cage. Every toss was recorded by a half-dozen TV cameras. Little

E.Y., dressed in purple Rockies warm-ups, had his game-face on, but his dad was grinning from ear to ear. Little E.Y. lived in New Brunswick, New Jersey with his mother, and Young, who wintered in Phoenix with his sister, didn't get to see him as often as he'd like.

"It's just a very special day," Young said in answer to a shouted question. "My whole family is here, which makes it even more special."

"Hey Eric," some grinning TV type shouted, "you anxious for the game to get started?"

Young's grin widened for a brief instant. "I can wait. I'm having a wonderful time playing catch with my little boy. I'm sure I'll get a little nervous when I step up to the plate. That's gonna be an indescribable feeling."

Back at the gates, clots of people in search of opening-day programs were creating gridlock. No one knew of Todd Zeo's heroic feat of distributing 200,000 programs throughout the stadium, so most everyone stopped at the vendors just inside the gate. Many pulled out wads of cash and bought 10 or 15 of the slick, bulky magazines.

Mark Zessin groaned and slapped his forehead as he watched the jam-up worsen. "Egress is a little slower than we'd like," he understated in a nasal Chicago accent. "Oh, well, as long as they don't get pissed off."

No need to worry. It was packed and steamy in the concourses as throngs of people inched toward their seats, but there were many more smiles in evidence than frowns. Even fans who were stuck high atop the temporary bleachers beyond the centerfield wall weren't complaining. Martin and Barbara Johnson from the mountain town of Bailey were wedged onto an aluminum bench in the back row of the highest bleachers. They had as good a view of the Continental Divide as they did of the field, which was dizzyingly far below.

"This is infinitely better than the other option, which is no seat at all," Martin said with a shrug.

In the Rockies clubhouse, 37-year-old pitcher Bryn Smith, a

battle-scarred veteran with a patina of Southern California cool, was trying to keep his emotions in check as he paced around in a black T-shirt and jockstrap. In two hours, he was going out there to pitch and he was "climbing up one wall and down the other." So he grabbed his Walkman and his favorite tape "Exit, Stage Left" by the hard-rock band, Rush, and retreated to the trainer's table. With the music crashing in his ears at full volume, he fell sound asleep for 50 minutes.

It was nearly time for the opening ceremonies, and the stands were filling up. In the VIP section behind home plate, Sam Supplizio and Larry Varnell settled into their seats. The two men had chaired the Colorado Baseball Commission during the dark days when it had looked as though Denver would never get a team. Neither one could stop smiling as they watched marching bands forming and cameras jockeying for position down on the field.

"This is absolutely glorious," said Supplizio, a former big-league ballplayer who was to leave Denver the following day to act as outfield coach for the California Angels. "A guy behind me just now said 'you've got goosebumps on your neck,' and I told him they've been there for two days."

A few rows behind Supplizio and Varnell, in a seat dead behind home plate, an elderly black man with enormous hands sat ramrod straight. His eyes were brimming with tears as the Rockies were introduced to the wildly cheering crowd. It was 2:34 p.m., and when manager Don Baylor was introduced to thunderous applause, the man—Baylor's father, George—jumped to his feet and clapped.

George had seen Don play in three World Series and countless regular season games. He'd witnessed any number of his son's on-field heroics, but he'd never felt anything quite like the emotion that welled up in him as he watched 43-year-old Don Baylor presented to the crowd as the manager of a major league baseball team. "This is just a dream, a dream, just a dream," he said. "It's an almighty blessing."

On the field, folk-pop icon Dan Fogleberg prepared to sing the national anthem, a Rockies cap pulled low over his pony-tailed head. Nearby, Rockies general manager Bob Gebhard paced back and forth near the home-team dugout, sucking on what must have been his 40th cigarette of the day. Gebhard admitted freely that he had a bad case of nerves that had kept him awake the previous night, except for "three 45-minute spurts" of sleep.

The moment the entire Mountain Time Zone had been waiting for finally arrived at 3:04 p.m. The public address announcer boomed, "Ladies and gentlemen, your 1993 Colorado Rockies!" and the stadium shook with the cheers. High above the right field line, I perched briefly with my wife, brother and two close friends, Dan and Ann Gardner of Colorado Springs. As the Rockies settled into their positions Dan, an exuberant sort, leapt to his feet and let out a war whoop. "YEAH!!!!" he bellowed, well on his way to making himself hopelessly hoarse. "We finally got it!"

On the pitcher's mound, Bryn Smith had somehow found his composure. His first pitch, a fastball to Mike Lansing, was low and outside, but the crowd was making so much noise that no one cared or even noticed. Smith, glaring at catcher Joe Giradi, concentrated with all his might. He surrendered one single in the first inning, but got out of the inning without allowing a run.

As the Rockies trotted back to their dugout to prepare their first at-bats in their home stadium, Dallas Jensen of Denver stomped away from his seat in left field and marched purposefully toward the Rockies Guest Relations booth on the concourse behind home plate. He waited in line for a few moments, and when he got to the window, he bellowed out his complaint. "I bought season tickets. I paid good money for them," he said. "I get to my seat, and I find I'm directly behind the foul pole—a completely obstructed view."

A harried woman in a purple Guest Relations blazer tried to placate Jensen, telling him to wait while she found him another seat. It was at that moment that the crowd let loose with a roar the likes of which the city had seldom heard. Jensen didn't know it yet, but he had just missed a once-in-a-lifetime moment.

It was all the work of Eric Young, the leadoff hitter. He approached the plate carrying his 32-ounce black bat, batting gloves velcroed to his wrists, heart pumping. Young had been a star pass receiver on the Rutgers University football team, and had played before some huge, frenzied crowds. But this was something beyond his experience. The noise was deafening. It was hard to breathe.

He knew a lot rested on his shoulders. The Rockies had opened the season with two games against the Mets in New York. They had played poorly and lost both games, scoring only one run in the process. The time to set the tone was now, and he was the man with the chance to do it. Young squinted out toward young Expos pitcher, Kent Bottenfield. He knew Bottenfield would be nervous too. Throwing strikes might be hard under the circumstances. The best thing to do would be to watch some pitches and hope for a walk.

Young took a deep breath, trying to steady himself, and dug in. Bottenfield threw a perfect strike, then another. Young almost swung, but kept his bat back, waiting. His heart wasn't settling down much. He stepped out of the box and took a few more deep breaths, puffing out his cheeks. Bottenfield threw a ball, then another, then another. Young could sense the walk he wanted. Get on base and swipe a bag. That would really get things going. But he had to be ready to swing in case Bottenfield threw a strike. He knew the pitch would be a fast ball in this situation. He just wanted it to *be* a ball, or if it wasn't, to hit it hard someplace and get on base so his buddy, Alex Cole, could do some damage. He heaved a sigh, then dug into the batter's box.

The pitch was a fast ball, just as he knew it would be. Young swung hard. It was 3:18 p.m. when the ball hit the fat part of his bat, rose high in the air and jumped out toward left center field. Damn! Hit it good but got under it a little. It was going to be a long fly-out. So he put his head down and sprinted toward first base. He had to run hard. Those guys in the outfield had to be nervous too. The midafternoon light and the white ball against the shirts in the upper deck might make them lose the ball. He heard the crowd roaring as he rounded first base, the sound growing in pitch and intensity. Later, he'd swear it was the force of that noise that carried the ball farther than it had any right to go.

As he neared second base, he looked up for third-base coach Jerry Royster's sign—should he stop at second or keep running? At that moment he heard the crowd's roar deepen and intensify yet again. He saw the second-base umpire give the circular home-run motion with his index finger. Young didn't think his heart could race any faster, but he felt it speed up as it dawned on him: *It's history,* he thought. *I just made history.* Chills coursed through his body as he crossed home plate, felt his teammates slap his helmet, heard the fans screaming "E.Y.! E.Y.! You're the man!!" It was hard not to cry.

Eric Young was right. His home run made history, in Denver at least, and he'll forever be a favorite in the hearts of Colorado's baseball fans. But then, his home run was just the first crystalline memory in what would become an endless series of such moments in 1993.

CHAPTER ONE

YEARS OF LONGING

For me, the 1993 baseball season was an eight-month-long fantasy, an unprecedented opportunity to climb inside the game and experience it from several new perspectives.

I was raised on the South Side of Chicago as an avid White Sox fan. The real estate company where my father worked had season tickets, and he somehow talked his way into being the guardian of those four, front-row seats in the upper deck just to the first base side of home plate. We saw a lot of games from that sweet perch over the years. One of my strongest sensory memories from childhood is the smell of ballpark hamburgers cooking in rancid grease at old Comiskey Park.

So when Denver was awarded a National League expansion franchise on July 5, 1991, I began firing a salvo of memos at my editors at *The Denver Post*. What a perfect opportunity a first-year expansion club provided for exploring the inner-workings of baseball from a non-sports point of view. There were so many different angles of exploration. What was it about this game, around which an entire culture had grown, that so fascinated people? And what went on behind the scenes, in those little byways and folkways no one ever explored, or had come to take for granted?

It took some doing, but I convinced the editors to let me spend the Rockies' first year hanging around the ballpark, trying to get a feel for the hidden side of baseball. I wasn't looking for dirt necessarily, though I found some. I was seeking something I thought was more interesting, though harder to define. It involved searching throughout Mile High Stadium for quirky stories, like how the organist was hired and why mud was rubbed into baseballs. It involved spending time in the Rockies clubhouse, trying to dissect the prickly relationship between ballplayers and sportswriters, and to find out who was giving the players tobacco. It also meant going on a few road trips with the team, to see how the millionaire gypsy caravan operated, and to divine what I could about Denver's budding baseball culture through the experiences of other baseball cities.

Beginning in 1991, I sensed, as did many others, that baseball in Denver was going to be a unique phenomenon. The city pulsated with excitement from the day the Rockies were born through the last out at the last home game on September 26. I wanted to be a part of that, but I also wanted to take it apart and see why it was so.

Who would have thought that in one season nearly 4.5 million people would pay to see a major league baseball game in Denver, Colorado? Even the most wildly optimistic projections before the 1993 season began showed the Rockies with a shot at hitting 3 million.

"I look back through my files and I'm amazed, really," said John McHale, the Rockies executive vice president for baseball operations, an hour before the team's final home game of the inaugural season. "All the attendance projections I could find from as late as a year ago showed us drawing from 1.9 to 2.2 million. As the season ticket orders grew and the presale orders came in early this year, it became clear we'd do pretty good. By January, it was clear we had an excellent chance to hit 3 million. But it wasn't until we were well into the season that I began thinking 4 million was a real possibility."

One morning in early May, I was interviewing Bernie Mullin, the senior vice president of business operations, in his 21st-floor office that looked out over the city and the snow-covered Continental Divide. I asked him, half jokingly, what the chances were of getting 4 million fans. He leaned across his desk, put a hand up to his mouth, and whispered, "Off the record? Slam dunk." Obviously, he wasn't kidding.

How to put this in some perspective? With a metropolitan area population of 2 million, Denver is one of the smallest sports markets in the nation. Only Cincinnati and Milwaukee's metro areas are smaller, but both those cities can draw on much larger population bases outside the immediate urbanized area. That was always the primary reason given when the Lords of Baseball passed over Denver's bids to win a big-league franchise. There was no way, they reasoned, such a small population so thinly spread over so vast an area could ever support a team, either with attendance or the kind of radio and television ratings needed to pour money into the coffers.

They were wrong. But then, everyone was wrong. Even the most cockeyed optimists were off by a couple of million people. Trying to make some sense of this, hoping to answer the essential *why*, I looked first to the past. I sought out Frank Haraway and Bob Howsam, two of the grand old men of Denver sports. Each had 50-plus years of perspective on sports in Denver. Surely they'd know if anything in the city's sports history foretold how ridiculously successful big-league baseball would be here.

"Well, let me tell you," said Haraway, a 76-year-old retired *Denver Post* sportswriter who served as the Rockies official scorer in 1993. "I always felt that major league sports people back east pretty much looked down the groove of their nose at us, and imagined that all we did out here was dodge behind trees and shoot Indians. Yet there were times when major league exhibitions drew extremely well here, and the Broncos proved beyond any doubt that Denver would turn out for a top-flight professional team.

"I believe the Broncos have had sellouts—76,000 fans—for every game since 1969. That really is a phenomenal draw, and that's when Denver really got into the big leagues as far as draw goes."

Also, Haraway said, Denver has always been a baseball hub for the surrounding region, with its minor league teams drawing far better than anyone ever had a right to expect.

If there was such a person as Mr. Baseball in Denver, it was Bob Howsam, a mild-mannered man of 75 who helped bring professional baseball back to Colorado after World War II, and built the Denver Bears into arguably the most successful minor league franchise ever. Howsam had retired to the mountain resort town of Glenwood Springs, but wound up spending much of the summer of 1993 in Denver, where he served as a senior consultant to Rockies chief executive, Jerry McMorris. Of all the brilliant and lucky moves the Rockies made that first year, hiring Howsam had to rank near the top. He had demonstrated through his success with the Bears, the St. Louis Browns, and later the great Cincinnati Reds so-called "Big Red Machine" teams of the 1970s, that he not only knew baseball but how to market it.

Howsam first got involved in baseball in 1947, when his father-in-law, U.S. Sen. Ed Johnson, asked him to take on the duties of executive secretary for the newly revived Western League, a Single A minor league. The league was brought back from the dead at the urging of Denver business elites, who felt the town needed a professional ballclub to prosper. Denver had had a team in an earlier incarnation of the Western League until 1932. It was the height of the Great Depression, and tough economic times put the team under.

"I was administrative assistant to Senator Ed in Washington following the the war," Howsam recalled. "He was appointed non-paid president of the Western League, and he had to select someone to run it day-to-day. He selected me. I had to draw up schedules, write a constitution, hire umpires and all of that. I came back out to Denver on a leave of absence for six months to do it. It was a demanding job."

Denver's franchise, the Bears, was owned by three men that first year: Will Nicholson, who later would become mayor, his brother Ed, and Charlie Boettcher, scion of one of the state's wealthiest families. "They had gotten the franchise and they thought all they had to do was open the doors and people would come in," Howsam said. "Well, it didn't work that way so right away they wanted to sell. So I talked my brother Earl and my dad Lee into coming in with me and we bought a controlling interest of the Denver Bears in 1948."

In 1947, the Bears were playing in old Merchants Park, a dreadful, rickety, clap-trap wooden stadium three miles south of downtown. The Howsams figured the first thing they had to do was build a new ballpark to attract fans. "So Senator Ed Johnson and my father, brother and I, we went out and sold $250,000 worth of bonds. We bought the old dump where the present Mile High Stadium is and built Bears Stadium there. We moved in on Aug. 19, 1948." At first, the stadium had one level with 10,000 seats between first and third base. By the end of 1949, the Howsams had put in seats along the length of both foul lines to bring capacity to 18,523.

The town responded by going baseball mad. In 1949, the Bears drew 463,039 fans, a phenomenal number for any minor league team, let alone a Class A club in the great western outback. In fact, the Bears that year outdrew two big-league teams—the St. Louis Browns and Philadelphia Phillies. "And they kept on drawing real well and led the minor leagues in attendance several times," Haraway said. "Denver was pretty much considered the envy of the minor leagues for the baseball support."

How did they do it? In a variety of ways, Howsam said, relishing the opportunity to remember those glorious early years. "What really brought them in at first, was the fact that we had a new stadium, which has great appeal for any sport. It was a beautiful place to go in the evening, old Bears Stadium. It had no roof, and you could look over and see the skyline. It just started to become something to do. It became as much a social event in those days as it was just a sports event. Exactly like the Rockies this year. In A ball, we drew as high as 14,000. That was unheard of."

Unlike their predecessors, the Howsams didn't just open the gates and wait for the fans. "It was merchandising really. That and the fact that it was new, that baseball had come back. And after the war, I found people really liked, needed and wanted to go out. They'd been cooped up and limited in doing a lot of things.

"Our advertising program was pretty aggressive. We had an advertisement with the Bears schedule on the side of every bus. Inside the bus there was an ad as well, where you could pull a schedule off. We also had schedules in the taxicabs. We had billboards in all the hotels, some of them five feet high. We had displays in all the restaurants. Really, no major league clubs did that much advertising in those days. They opened the gates, they expected people to come. We used to speak and go places and show films. We'd go up into Wyoming, Utah, New Mexico. Even in those days, believe it or not, we had a season ticket-holder from Tulsa, Oklahoma, and one from Chicago."

Howsam had a bit of the promotional showman in him as well. "We built in programs to have cities come in from all over the region. We sponsored baseball tournaments in three different divisions, so towns could compete against towns of comparable size. We gave each town the opportunity to put on a program while they were here, and get a plug or two on the radio. I'll never forget what Yuma (a small town on the eastern plains) did. In those days we had an 8-foot wire fence in front of the stands so the ball wouldn't hit the women, because we thought maybe they wanted to visit instead of watch the game. Anyway, Yuma brought in about 10 to 12 jackrabbits and they tied $5, $10 and $20 bills around the animals' necks. They turned them loose on the field, and whatever player caught the rabbit got to keep the money. Well, you know wild jackrabbits and how they can go. They took off and they were jumping all over the place, up on that fence and everything. I know it sounds ridiculous today, but to our players, $10, $15 meant something. And they were diving after those jackrabbits. I thought I was going to lose my ballclub. I thought they'd break their backs or arms or heads or whatever. It was the darndest thing you ever saw. I was so glad (when it was over)."

When Howsam thought back on it, those city promotional tournaments were a sure sign, 40 years before the Rockies were born, that a baseball franchise in Denver could be a strong regional attraction. "Over the years we did that, we had over 100 cities come in here. And I mean entire towns. When Yuma came in, there were about 1,600 people in the community and over 1,400 of them came, a trip of 140 miles each way. The town of Windsor, population of, I believe it was 74, had 73 at the ballgame. The only person who stayed behind was the justice of the peace, just to keep watch over the town."

Eventually, however, support for the Bears began to slip. As Denver baseball fans became increasingly sophisticated, they longed for a higher caliber of play. In 1955, they got it. The big-league Philadelphia Athletics moved to Kansas City that year, and the Howsams bought the New York Yankee's Triple A Kansas City farm club for $90,000 and moved it to Denver. That was the start of some glorious years of minor league ball in Denver. The Yankees were a powerhouse team in those years, and their minor-league club was stocked with talent. Denver fans got to watch the likes of Tony Kubek, Bobby Richardson, Roger Maris, Marv Throneberry, Whitey Herzog, Don Larsen and Ralph Terry. "I know when I left baseball in Denver in the early 1960s, there were 47 major leaguers who had played here," Howsam said.

In the 1960s and 1970s, The Bears switched affiliations several times, but always seemed to field competitive teams with future major league stars on the rosters. In the early 1980s, the Bears were affiliated with the Montreal Expos, and fielded such players as Tim Wallach and Tim Raines. Later, the Cincinnati Reds used Denver as a Triple A feeder, and Bears fans got to watch Eric Davis, Kal Daniels, Paul O'Neill, Barry Larkin, Chris Sabo and Rob Dibble.

Another solid hint that Denver could be a spectacular baseball town came every July Fourth, when the Bears (and later the atrociously renamed Zephyrs) sold out the stadium for a game followed by a whale of a fireworks show. The Fourth-of-July fireworks game always drew Denver's biggest baseball crowd of the year. In fact, the Bears set the minor league attendance record for a single game on July 4, 1982, when a crowd officially listed at 65,666 packed Mile

High Stadium. But the official attendance figure was deceptively low, because the club lied about attendance to keep the fire department from coming unglued.

Jim Burris, who was the Bears general manager from 1965 to 1984, couldn't keep from chuckling when he remembered the 1982 record setter. "Oftentimes, a minor league team will inflate its crowd count, though doing so is kind of like cheating at solitaire," he said. "But this was one time where we actually under-counted." As Burris remembered it, July 4, 1982, was the first time the Bears gave away tickets through the King Soopers grocery store chain. Response was overwhelming.

"Three, four hours before game time, my son Bob, who was the business manager, came up to me and said, 'I'm afraid we are in trouble. There are more people out there than the fire department will allow into the ballpark.'" For safety reasons, certain sections of the stands were supposed to stay empty during fireworks displays. But when Burris saw "people lined up all the way to the street in all directions," he decided to let them in and damn the consequences.

"My best guess is we had 71,000 people in here that night, but that'll never show up in the record books," he said. "And everything went just fine."

Though the holiday games had always drawn healthy crowds, the numbers didn't explode until 1980. Attendance was spurred by the July Fourth game the previous year, when 38,490 witnessed perhaps the most thrilling baseball game in Denver history. "We didn't have a real good ball club that year and in that game we fell hopelessly behind early," Burris remembered. "It was something like 10-0 in the third inning. We went into the ninth down 14-7. Then, with two outs in the bottom of the ninth, we scored nine runs to win it, the last three on a home run by a journeyman named Jim Cox. The place went crazy." So exciting was that game, Burris said, that it created an instant July Fourth tradition, and holiday crowds during the next decade averaged better than 50,000.

Burris and Gary Jones, Denver's stadium operations manager

since 1967, also remembered a July Fourth game—sometime in the mid-1960s—when fireworks caught the left field fence on fire. "There was this huge wooden fence out there before the east stands were built, and it just went up like nothing," Jones said. "Luckily, no one was hurt."

Burris' favorite story involved a blunder by a grounds crew. "It was the late 1960s, July Fourth, a perfect day, not a cloud in the sky. Things looked good, so I headed out to Centennial Race Track for the day. But evidently, the grounds crew turned on the water and left for a long lunch. I suspect there may have been a couple of beers involved. Well, left field looked like a lake when I got to the park. God, I thought, how could we explain it if we had to cancel a game because of a wet field when there wasn't a cloud in the sky?" But luckily, the crew managed to get enough water off the field so the game could be played.

So it came as no surprise to those with some historical perspective that the Rockies drew well in 1993. But 4.5 million? "I thought baseball would do well, but to be perfectly honest about it, my opinion was they would draw somewhere between 2.5 and 3 million," Frank Haraway said the week after the season ended. "I still just can't believe it. I'd go out there to the stadium, and I didn't miss a game all year, and I couldn't believe there was 50,000 to 60,000 every game. And I says, Jesus, this will taper off somewhere, but it never let up. They never went under 40,000 for one game."

Haraway said he had spent a fair amount of time mulling over the reasons for the phenomenal draw. "It's got to be partly the fact that there's no other team in the region. They tried hard to sell that idea to major league baseball owners when the idea of expansion came up, that there was no major league team any closer than Kansas City, which is 675 miles from here. But they always seemed to get around to the idea that there was not enough population out here to get the response and the money from TV and radio coverage, or to keep the ballpark attendance up to the level they would need. They just felt the population was not dense enough here.

You've got to be honest about it. Nobody thought that Denver, or any other city, would draw 4.5 million."

Bob Howsam agreed that geography played a major role. But lucky timing had something to do with it as well, he thought. "It just happened to come at the right time, and the stadium was large enough, and this region is prospering economically right now. People in the mountain region have some dollars in their pockets to spend on entertainment.

"The other thing to remember is that people like to go where there are crowds. I used to walk around and just listen to people talk. I'd hear it all the time: 'I don't know much about what's going on, but isn't it nice to be out here with the crowd?'"

Geography, pent-up demand, a solid history of supporting big-league sports franchises, and even minor league baseball. Those factors all helped explain why the Rockies drew so well in 1993. Perhaps demographics had something to do with it as well.

According to Bernie Mullin, national research conducted for major league baseball has shown that the typical baseball fan is a male, 15 to 45 years old, who works a white collar job. Over the years, however, the number of female fans has been growing steadily. If that data is accurate, then the Denver metropolitan area provided fertile ground for cultivating fans. Colorado's front range is younger, better educated, and more affluent than the country as a whole. There's also a disproportionately high number of single males, and a lower than average number of single females. A national ranking conducted in 1993 by a Denver-based firm called National Demographics and Lifestyles placed Denver in the top 30 metro areas nationally for the percentage of people participating in sports and outdoor recreation activities.

So there were some signs out there that baseball would do well in Denver. And they grew in frequency and intensity as the time neared when Denver was to make its most serious and concerted pitch for a big-league franchise. I began paying close attention to Denver's quest for baseball soon after moving to Colorado in the late 1980s. As I looked back on it during the 1993 season, I recognized that between 1989 and 1993 the region had sent at least three clear messages to the world that baseball was going to be a smash hit in Colorado.

Two signals were sent before Denver got a team: the surpisingly easy victory at the polls in 1990 of a sales tax hike to finance a new stadium, and the emotional welcome the National League Expansion Committee received at a rally in March 1991. The third signal, the raucous expansion draft-day party in downtown Denver's Currigan Hall, November 17, 1992, showed that thousands of people were eager to come out to cheer anyone remotely resembling a big-league ballplayer. Much of the weight of their adulation fell on David Nied, a 24-year-old pitcher who was the Rockies first draft pick. All that attention was a lot for a young man to handle.

But it took some doing for Denver to get to the point of having a Nied to cheer. Never mind that Denver had been a sports-and-fitness-crazy town for as far back as anyone could remember. The Lords of Baseball made it plain that they wouldn't take Denver's bid for baseball seriously until people opened their wallets. But in 1989, when the National League announced it would add two teams for the 1993 season, long-time baseball backers sensed a real opportunity hovering there on the horizon. If Denver blew this chance, who knew when another one might happen along?

Baseball owners in general insisted that one essential criterion for winning an expansion franchise was a baseball-only stadium, something Denver didn't have. So Denver baseball boosters decided that the best way to impress the powers-that-be would be for residents of the Front Range to approve a modest one-tenth of one percent sales tax increase to pay for a new, baseball-only stadium. In their characteristicaly capricious manner, major league team owners, who have the ultimate say in such matters, later decided that Miami's bid for a franchise was perfectly fine, even though the Marlins were to share Joe Robbie Stadium with the NFL Dolphins. By then, it was too late for Denver to backtrack. Many in Denver thought Mile High Stadium was a perfectly adequate ballyard.

Remember, it had been built for baseball by the Howsam family in 1948, but Denver's bid was going nowhere if it included a proposal to share Mile High Stadium with the Broncos.

In 1989, the state legislature created the Colorado Baseball Commission to promote Denver as a big-league city. Appointed as co-chair of the commission was Larry Varnell, a Central Bank executive and former minor league ballplayer who had been out on the hustings trying to bring a big-league team to Denver since the mid-1970s. Varnell had seen Denver fall short on several occasions. The most notable was in 1980, when oil magnate Marvin Davis came ever so close to snatching the Oakland Athletics. But the deal fell through at the last minute, leaving the dreams of local baseball fans dashed.

So Varnell wasn't going to let this chance pass. His commission got a penny for every $10-sales-tax increase proposal placed on the August 14, 1990 ballot. Voters in six front range counties—Denver, Adams, Jefferson, Boulder, Arapahoe and Douglas—were to vote on the tax increase which, along with an unspecified contribution from the private sector, would pay for a ballpark to be ready for the 1995 season.

When he looked back at that loosely organized campaign from the comfort of 1993, Varnell had to laugh. After all, everything had worked out just fine. But for a while in the spring and summer of 1990, it had looked as though the vote was doomed to fail. Polls that spring showed public sentiment running 2-1 against the stadium tax. It looked so bad in late June that baseball commission member Kathi Williams, a state representative from suburban Westminster, suggested pulling the stadium question off the ballot. Williams reasoned that if a "no" vote would kill Denver's chances for a big-league ball team, then the matter shouldn't be put to a vote until it was reworked and made acceptable to the public. Williams was quickly shouted down by her fellow panelists, but she seemed to have a legitimate point. Fundraising during the spring lagged far behind what political consultants said was needed to run a successful campaign. Early in 1990, organizers said they hoped to rake in $1 million for the campaign. As money trickled in, they revised that figure downward to $750,000, then to $650,000. By early June, with only six weeks left in the campaign, just $50,000 to $80,000 had been raised. Hitting the $400,000 level suddenly seemed overly optimistic.

Then in early July, cable-TV magnate, Bill Daniels, kicked in $100,000, and after that money started pouring in. By election day, the campaign had raised close to $500,000. The advertising campaign was straightforward and effective. Bus bench advertising read, "Imagine if Denver was playing the Dodgers today." It conjured up nice, concrete images.

But Varnell and others spent a lot of time out on the hustings warning against the initiative's failure. Such a failure, Varnell cautioned in endless stops along the rubber-chicken circuit, would kill Denver's chances outright, and possibly forever.

"During that effort, seems like I was speaking two, three times a week over the six-county area. I made a lot of promises, with my fingers crossed, about how well this team was going to be supported. I guess I probably thought down deep inside that the numbers I was promising could happen (two million in annual attendance). But of course it's turned out far better than I hoped or promised."

Despite jitters down to the last minute that the vote would fail, the stadium tax increase passed by a comfortable 54 percent to 46 percent margin, though it was voted down in Denver proper. So it was that on August 15, 1990, the day after the vote, the city of Denver was a serious contender for an expansion team.

The political machinations involved in bringing baseball to Denver from that point forward were complex and tortured. Much of what occurred was behind closed doors. But anyone who was in the 13-story atrium of the United Bank building at noon on March 26, 1991, could look back on that hour as the defining moment in Denver's courtship of major league baseball's mammoth egos. A rousing, unrehearsed baseball rally on that day provided the National League Expansion Committee with a sneak preview of Colorado baseball mania.

The rally had been hastily called just a few days before in direct defiance of the committee's order to stage no demonstrations. It represented a bold gamble by local boosters, who knew the Denver ownership group was less financially solid than those in some other cities.

I wandered over to the rally, as did many others, as a diehard baseball fan on a lunch break, hoping to do my small part to sway those unapproachable millionaires who held our futures in their hands. Just about every other male in my office was there as well. We walked over as a group not knowing what to expect. Maybe no one would show up. At most we expected a few hundred others like us. But we had trouble getting through the doors. The glass-walled atrium was stuffed full of people—at least 2,000 of them—wearing baseball caps and T-shirts, waving pennants and buzzing as they awaited the committee's arrival for a meeting with the prospective ownership group. Up on a slapped-together stage, long-time Denver Zephyrs radio announcer Norm Jones tried to focus the crowd's attention. But the people were already locked in on the 17th Street entrance, craning their necks to see when the bus carrying the bigwigs would arrive.

When it pulled up shortly after 12:30 p.m., a chant welled up from somewhere in the crowd. It seemed to begin spontaneously. As the committee, escorted by the Denver ownership group and various politicos, entered the building, the first thing they heard was 2,000 people chanting "BASEBALL, BASEBALL, BASEBALL, BASEBALL." They looked startled at first. But then, one by one, I could see them start grinning—Fred Wilpon of the Mets, Bill Giles of the Phillies, Doug Danforth of the Pirates, and league president Bill White. As the group approached the stage, Jones led the crowd in a rousing rendition of "Take Me Out to the Ballgame," followed by a deafening cheer. Close-in witnesses reported seeing a couple of committee members moved to tears. I know I felt a lump in my throat, and so, it seemed, did everyone in the place. The stunned committee members were presented a large, poster-board ticket symbolizing the 21,000 season ticket commitments (including $50 deposit) the non-existent team had received to date.

"I don't get cheered like that in Pittsburgh's stadium, I can tell you that," Danforth told *The Denver Post* later that day. And Denver Mayor Federico Peña, who was up there on the stage with the committee, said the rally "was a very positive emotional jolt for them. They got a sense of the passion this community has for baseball and for sports."

The committee spent no more than five minutes on the stage before heading up to some 41st-floor law offices to talk turkey with the ownership group. As they walked through the edge of the crowd, and then rode up a long escalator to a pedestrian bridge leading to the office tower, the crowd cheered them so loudly that I feared the glass in the atrium would come crashing down. Denver had hit a home run. That visit, highlighted by the forbidden rally, sealed the deal. The city was forced to wait on tenterhooks until July 5, but it was all but decided on March 26.

In the ensuing 20 months, baseball became a major topic in the Denver media. But to many, the story was lost in the fog of abstraction. The Rockies drafted their first amateur players and sent them off to Bend, Oregon to play in a low-level minor league. Still, it all seemed pretty distant to most people. Those draftees were kids just out of high school who wouldn't see action in Denver for years, if ever. When the Rockies unveiled their white-with-purple-pinstripes uniforms at the July 4, 1992 game between the Cuban and U.S. Olympic baseball teams, they had to recruit minor leaguers to model them. The team existed as an organizational structure. But there were no players.

That all changed on November 17, 1992, the day of the expansion draft. The draft gave the Rockies and the Florida Marlins, operating under a complex and arcane set of rules, the chance to choose players from the 26 established big-league clubs. Expansion teams in the past have started out at a great disadvantage. Not only have they not had any players, they've had no system of farm teams full of young prospects with which to stock a big-league club. In the past, most expansion teams have tried to put at least a semi-respectable team on the field their first season, but have used the expansion draft to load up on prospects.

The 1993 expansion draft, however, afforded the Colorado Rockies and Florida Marlins some unusual opportunities. For the first time, teams from both the American and National Leagues were required to make players available. Until now, only teams from the league that was adding teams had to open their rosters for raiding by the newcomers. Although the two leagues were, in reality, interdependent, club owners were loath to part with their talent, even if it did mean bigger profits down the road. After all, expansion wasn't a benevolent gift to the cities so blessed. It was all about making some very rich people—the owners—a little bit richer.

In any case, under this new system, each of the 26 existing major league baseball organizations could protect its top 15 players during the first round of the draft. But that left a lot of good players hanging out there, more than there had been in the previous expansions: in 1961, when the Los Angeles Angels and a new incarnation of the Washington Senators were added to the American League; 1962, when the Mets and Houston Colt 45s joined the National League; 1969, when the San Diego Padres and Montreal Expos went to the National League, and the Seattle Pilots and Kansas City Royals to the American League; and 1977, when the Seattle Mariners (the Pilots left for Milwaukee after one season) and Toronto Blue Jays joined the American League.

The Rockies won a coin toss allowing them the first overall pick on draft day. Since pitching is always the hardest commodity to come by, the team's brain trust settled on David Nied, a 24-year-old Atlanta Braves phenom, as the top choice. Nied wouldn't quite be the first Rockies player. The day before, the team had announced the free-agent signing of Andres Galarraga, once an excellent power-hitting first baseman who at 31 now appeared to be on the downside of his career. Don Baylor, the venerable Rockies manager, had served as the St. Louis Cardinals' hitting coach in 1992, when Galarraga was with that team, and he had seen "The Big Cat" finish the season strong. So the Rockies signed him up.

Even though Galarraga might have been the first flesh-and-blood player, Nied was the focus of far more attention. For days, the papers had been full of stories speculating that he'd be the first pick, and labeling him a sure-fire superstar, destined to be the club's number-one starting pitcher. Nied had marched through the Braves farm system like Sherman en route to Atlanta, and in September of 1992 he had gotten the call from the big club. He pitched in three games, a total of 23 innings, and won all three.

Armed with impressive stats, Nied went into the off-season convinced the Braves would protect him from the draft. But the Atlanta organization was overflowing with hot prospects, so Nied was left unprotected. Although playing for a winning team would have been fun, Nied sensed that coming to Colorado would be a golden opportunity for a young pitcher. In fact, the thought excited him. So, when Rockies general manager Bob Gebhard called Nied on November 16 and told him he would indeed be the first pick the following day, Nied was "psyched." And when Gebhard asked him if he'd be willing to fly into Denver on draft day to join a little draft party, he was more than happy to oblige.

"I came on down, and I had no idea what I was getting into," Nied recalled later. "I'd never been to Denver and I had no idea what kind of excitement level there was here. I figured maybe 200, 300 people and 10 or 15 media would be at this party . . . I had no idea." Even months later, Nied couldn't talk about it without a dazed look of wonderment crossing his face.

He was taken directly from Stapleton Airport to Currigan Hall, a cavernous and outmoded convention facility on the fringe of downtown. If he expected a few hundred people, as he said, then he was in for a big surprise. At least 4,000 fans had jammed bleachers erected in the hall, to watch the draft on big-screen TVs and revel in the moment. Some people milled around a miniature replica of the Coors Field, the publicly financed, baseball-only stadium to be built on the edge of downtown and ready for Opening Day 1995. Others browsed through collections of baseball memorabilia, munched on hotdogs, peanuts, Crackerjacks and other ballpark food, or tried their luck at a carnival of booths featuring batting cages and pitching radar guns.

They couldn't believe their eyes when Nied, in the flesh, appeared before them, a Rockies home jersey buttoned over his business suit. They weren't alone in their wonderment. Nied couldn't believe his eyes, either. "I was nervous. It was like, wait a minute, this isn't what you're supposed to be doing during the offseason," he said. "It was pretty hectic. It was a situation I'd never been in, much less with the spotlight of being in the big leagues."

Nied, who had been in the World Series with the Braves (he never got in a game) just a month before, said this was far more overwhelming. "Everyone wasn't coming my way at the series, they were going everybody else's way. This was a different type of a situation. I mean, I was in the spotlight, big-time. I think a lot of them, they knew my name but they didn't really know who I was. They were just so happy about getting a team. It was pretty crazy. Don't get me wrong, people treated me great. But it was a little hard to handle."

It wasn't going to get any easier. Nied, an affable, outgoing young man, had just seen his life turn topsy-turvy in Denver, and he was not ready for what was in store. From November 17 through the club's first spring training, all of Colorado's pent-up desire for baseball would be heaved onto Nied's shoulders. He would have precious little time to himself, or for his fiancee, Malissa Murray. He became the Rockies poster boy, symbol of this fresh-faced young team. Everyone wanted a piece of him.

Late in the season, a few months removed from that crazy time, I asked Nied if the glare of the spotlight early on had bothered or distracted him. "Yeah, pretty much, because I'd never been involved in something like that. Sometimes I didn't feel like it was fair, because I'd rather have waited until I'd been in the big leagues awhile and gotten established before getting a lot of publicity. I didn't like it from that standpoint. I knew it would be tough, but it was just something I was going to have to go through.

"All of a sudden, everybody kinda looked at me different. And I'm just . . . I'm not gonna say I'm a regular pitcher, but my stuff's not that different from anybody else's. I'm just one of the guys, and that's the way I'd like to be treated. Once they kinda put me on a pedestal, seemed like they were trying to separate me from everyone else. And it wasn't true. I just want to be one of the guys, one of the twenty-five guys on the team."

From draft day, the pace of Nied's life quickened. He was recruited to join the Rockies winter caravan—a promotional bus tour stopping at every podunk town shopping center and sporting goods store—through several states contiguous to Colorado. He cheerfully obliged, but the grind wore him down, mentally if not physically. And then there were the endless interview requests. "It seemed like a lot of my off-season was spent caravaning, or taking a picture for a magazine or talking to somebody from a magazine. I didn't realize there was so many sports magazines, baseball magazines, baseball card collectors' magazines, or that there was as much media in Denver as there was. I had no idea.

"I thought it would slow down eventually, but it didn't. I thought maybe spring training would settle it down, but it just got worse. The heat just got more magnified and more magnified. I mean, there's nothing wrong with that, but it just went on, on into spring training, on into the first game. More and more, everybody wanted to know about the Rockies and what was going on, and the same with me. How I was feeling, and stuff like that."

Nied might not agree, but injuring his elbow in June might have been the best thing that happened to him all year, because it got him out of the spotlight. He'd been struggling on the mound, his confidence had been shaken, and after every successive bad outing, the reporters would be bunched around his locker, asking, "What's wrong, David? Pressure getting to you?" By the time he returned to the line-up in September, fans and the media had shifted their attention elsewhere. There was Andres Galarraga's quest for the batting title to track, and the puzzling failure of pitcher Greg Harris, acquired in a trade at mid-season, to mull over.

"I was just kinda glad to get out of the spotlight a little while," Nied said at the end of the season. "You know, there's nothing wrong with that. It just seemed like whatever I said and whatever I did was making headlines. On the field, off the field. I had been just a little over a month in the big leagues before I came here, and I was being treated like the most valuable player of the World Series or something."

I asked Nied whether all the external pressures had something to do with his sub-par performance in April and May. His answer was an emphatic *no.* "That was just making some bad pitches at bad times. My stuff was fine. Mentally, I was OK. The game doesn't change once you get out there on the mound, so none of that other stuff was affecting me. I just made some mistakes. You go through that once in a while. It's just that it all happened in a six-game period. You have streaks like that and I just hit a bad streak right then."

But a few minutes later, he seemed to contradict himself. "I want to come into spring training next year ready to go, physically and mentally. Last year I think I was physically ready but mentally I might have been a little bit drained from all the off–season stuff. It was like everything was a high, high, high. I was setting myself up for a fall, it seemed like."

It probably worked to his disadvantage in the end, but Nied had a winter-long sneak preview of what was in store for the Colorado Rockies. The rest of the team would have to wait until spring training rolled around to get a taste of Rockiesmania.

CHAPTER TWO

TUCSON TRANSFORMATION

Finally, after years of waiting and then months of abstraction, the time had come for mountain states baseball fans to see their team in the flesh. It was February 1993, and the Rockies were assembling in Tucson for their first spring training. Thousands of fans weren't far behind. Nor was the media pack that would follow this team's every move from February 21 until the end of the season on October 3 in Atlanta.

If I was going to follow the Rockies and chronicle Denver baseball in its fledgling season, then obviously I was going to have to start in Tucson. I had a lot to learn, and this was a perfect place for my first lessons. How did a new team get itself prepared to start playing ball? How would the players react to the media onslaught? Was spring training still that wonderful, sleepy ramble through baseball's past that all the newspaper travel sections led readers to believe? What was it like to be there in Tucson when fans got to see their team on the field for the first time? And finally, I wanted to follow the Rockies across Arizona to Yuma for their first road trip. It would give me a chance to visit a small town with a sad story to tell, a story that provided a stark counterpoint to the excitement sweeping Denver.

Planning for spring training was a major undertaking, especially considering that this was to be the first time the Rockies would take the field. Those players had to get everything from their wristbands to their jockstraps somewhere, and it wasn't coming out of their own pockets, that much was for sure. The planning had begun the previous summer, months before the Rockies had any players to call their own.

It was the kind of gritty detail work that some people thrive on but most people hate. It consisted of making lists, adding to them, then double- and triple-checking them for glaring omissions. What had to be ordered to get this team off the ground? Some of it was easy. Uniforms, of course, and numbers to sew on them. Baseballs. And once the expansion draft had occurred and the team had some players, equipment manager, Dan "Chico" McGinn, had to contact each player to get the specifications for their custom-made bats, fielding gloves, batting gloves, sliding gloves, batting helmets, wrist bands, headbands, jockstraps, protective cups, bat weights, sunglasses, spikes and rubber cleats for artificial turf.

It was a hefty list, made more so by the fact that the Rockies had invited 63 players to camp. And ordering equipment was but one facet of the start-up. In every way imaginable, Colorado's big-league baseball team was starting from scratch. There was no clubhouse atmosphere, no team leaders. Memorabilia brokers didn't know yet what types of Rockies effluvia would entice the pack rats into their stores. How much, after all, was a David Nied autograph worth before he'd ever faced a batter in Denver?

In June 1992, when the Colorado Rockies hired McGinn as their equipment manager, the team had a logo, offices and a place to play during the 1993 and 1994 seasons. And that was about it. McGinn had worked as a batboy and later an assistant equipment manager for the Minnesota Twins for eight years. So he knew the territory and knew he had his work cut out for him.

"This is very much different from anything I did for the Twins. I mean, I've had to order everything from hangers on up," McGinn said one warm morning in early February, as he stood amid a pile of boxes and duffle bags in the Rockies clubhouse in Mile High Stadium. It wasn't the best time to chat with McGinn, but he was a gruff type and there weren't many good times. This was a particularly bad day, however, because the last truck for Tucson was rolling out that afternoon, and he had to make sure everything was on it.

"Starting last June, I made a checklist of my own—a master sheet—from uniforms, bats and balls on down to cleaning supplies, coolers, refrigerators, microwaves, all that type of stuff." List in hand, McGinn headed to baseball's annual winter meetings in Louisville, Kentucky, in December. "It's a trade show. Everybody is there, from Bazooka gum to somebody trying to sell you a T-shirt, to all the major equipment manufacturers. It's crazy."

In addition to uniforms, game equipment and hangers, McGinn ordered mops, buckets, cleansers, vacuum cleaners and stain-removing chemicals for use in the industrial-strength clubhouse washing machines. Other clubhouse purchases included portable compact disc players to provide motivational music, toaster ovens, microwaves, refrigerators, coffeemakers, and huge plastic drink dispensers.

For the training room, McGinn ordered an exotic assortment of salves and ointments, crutches, bandages, a light table for viewing X-rays, athlete's foot remedies and an exercise bicycle. And for the video room (yes, the video room) two video cameras, two VCRs, four color TVs and cases of blank videocassettes. As baseball has grown increasingly high-tech, hitters have come to rely on videotapes to study their swings, as well as the motions of opposing pitchers. By studying their swings, hitters and their coaches can discover odd hitches that might develop and lead to a batting slump. Rockies slugger, Andres Galarraga, said that watching a videotape of his swing with Don Baylor turned his declining career around.

It sounded like a huge load of stuff, and it was. The clubhouse looked like hell the day I stopped by, with boxes and equipment piled everywhere. Several brawny guys were loading the boxes into an NW Transport (team owner Jerry McMorris' trucking company) tractor-trailer. But McGinn harbored no illusions that he had everything he needed. "You're gonna forget something, you just don't know what it is ahead of time," he acknowledged, spitting some SKOAL into a large plastic trash barrel. "See, the only thing is, I'm sitting here at a point where I'm just getting this stuff in. Next, I've got to get it to Tucson, then unload it, take a look, see what I've got and what I don't."

For players and coaches as well, this was to be a spring training with an added wrinkle, a cross between a job tryout and freshman orientation week. Few of the players knew each other or their coaches. Before starting the first workout for pitchers and catchers in mid-February, manager Don Baylor had each player stand up and say his name. Pitcher Bryn Smith passed out "Hello, my name is. . . ." stickers for everyone to slap on their chests. A photo of Rockies players warming up at Hi Corbett Field wearing the stickers was the lead photo in a big *Sports Illustrated* spread on the two expansion teams in early March.

"You might have heard some of the names, but when you've got 63 guys, it's almost like you're having a quiz every day," said catcher Joe Girardi, a four-year, major league veteran. "You see people, and you can't match the face with the name for a while. It's kind of difficult when you're catching a pitcher and you don't really know his name."

Girardi said he and a couple of other veterans were eager to assume leadership roles. This, he said, would help ease the atmosphere on a team where no one knew anyone else.

"It's a lot like starting at a new university," he said. "You really don't have the comfort zone you'd have if you were to come to an existing club, friendship-wise. We're lucky in the sense that when you spend eight hours together every day, you make friends pretty quickly. And we're gonna see each other these next seven weeks a lot. Friendships are definitely needed when you come to a new team, because the season is long and you are spending so much time together."

Larry Bearnarth, the Rockies pitching coach, had been around big-league baseball for 30 years. He pitched for the New York Mets in 1963, the team's second season. He said the social awkwardness on an expansion team was more pronounced 30 years ago than it was those first days in Tucson. "In the first couple of expansions, you had players coming from other teams who had been with one team forever. But baseball has changed a lot. Guys move around from team to team. There's always an adjustment when you meet a lot of new people, but a lot of these guys have been through different spring trainings, and they've learned to adjust."

Adjusting to each other wasn't going to be a problem, even if it was a bit awkward at first. But how well they'd adjust to the coming frenzy was yet to be determined. For many Rockies players and executives, the first inkling that this inaugural season was going to be a time of intense scrutiny came on picture day during the first week of spring training. Picture day is an ordeal professional ballplayers endure each year. It gives every newspaper, television station, card company and freelance yahoo a chance to pose the players in uniform for the head-shots that will grace the sports pages and broadcasts throughout the season. Although a royal pain to players and management, picture day is normally manageable, with perhaps a half-dozen media outlets snapping pictures and each player filming a public service announcement or two.

Picture day in Tucson was set for Saturday, February 27. I flew into Tucson February 26, and stopped by Hi Corbett Field to introduce myself to Rockies public relations director, Mike Swanson. I found Swanson, a lanky balding guy who usually had a slow, laconic manner, scurrying around the visitors clubhouse amid a tangle of electrical wire and a forest of klieg lights and tripods. He didn't look particularly happy.

"I have never seen anything like this. Never," Swanson said half apologetically as we shook hands. Swanny, as everyone called him, helped run the San Diego Padres PR operation during the team's 1984 trip to the World Series. But the national media blitz surrounding the World Series was nothing, he said, compared to the attention focused on the Rockies.

It had started a few days earlier, when the team's pitchers and catchers first took the field. There were so many reporters and TV cameras on the field that the players seemed outnumbered. "Don Baylor has been giving a brief interview, like two minutes, at the end of each workout," Swanson said, spitting a stream of tobacco juice into a handy receptacle. "He has it on the top step of the dugout. There have been at least eight TV cameras and probably 25 reporters at each one of those. And he says basically the same thing each time—you know, 'it was a good practice, the guys worked hard.' And they just eat it up. Unbelievable."

The visitors' clubhouse, where picture day was to be held, had the feel of an ancient catacomb. Although the Tucson weather was warm and dry, it felt damp and chilly in the clubhouse, with its metal lockers, cement floor and exposed pipes. The $4.3 million renovation of the Hi Corbett Field spring training complex that the Rockies had squeezed out of Tucson city government included a plush clubhouse for the Rockies. But no such accommodations were made for the visiting teams, who normally bused in and out of Tucson as fast as possible.

The cramped clubhouse proved a tough place to hold what turned out to be a mega-media event. Twenty-four different media outlets and baseball card companies showed up to shoot the Rockies. There were four Colorado newspapers, several Arizona papers, CBS, ESPN, five Colorado TV stations and countless card companies. It took four hours to cycle all the players through.

"None of these card guys have pictures of our guys wearing our uniforms," a harried Swanson said as he shepherded players through the maze. To compound the problem, the team at this early stage was still suffering from what Swanson termed "the expansion blues." Not only was this picture day, it was also uniform-fitting day. Everyone wanted photos of the Rockies in their spiffy-looking white-with-purple-pinstripes home uniforms. But so far, only a dozen home jerseys had been tailored. No player had a uniform to call his own. They held practices dressed in their black mesh, warm-up jerseys. So Swanson and his assistant Coley Brannon had to hurry players through the gauntlet of photographers, reclaim the jerseys and pass them on to others.

Third baseman Charlie Hayes, who looked like he had rolled out of bed seconds earlier, perched himself on a stool with a mock scowl on his face. "Y'all take all these pictures and then you use the same one every time," he said in a thick Mississippi drawl. The head-shots of Hayes that resulted from the session—cap pulled down low, jersey buttoned to the neck—looked sharp and professional. What they didn't show was that his uniform pants were unsnapped and his belt trailed to the floor.

As if the presence of so many video and still photographers didn't create enough chaos, the picture-fest was deemed a newsworthy event by Tucson and Denver television stations and newspapers. At one point, I saw a TV crew filming another TV crew that was shooting a photographer who was photographing another photographer taking a player's portrait.

No one even knew who these players were yet. With the exception of rookie phenom David Nied, first baseman Andres Galarraga and third baseman Hayes, few of the Rockies were familiar to any but the most devoted followers of the game. "Uhh, what's your name again?" a *Rocky Mountain News* photographer asked a youthful-looking player who perched on a stool before a blue backdrop. "Pedro Castellano," the player replied. "OK, thanks," the photog said. "What was that first name again?" "Pedro," the player replied again with no hint of impatience.

Most of the players seemed to take it all in stride, at least at first. But by the time they had run the gauntlet, they looked frazzled. Roberto Mejia, the 21-year–old second baseman from the Dominican Republic, exited the clubhouse and heaved a huge sigh when the last photo had been snapped. He walked into the dugout and onto the field. When he glanced up, his eyes fell upon yet another gaggle of photographers spread along the third base line, waiting for him. "Goddamn," he muttered, one of the few words in his English vocabulary.

For Swanson and the players, it was a day that couldn't end soon enough. But for souvenir vendors, this was another in a series of banner days. Clark Worthington, who won the novelties concession at Hi Corbett Field "because I know some people," said he'd been selling about $1,300-worth of Rockies items since the first players had straggled into town 10 days earlier. No matter how routine the drills scheduled for a given day, a couple of hundred people, many of them Coloradans, had wandered into the park and adjacent practice fields each day to get a look at this new team in the flesh.

Anticipating a huge influx of Coloradans once the spring training games began on March 6, Worthington had ordered boxcarloads of Rockies novelties. He projected he'd rake in $10,000 a day in sales through the first few days of April. "There are a lot of people from Colorado here already, I mean a lot, and they are buying," he said. Worthington had eight different styles of Rockies caps for sale, ranging in price from $15 to $25. The biggest seller by far was a white cap with the purple, interlocking "CR" logo and the words, "Spring training, Tucson, 1993," stitched below.

Rockies general manager Bob Gebhard fretted that the attention would prove a distraction to his fledgling team. "Everyone's gonna be nervous and uptight, even the veterans," he said, surveying the scene with a squint, the ever-present cigarette wedged between his thumb and index finger. "This is part of history being made here."

Gebhard had anticipated unusual media and fan interest in the Rockies, but the extent of it had caught him by surprise. "We came out here the first day, when it was just the pitchers and catchers, and there must have been 15 TV cameras," he said. "For just pitchers and catchers, for crying out loud."

David Nied had been through moments like this before, but he still had a wide-eyed look about him on picture day. "I saw what all this was going to be like on draft day, and I've kind of grown accustomed to it," he said following the day's event. Nied was seated in the Rockies dugout, a bat between his knees. He had been on his way to the shower and an afternoon to himself, but had consented almost cheerfully to one last interview request. As soon as he sat down with me, several other reporters gathered 'round, and what was to have been a five-minute session dragged on for almost half an hour.

Nied could see the hype getting to some of his uninitiated teammates. "Some of the rest of the guys, they didn't realize what it was going to be like. They're just saying 'wow.'"

Sitting there on a bright spring day in Tucson, Nied couldn't have known how his year would play out. But he was confident that all the attention wouldn't change him. "I can handle it. I'm a pretty normal guy," he said. "I mean, I'm not a jerk or anything."

Undoubtedly, the novelty of the Rockies explained much of the hyped-up atmosphere. But veteran players and others who had been around the game awhile told me that spring training had been heading in this direction, inexorably and lamentably, for years throughout big-league baseball.

Behind its facade of laid-back, pastoral charm, spring training by 1993 had become a high-powered industry unto itself. Gone were the days when overweight players lumbered into camp, played themselves into shape during the day, then hit the bars until the wee hours. Players knew they had better show up ready to play. After all, millions of dollars in salaries hung in the balance. Today, players for the most part report for spring training in fighting trim. "Some of these guys show up now, and they've got no fat on them at all," marveled Rockies hitting instructor, Amos Otis, a star outfielder for the Kansas City Royals for 17 years during the 1970s and 1980s. "It's a combination of things. Mostly it's the money involved, which makes the competition for the jobs a lot more intense. Guys know they've got a better shot if they show up in shape."

Gone as well were the days when fans, for the small sum of a buck or two, got to rub shoulders with normally unapproachable stars, then sat practically on top of the field to watch teams battle languidly under the desert sun. The old, rickety, spring-training parks of the past were being replaced by much larger and sleeker mini-stadiums. Ticket prices were higher, and most of the seats were reserved.

From the perspective of team owners, of course, all this was fine and dandy. Teams no longer resigned themselves to losing money on the seven-week training camp. It had become a money-making enterprise for all involved. Added national exposure through cable TV, and endless romanticizing about spring training in the media increased crowds exponentially during the 1980s. Among the throngs were still innocent, wide-eyed kids seeking their heroes' autographs. But there were plenty of pit vipers as well. Players and coaches said they'd seen too many instances of mercenary-style memorabilia brokers stampeding over the kids in pursuit of the riches autographs could bring.

As a result, all fans had been pushed back somewhat at most big-league camps. "It's a lot harder for the fans to get close to the players during spring training than it used to be," Otis said following practice one day. "Spring trainings I used to go to as a player, we'd get out of the clubhouse and man, there'd be a mob out there—couple of hundred people waiting for autographs. You'd stand around for an hour-and-a-half signing autographs. Today you come out of the clubhouse, you may see 25 or 30 people, but it's not because the fans don't want to come out. It's because security keeps them away."

The Rockies were trying to do things a bit differently. As an expansion team with few big-name stars and a desire to please, the team wanted to keep the players accessible. "We've tried to make an effort here in our first camp to expose the fans to the players," said Bob Gebhard, standing on the field as his players ran wind sprints around him. "Clubs have to recognize that we need that fan base to survive, and that the good relationship between fans and players is so important."

Pitcher Bryn Smith, at 37 the oldest Rockies player, agreed with Gebhard. An outgoing sort, he enjoyed rubbing elbows with the fans. "If you're any type of a baseball fan, spring training is still the best chance to get close to the players and see we do talk and do walk, and are just regular human beings," he said, as he stood near the outfield fence signing autographs.

Rockies fans in Tucson could stand just outside the indoor batting cages and listen to the resounding crack of wood against horsehide. They could hear the players joking and cursing and grunting as they exerted themselves. Fans also could wait at the clubhouse door and ask for autographs as players emerged. The clubhouse exit opened onto the Hi Corbett Field concourse, and the players parked their BMWs and Lexuses and other pricey cars in an unsecured lot alongside the regular folks.

While the Rockies represented a throwback in this positive sense, the team proved in other ways to be on the cutting edge of spring training philosophy. Take marketing and money, for example. Tickets ranged in price from $4 to $7, a reasonable entertainment value, but hardly the bargain of days gone by. Team officials marketed spring training aggressively, advertising spring packages in Denver and other mountain states. The result: ticket sales approached 7,000 per game for the 18 games in Tucson, compared to the 4,500 the Cleveland Indians drew during their last few seasons at Hi Corbett.

The Rockies planned to turn a tidy profit from spring training. "Most teams in baseball have switched in recent years from losing money on spring training to making it a profit center in and of itself," said Bernie Mullin, then the Rockies vice president for business operations. "You start paying the same attention to the spring training operation that you do to the regular season operation. You go out and maximize revenues. You make money off signage on the outfield walls, advertising sales in the programs, ticket sales and everything else. In the past, a lot of clubs just opened up the gates and whatever came in, came in. What happens these days is the club starts getting more involved in putting everything together. Like the stadium deal here. In the past, teams were involved only to the extent that they'd say, 'We want a concession operation that's good, high-quality food at reasonable prices.' Today, we'd like to have a piece of it."

What that meant, Mullin explained, was diverting a bit of each "revenue stream" that trickled past into the team's coffers. The Rockies didn't hesitate to take pieces of a lot of different things that first spring, and not just food, beer, and souvenir sales inside the park. For example, a small percentage of each Rockies vacation package sold by Professional Travel in Denver went to the team. It was impossible to find out from the Rockies or Professional Travel president, Ed Adams, how much the team made off this deal, because team brass considered this information proprietary and weren't willing to discuss it.

This much I did learn: Professional Travel sold in the neighborhood of 150 packages. They included airfare, game tickets, hotel, and the chance to rub elbows with players, Gebhard, Mullin, and owner Jerry McMorris at team functions at the Viscount Suites Hotel. Adams said his company also made individual travel arrangements to Tucson for "hundreds and hundreds of Coloradans."

It was fascinating, and a bit sad, to see how large an industry spring training had become, and how many facets there were to it. Baseball wasn't the simple game it had once been. Everyone was working an angle, looking for a way to make a buck, or to promote their products by hitching them somehow to baseball's star.

Ballplayers in the 1990s are more than athletes, whether they like it or not. They are also consumers of and pitchmen for sports equipment. They are highly visible media stars, and provide savvy manufacturers with opportunities for free advertising as well—headbands and wristbands with Reebok emblazoned in large letters, Nike T-shirts and so forth. Hidden in all the high-tech marketing, however, are some old-fashioned practices that showed me the soul of baseball hadn't yet been sold lock, stock and barrel to the devil.

On the Sunday after picture day, Tucson awoke to a drenching downpour that lasted most of the day. Players showed up at the field, but stayed in the clubhouse or took a few hacks in the indoor batting cage. Outside the clubhouse door, in a sheltered spot under the right field bleachers, two men were hard at work beside a white van.

They were surrounded by stacks of cardboard boxes. Inside each box were brand new baseball gloves, smelling of good, tanned leather.

Bob Clevenhagen, a squat, graying man with a Missouri twang and a ready smile, sat in a folding chair, deftly lacing gloves together. On his belt he wore a pouch full of tools he had designed for his specialized task. Clevenhagen was the only glove designer for Rawlings, the lone remaining U.S.-based manufacturer of baseball fielding gloves. Rawlings supplied about half the gloves used by big-league ballplayers. Clevenhagen made the rounds of each big-league club each spring, taking orders and handing out gloves for players under contract to Rawlings to try out. Accompanying Clevenhagen was Jim Hughes, who tracked inventory as players emerged from the clubhouse to select gloves to try on the field.

I asked Clevenhagen what a glove designer does. He experiments, trying to come up with gloves that will make fielding easier. "I try to change materials to make the gloves easier to break in," he said as he tightened the laces on catcher Joe Girardi's dusty, well-worn mitt. "Gloves today are sturdier and have deeper pockets than a few years ago. What we've done is make it so the glove catches the ball, not the person. The days of the old, flat glove are gone."

Clevenhagen was only the third glove designer in Rawlings' almost 100-year history. The first two designers were a father and then his son. "I used to run the manufacturing end of the operation. When the last guy got ready to retire eight years ago, he named me as his successor. I guess I'm lucky he never had a son."

In his van, Clevenhagen carried about 40 different models of Rawlings gloves. There were gloves for each fielding position. First-baseman's gloves are huge and clam-shaped, making it easier to scoop low throws out of the dirt. Pitchers' gloves have solid webbing in the pocket, so hitters can't see how the pitcher is gripping the ball. Third baseman's gloves are wide and fairly shallow, and the shortstops' gloves are deeper. Catchers' mitts come in a variety of sizes, from the huge pillow-like unit for handling the elusive knuckleball, to the more traditional, hinged and padded glove most catchers use each day.

Clevenhagen also had a variety of gloves for left- and right-handed players, and each type came in blue, brown or black. All gloves used to be brown, he explained, but black have been gaining in popularity over the past five years, and now about half of all players choose black gloves. Clevenhagen frequently custom-laced gloves for players with their own particular sense of style. Rockies outfielder Jerald Clark, for instance, requested a black glove with brown laces.

Occasionally, Clevenhagen custom-laced a glove for his own purposes. The year before, when Rockies catcher Joe Girardi played for the Chicago Cubs, Clevenhagen talked him into using a new, experimental model catcher's mitt. "It was brown, but I put black laces in it, just to see if he was using it. With the black laces, I could watch a Cubs game on WGN and see whether he was using the glove or not. Most people wouldn't have noticed it, but I was watching carefully."

Anything you might possibly want to know about a baseball glove, Clevenhagen could tell you. Curious about all that padding in a catcher's mitt? "The padding is what we call a felt, but it's actually fine thread all packed together—stuff that's swept off garment factory floors. It's what they've used for padding since they started making gloves, except there used to be asbestos in it and there isn't anymore."

Until Clevenhagen paid his annual visit, players were using last year's gloves. "They want the new one during spring training so they can start breaking it in," he said. There's a reason for that. I tried on a first baseman's glove and it felt stiff and unyielding. "Yeah, but they break in a lot quicker than they used to," he said. "Big leaguers just play their gloves into shape. They don't have to oil them or anything like that. The leather has more oil in it than in the past. In the old days, they didn't know how to tan the leather with oil in it."

Clevenhagen said most players keep two gloves on hand and use them for one season, or two at the most. Catchers' gloves take more of a pounding and rarely last more than a year. Some players, however, develop a strong attachment to a particular mitt and use it until it falls apart. Amos Otis, Clevenhagen told me, was famous for using the same glove for 17 years.

"Yeah, it was the only glove I used in the major leagues and the minor leagues," Otis recalled. "I got attached to it and it felt comfortable. It was something I could put my hand in four months later without even breaking it in. By the end of my career, you could see my palm through it, that's how wore out it was. But I never caught a ball there; I caught the ball in the web.

"I got seven or eight gloves from Rawlings every year, and I gave them to kids throughout the neighborhoods in Kansas City. I kept them in the trunk of my car, and a lot of times I'd just stop, see kids playing ball and hand them out. In the 17 years I got gloves, I gave every one of them away."

Otis's glove now resides in the Kansas City sports hall of fame. But during Otis's career, it was stolen from him three times. Each time, he got it back. "The first time was after Joe Garragiola showed it on the NBC game of the week. The next trip we went into Boston and it was stolen. Then it just showed up in New York. Somebody mailed it back to me four days later. I guess I'll never know why. Another time in Milwaukee, someone broke into the clubhouse and stole everything. I said, 'I probably won't get it this time.' But when the equipment man was going to put out the trash, he found the glove in the trash. The glove looked so raggedy the thieves didn't want it.

"The same thing happened in Fort Myers (Florida) in spring training. Somebody broke in and stole all the new stuff. So I just walked over to the trash can, and sure enough, there it was."

For 10 days, from February 22 until March 3, obsessively–dedicated fans and bored-looking sportswriters hung around spring training watching drills and workouts. Seeing the players practice sliding, fielding bunts, calling for pop-ups and turning the double-play was interesting for a couple of days. But even a devoted baseball fan like me grew bored with it after awhile. So when March 3 rolled around, people's pulses quickened a bit. It was the day of the first intersquad game.

About 200 people wandered into the stands and watched the game under cloudless, light blue skies. Players approached the game with real intensity, and the smattering of fans cheered the nice plays with enthusiasm. It was baseball distilled to its essence—no scoreboard, no public address system, just six innings of guys playing hard, trying to impress the brass and win jobs on the big club. It was one of the only moments of the season where baseball took precedence over hype.

Three days later, the real frenzy began. Sure, picture day had been hectic, and the players had gotten a taste of how intense the media scrutiny would be during the season. But on March 6, the day of the Rockies first exhibition game against another team, the San Francisco Giants, the fans became a factor as well. And, their presence was overwhelming, just as when the expansion committee visited Denver, and on draft day in Currigan Hall.

By the thousands, fans from Colorado made the trek to Tucson for that first game, filling up hotels and packing bars and restaurants. Tucson was buzzing, almost as if the World Series had come to town.

"At least 50 percent of the 7,726 tickets we've sold for today are to people in the Denver area," said ticket manager Tom Sullivan, moments before the Hi Corbett Field opened for the first game. "Actually, it's the same for all the spring training games. There are going to be a lot of Coloradans down here in Tucson all month."

Pat Milstein of Denver had first-hand knowledge of the great trek southward. "I was on a United Airlines flight coming down here from Denver yesterday morning," Milstein said two hours before the first pitch. "The flight attendant got on the P.A. and asked how many people on the plane were headed down to see the Rockies game. Just about everybody cheered."

It was a big day for Denver's grand old men of baseball. Bob Howsam and Larry Varnell reveled in the moment as they sat under a huge, white tent the Rockies had set up on their practice fields for a VIP cookout before the game.

"This is the day we've been dreaming about for 30 years," Howsam said, beaming. "We've been through so many disappointments. We never gave up hope, but it did seem like a long shot at times."

Among the Coloradans in attendance, there may have been people who had waited longer for big-league baseball to come to Colorado, but no one waited with more ardor than Barrie Sullivan. For Sullivan, a 54-year-old Denver lawyer, the Rockies first-ever exhibition game ranked right up there with his first game in Fenway Park at age eight, and his first Red Sox World Series game in 1975, as the biggest thrills in his lifelong obsession with baseball.

As he basked under a blistering sun in the 14th row of Hi Corbett Field near home plate, Sullivan had a look of stunned rapture on his face, like a pilgrim who at long last had reached his shrine. While that description might sound exaggerated, Sullivan wouldn't scoff at it. A native of Quincy, Massachusetts, Sullivan described the Boston Red Sox as "my religion," and baseball as a not altogether healthy, lifetime addiction.

As Sullivan explained it, being a Red Sox fan was a form of slow torture, and over the years the team's uncanny ability to fail at the worst possible moments had tarnished his love a bit. "Never forget, never forgive. That's been my motto since they blew the sixth game of the 1986 World Series (and then lost the series in seven to the New York Mets)," Sullivan said, as he watched the interminable pre-game festivities.

He had arrived at the park at 11:00 a.m for the 1:05 p.m. start, decked out in a purple Rockies polo shirt and a Rockies cap. Moments before game time, Sullivan's wife, Sandy, and their four-year-old son, Joseph, arrived, and they settled into their seats.

As always, Sullivan wore a large, clunky-looking ring on his right ring finger. It was a Red Sox World Series ring from 1967, the year Boston lost the series in seven games to the St. Louis Cardinals. The ring belonged to Al Lakeman, the team's bullpen coach, who died in 1980. "I bought it at an auction and it fit perfectly, so I wear it all the time," he said.

Sullivan didn't pretend for a moment that he'd ever get the Red

Sox entirely out of his system, but he insisted that he was ready to divide his allegiance. And when the Rockies put on an inspired show in their easy 7-2 win over the Giants, Sullivan looked ready to change horses right then and there. Many in the already-friendly, sell-out crowd seemed a bit surprised by the Rockies' prowess, and lavished several standing ovations on the team.

Unlike Howsam and other long-time Denver baseball boosters, Sullivan hadn't waited 30 years for baseball to come to Denver—he moved to Colorado in the mid-1970s—but it seemed longer than that. Since 1979, he and Sandy had come to Arizona each spring to watch major league teams train.

"It's just impossible to explain how wonderful it feels to be here seeing our own Colorado team," he said. "I always said, even after the franchise was awarded to Denver, that I wouldn't believe it until I saw the team take the field. Well, here they are."

To keep tabs on the Rockies through the regular season, Sullivan had bought eight season tickets at Mile High Stadium—six behind the Rockies dugout, and two down the right field line, in the front row directly behind the Rockies bullpen. "I want my son to be able to see the players up close without anyone telling him he can't be in the front row," Sullivan said.

He also confided, as he sat there watching the Rockies coast to victory, that he planned to close his law office for the home opener April 9th—Good Friday. "It's a religious holiday in the strictest sense of the word. For me, because it's opening day. For others, because it's Good Friday."

Following that thoroughly satisfying debut, the Rockies bid adieu to their adoring fans and boarded buses for Yuma, where the San Diego Padres awaited them. Everywhere I traveled with the Rockies that first season, there were valuable lessons to be learned about the relationship between professional ballclubs and the surrounding communities. The first, and one of the most sobering, came in Yuma, a desolate desert outpost 240 miles west across the vastness of southern Arizona.

The Rockies' happy caravan pulled into Yuma the morning after that first exhibition game. Colorado baseball fans were so pumped up about the impending arrival of baseball that several dozen made the four-hour trek to see the Rockies play a two-game, weekend set against the Padres. For Coloradans, it was another of those giddy moments at the start of a love affair. But they found the mood in Yuma decidedly less upbeat. Never a garden spot, with its low-slung, military barracks-style housing and its bleak, dusty vistas, it was a town as depressed about big-league baseball as Denver was ecstatic.

It was divorce time in Yuma, a military and retirement town of 55,000 midway between Phoenix and San Diego. After 24 years as the spring training home of the San Diego Padres, the city was about to lose its connection to the big time. Following the 1993 spring season, the Padres were pulling up stakes and heading 170 miles east to Peoria, a Phoenix suburb. To year-round Yuma residents, the team's departure was like a kick in the solar plexus. It was almost as if the town's only bridge to the outside world was being dynamited.

"We think we're a real viable spring training market, but we couldn't overcome the obstacle of being three hours from Phoenix," said Gary Magrino, a local businessman. Magrino headed the baseball committee of the Caballeros de Yuma, an arm of the Yuma County Chamber of Commerce. The odds of wooing another team were slim, Magrino acknowledged. So there was the bittersweet scent of a fractured relationship lingering in the air.

Losing the Padres was going to put a small but noticeable dent in Yuma's economy. With the Padres hometown just three hours to the west, Yuma had come to count on the annual spring influx of money-laden Californians crossing the desert for a sneak preview of their boys of summer.

A study commissioned in 1992 by the Caballeros estimated that baseball fans brought $4.5 million into the Yuma economy each spring. That was just two percent of the roughly $200 million winter visitors spent in Yuma each year, but it hurt nevertheless, said Butch Opsahl, the chamber's president.

What Yuma was really losing was less tangible, and its loss hurt more than a lack of money ever could. As the Rockies took infield practice before Sunday's game at Desert Sun Stadium, two 12-year-old peanut vendors talked about the mourning that was soon to begin.

"It'll be a little different, that's for sure," said Nathan Zack, as he dispensed a 50-cent bag of peanuts. "I guess I'll have more time to play basketball." Zack had been saving for a year to buy himself a computer, and counted on the $20 he made each game to pad his piggy bank. He was going to have to sell like a madman that spring to earn the computer before the money well ran dry.

Zack and fellow-vendor, Tyler Lord, said they were angry at the Padres organization, but vowed to remain loyal to the team. "I'll probably be even more interested in them than I am now," Zack said. "But I'm not going to forgive them anyway."

It hurts when a big city loses a sports franchise. But people survive—they adjust and at times even thrive. And there are plenty of other diversions in a city. That was not the case in Yuma. No one there was pretending that the Padres' departure was insignificant. Yuma is a long way from anywhere else. For excitement, local residents can drive south 20 miles into Mexico and bet legally on college basketball, or major league baseball for that matter. But there's not much else. The climate in winter is agreeable, dry and warm virtually all the time. Once the snowbirds depart, however, the endless succession of 100-plus-degree days begins. The local phone book contains a glossy insert instructing people on desert survival and what to do if caught in a dust storm.

It may have been for just seven weeks each spring, but the Padres gave Yuma a sense of belonging to something bigger, Opsahl said. "If you look at the size of this community, and the fact that we've handled this so well for 24 years, well, it gives us confidence that we can do big things here, and do them well," he said.

Magrino said what he'd miss most of all was personal contact with the Padres. "This is a good, down-home town. Over the years, we've gotten to know the people on this team. Their babies are born in our hospitals. We've handled their emergencies. Now, they're going to be gone. It's sad, but life goes on."

Sure, life would continue, but February and March of 1994 were going to be grim months in the desert of southwest Arizona. I felt like I was accompanying a baseball Ebenezer Scrooge, as a spirit led us on a journey into the world of Denver's baseball future. Beware, Denver, the ethereal spirit seemed to whisper. Things may look rosy now, but there's no way to know if what happened to Yuma might happen to you.

CHAPTER THREE

READY OR NOT . . .

After the trip to Yuma, it was time for me to head back to Denver. I wanted to see how the city was preparing for the big day when the Rockies arrived, bathed in as-yet unearned glory. What more logical place to start than the city's many sports bars?

If, as promised, the Colorado Rockies were going to pump loads of cash into the metro-area economy, then the lucky souls who owned sports bars figured to pocket a hefty chunk of it. Bar owners began planning for the coming of baseball as soon as National League president Bill White announced on July 5, 1991, that Denver had won the contest for a big-league franchise. Savvy tavern owners knew that luring baseball customers required more than serving dollar draft beers and microwaved hot dogs.

Full-service bars also had to act as ticket brokers and transportation coordinators. No one knew in the early going that it would be virtually impossible for non-season-ticket holders to secure a box seat ticket to a Rockies game. But several forward-thinking bar owners advertised by word of mouth that they could get their regulars top-flight tickets for all but the most popular games. Connections they had cultivated over the years were going to pay off, big-time. A few also planned to run regular shuttle-bus service from their businesses to the gates of Mile High Stadium.

"There really are two kinds of sports bars," said Gil Whiteley, former baseball commission member and owner of Maxfield and Friends, a sports bar and off-track betting parlor a mile northeast of the stadium. "There are event bars, places that run buses, and where people with tickets to the game gather before and after. And then there are TV sports bars that draw people in to watch sports there."

Maxfield and Friends, Zang Brewing Co., and Brooklyn's, three sports bars close to Mile High, qualified as event bars. They figured to do booming business on days and nights of home games. Before the season started, the raspy-voiced Whiteley estimated his bar would rake in $3,000 to $4,000 on each of the Rockies' 81 home dates this season. Reality exceeded expectations.

At Brooklyn's, the closest of the three to the stadium, "All we have to do is open the door and we'll be barraged with people," said Manager Dave Keefe. "We're only two blocks away, and plenty of people know we're here."

Other bars planned to market themselves more aggressively. Zang and Maxfield and Friends ran free shuttle buses to all home games. Fiore's Restaurant, 15 miles southeast of Mile High Stadium, ran shuttles to 25 games. Fiore's shuttle cost $8, but that included a pizza dinner.

"I'm not trying to make a lot of money on this," said owner Barry Fiore, a lifelong baseball fanatic. "I'm doing it because I really think baseball, above all others, is a sane sport. All the rest are insane. They're all masochistic. In baseball, there is no intent to hurt anybody. In football, basketball, soccer, hockey, you gotta hurt somebody. Baseball is the only one that takes a lot of intelligence to play."

Fiore acted as secretary/treasurer for a consortium of fans that held 40 prime inaugural-season tickets to Rockies games. Fiore had talked his group into buying a block of season tickets during the last three years of minor league ball in Denver. Zephyrs season-ticket holders got first crack at good seats for the Rockies, so Fiore & Co.

were sitting pretty. Loyal customers who needed a ticket for a particular game knew they could turn to Fiore, who sold the tickets at face value.

Fiore was, without question, the only barowner in Colorado who also held four season tickets to Chicago Cubs games at Wrigley Field. He'd had his four tickets to all 81 Cubs home games "for a long, long time now," and his friends and customers could get those tickets if they were heading to the Windy City.

The more savvy sports-bar owners were spending money to make money. Fiore figured he'd invested $15,000 getting his place ready for baseball. He installed two Sharp projection system, big-screen TVs, bringing his total to three. "We've got to have both the Rockies and the Cubs on the big screen if they're playing at the same time," he said.

In the weeks leading up to April 9, the Rockies, Denver, and some of their contractors were preparing for opening day and the months beyond. Baseball, far more than the casual fan may have realized, viewed itself as an entertainment industry more than a sport. Newspaper sports pages focussed exclusively on the games and issues directly related to them, such as labor disputes, player salaries, trades and injuries. They didn't cover the extensive planning that went into everything from deciding which songs to play between innings, to exactly how an usher was to treat an unruly customer.

In late March, I decided to drop by a training session run by Andy Frain Services, the ushering company hired by the city to handle crowd control operations at Mile High Stadium. In the interest of fairness, I must make a confession here. I have a long-standing, deeply ingrained prejudice against Andy Frains. Over the years of my childhood and adolescence, I had many a run-in with the Frains at Comiskey Park. And it wasn't just me. My father, a mild-mannered sort with a deeply submerged rebellious streak, snarlingly referred to Andy Frain ushers as "The Hitler Youth."

One of my dad's favorite stories about Andy Frains dated back to the mid-1980s, when he decided to take his 9-year-old grandson, my nephew Matthew, to a Sox game on a bitterly cold April day. He bought a couple of tickets at the gate, and was dismayed to find the seats were tucked far back in the upper deck of old Comiskey Park, deep in the shade and not sheltered from the wind. Matthew, a skinny lad, was shivering hard enough to shatter his teeth. So after about the fourth inning, my father looked around, and spotting some seats in the sun, decided to move. The new seats were in the same price category as the seats they had left, so my father didn't anticipate any trouble. After all, who would possibly want to hassle a grandfather and grandson, out to enjoy a day together at the ballpark? Boy, was he naive.

They settled in, enjoying the sun's warmth, when an Andy Frains usher came scampering down the aisle. "Can I see your tickets?" My father explained that these weren't their seats, but they had bought $8 seats and these were $8 seats. Since the game was almost half over, he reasoned, and there were plenty of empty seats, he thought he'd get his freezing grandson into the sun. The usher would have none of it. "You'll have to move back to your seats," he said. "No deal," my father replied, "unless you can give me a better reason than that." So the usher left, and returned moments later with a couple of burly security guards, off-duty Chicago cops in no mood for a reasoned discussion. Before they knew it, my father and Matthew were pitched out into the street.

Of course, my father milked that outrage for all it was worth, firing off a series of angry letters to the White Sox, demanding redress. He got it, in the form of a pair of field-level seats to a future game. The fellow who sent him the tickets made the mistake of telling my father to contact him whenever he needed assistance. My father must have called the guy a half-dozen times that year to request more prime seats, before the team got wise to his scam and finally put an end to it.

The incident further ingrained my father's—and indeed my whole family's—hostility toward Andy Frains. But Andy Frains had always been easy to hate. Back in the 1960s in Chicago, the company seemed to hire almost exclusively gangly teenagers whose veneer of civility failed to mask their nasty attitudes. They got a kick out of the smidgin of authority vested in them by the silly looking blue suits and white gloves they were forced to wear. Rough-hewn White Sox fans got great pleasure out of dousing those silly uniforms with beers launched from the upper deck.

So when I headed to the stadium press box for this training session, I knew what to expect: a hard-nosed outfit that viewed ushering (which Frain now calls "crowd engineering") as something akin to a high-risk, police tactical squad operation. I wasn't disappointed, but was surprised to find myself taking a liking to the Frain bosses nevertheless.

The session was led by Mark Zessin, the top Andy Frain official in Denver. The company had moved into Denver in 1985, first to run security at Stapleton International Airport, and then expanding its services to the Denver Broncos and University of Colorado Buffaloes football games in 1991.

Zessin, a rumpled, balding guy in his late 30s, paced back and forth in the huge auxiliary press box, his booming Chicago-accented voice bouncing off the walls. The 100 trainees in attendance hung on his every word. He had the natural magnetism of a born despot.

"I shouldn't tell you this, but you know my claim to fame? At the first night game ever in Wrigley Field in 1988, I gave Lenny Dykstra of the Mets a beer bath. I was there as a fan, and when he came back to the wall for a fly ball, I dumped my beer right on his head." One of the trainees gave Zessin a high-five. Then the boss got down to business.

"If you look like you know what you're doing, people automatically assume you do," he barked. "It's like acting, and your uniform is your costume. Some of you younger people, you'll have to get used to bossing around people three, four times your age. Maybe you'll have to tell the vice president of United Bank to MOVE!!" He bellowed out that last word, and most everyone jumped noticeably. "Your voice and how you use it is so important. You may be thinking to yourself, 'I don't know what I'm saying,' but if you say it loud enough, people will believe it."

Zessin repeatedly stressed that Andy Frain practices "the Disney approach to customer service," which presumably meant pushing people around, but doing so in nice clothes and with a smile on your face. "The policy is called C.A.S.H.: Courtesy, Appearance, Service, Honesty. You're a sales representative, and what you're selling is a good time. Treat everyone fairly and equitably, no matter what this person might look like or smell like. If five guys with KKK hats show up, you service them, as long as they've paid." (When I asked Zessin about the nasty Frains of my youth, he grinned and said "Juvenile delinquents make the best cops.")

Zessin donned a blue Andy Frain windbreaker and led half the group down to the lower level box seats near the right field corner. Here, he lectured them on Frain's crowd control policies and techniques:

—Vendors shouldn't sell to a fan who isn't seated. If vendors try to do so (and they will, he promised, since they're on commission), the usher is to address the fan and have him or her sit down first.

—Anyone who doesn't have a ticket stub should be removed from his seat. "If you look in your section, and you see someone's face you don't remember seating, ask for their ticket," he said, his drill-sergeant's voice echoing off the acres of orange seats. "They'll give you all sorts of excuses, and believe me I've heard 'em all. If they tell you the other guy has the stubs and he's up buying beer, you ask that person to leave the seat and walk to the top of the aisle with you until the person with the stubs returns."

—Do not let people move into more expensive seats, or into better seats in the same price range. This is called weaseling. "If the people in the $16 seats wanted to sit next to someone paying $12, they'd have paid $12."

—To remove a recalcitrant fan from a seat, move directly in front of the person, blocking his or her view. "Now by standing there, you're blocking not only his view, but all the people behind him, too. So all of a sudden you've got 20 people on your side. This way, you take care of the problem without calling the guy a maggot, without having to drag him out, without any kicking or screaming."

Using these techniques quickly and efficiently, Zessin said, "is how we made our reputation at Andy Frain." Then turning to me, he said, "You said you're from Chicago, so tell me: am I right?"

"Yeah," I acknowledged. "And I hated it when I was a kid. I hated you guys."

Zessin smiled and opened his arms wide toward the trainees. "So you see?"

To be fair, Zessin also spent a lot of time stressing to his trainees that the company's main goal was to be solicitous of the fans, to make sure they were having a good time. Andy Frain literature given to trainees urged them to employ personal touches, like welcoming people to the park and high-fiving kids who caught foul balls. Zessin pleaded with the trainees to go out of their way to help fans—finding vendors, cleaning seats and "making sure they have an overwhelmingly positive baseball experience."

By 1993, most big-league baseball teams were hiring their own ushering crews, often retired people or high-school kids. Other than the Rockies, only the Chicago White Sox and Cleveland Indians, teams with fans renowned for their rowdiness, employed the Andy Frain service.

The typical Frain ushers worked another full- or part-time job, but needed a little extra income to make ends meet. At $4.25 an hour minimum wage, no one was going to get rich ushering. But hard-core baseball fans who took the jobs got to watch at least parts of many games, and not only did they get in free, they got paid for it.

Over the course of the season, the Rockies would take some heat for the heavy-handed tactics the Frains were known to employ. There were little things that irritated the fans, like ushers refusing to let people walk down an aisle to their seat during the national anthem. All in all, however, the ushers handled the crowds well, and complaints were relatively rare.

With 10 days to go before the home opener, I paid a visit to Mile High Stadium to see how work on renovations for big-league baseball were progressing. Denver city government and the Rockies had spent $1 million on Mile High over the previous seven months, readying the 76,037-seat stadium for two years of major league baseball. The city kicked in $600,000; the Rockies, $400,000.

Plenty of work remained in the short time left before Opening Day. I could see dozens of workers crawling over the stadium, applying finish to benches in the south stands, building 4,000 temporary bleacher seats for the first game, installing phone lines, putting in a new, polyurethane warning track around the perimeter of the field, removing clumps of Poa grass from the outfield and replacing them with Prescription Athletic Turf. New foul poles and outfield fences were being erected as well.

"It's been a lot of work, but the only major thing left is building the sets of temporary seating around the stadium to get this (opening day attendance) record in place," said Kevin Carlon, the Rockies young and super-serious director of stadium operations.

The record was something the Rockies were hell-bent on establishing, even if some fans in the temporary seats had to watch the action on video monitors. By building temporary bleachers to hold another 4,000 fans, the club figured to break the record of 78,672, set by the Los Angeles Dodgers in 1958. They did, drawing 80,227 on opening day.

To squeeze in enough seats, the Rockies built three sets of bleachers, high above the center-field fence, in right-center and in left field's foul territory. They also put five rows of seats on the field in foul territory beyond first and third bases. The bleachers, as it turned out, were completed just two hours before the first fan entered the stadium on April 9.

Those temporary fixes ordered by the Rockies were minor when compared to the renovations major league baseball required prior to the first regular-season pitch. The biggest job, surprisingly enough, was installing a $250,000 warning track to alert fielders of an approaching wall or fence. In some parks, warning tracks were made of dirt, in others, of an artificial surface. In theory, the track felt different underfoot from grass, and therefore warned a player chasing a ball to slow down or brace for a collision. The old minor league warning track at Mile High was a strip of asphalt, which Carlon said "definitely wasn't up to major league standards."

The new track was a springy, rough-surfaced, dark-red urethane, identical to those at Baltimore's new Oriole Park at Camden Yards, and Miami's Joe Robbie Stadium. "In Coors Field (where the Rockies are to start playing in 1995), we'll have an organic warning track of crushed brick," Carlon said. But that wouldn't work in Mile High, because the 21,000-seat east stands—all 13 stories and nine million pounds—moved in 145 feet for football games. The stands were floated in on pans of water, a low-tech solution that made a high-tech contraption work. "But if we have dirt down there," Carlon said, "dirt would fall in the pans, clog up the works and prevent the stands from moving."

The economics of baseball also prompted the Rockies to build new outfield walls. When the minor league Zephyrs played at Mile High, the 12-foot-high fences were covered with green padding. But the padding obliterated views of the playing field from the first 15 rows, rendering hundreds of seats useless. Loath to sacrifice a single seat, the Rockies padded the fence up to 6 feet, 8 inches off the ground. Above that, the team installed a wide-mesh fence to a height of 12 feet. This allowed people in those first 15 rows and $5 seats to see the action.

Baseball powers-that-be required the Rockies to install new foul poles at Mile High, to replace the rinky-dink models that had served the Zephyrs and Bears well for four decades. The Zephyrs used painted strips of wood extending above the walls. The Rockies installed flagpoles 65 feet tall, held in the ground by mammoth hinges.

Other changes weren't visible to fans. The baseball press box, on the private-box level behind home plate, was enlarged and modernized. But it still was far too small to hold the dozens of reporters, and others with tenuous connections to the games who somehow managed to acquire credentials. Many people were placed instead in the auxiliary press box, a facility far superior to the main box. During the football season, it served as the main press box, and had

room for a couple of hundred writers. Its only drawbacks for baseball were its location—down the right field line instead of behind
home plate—and the fact that its windows wouldn't open. During
summer day games it got stiflingly hot, and flies seemed to love
buzzing against the windows.

Some additions were made for the players' benefit as well. A
room above the clubhouse, in the park's northeast corner, was con-
verted to an indoor batting and pitching cage with a weight room
alongside. But most important to the players, a bathroom was built
into each dugout. In stadiums built for baseball, dugouts are connected to the clubhouses by tunnels, and there's usually a bathroom
at the end of the tunnel closest to the dugout. Until 1993, that
wasn't the case in Mile High. Players had to walk to the left field
corner to get to a real toilet.

"Before, they had these very primitive porta-potties in the
dugouts," Carlon said. "They worked, but no one liked using them
much. We've improved that situation a little bit."

So toilets, foul poles and fences were in place. It was time to
play ball.

All over town, media outlets had been psyching themselves up
for months to cover baseball exhaustively. By the time April 9 rolled
around, there was very little interested fans couldn't know about
their team. This was saturation coverage at its worst, and it was
costing a bundle.

Even during the weeks leading up to the regular season, the
media seemed to be going hog-wild over the Rockies. There were
specials on TV, special sections in the newspapers, endless blathering
on radio and TV sports talk shows. But to anyone who thought this
was too much, there was a simple warning: wait, it was going to get
worse—much worse.

Even if you wanted to be as far as possible from Denver on
April 9, say, on the other side of the globe, you would have found
escape from the media overkill impossible. The April 9 home
opener was televised nationally—in Japan. By the time opening day

rolled around and all requests were honored, the Rockies had granted 697 media credentials for the opening weekend. The combined seating capacity of the press boxes was roughly 150, so a lot of those media-types were left to roam the stands.

"I thought I had an idea of how crazy this would be, but I wasn't even close," Mike Swanson groaned over the phone from Tucson during the last week of spring training, as he prepared for another marathon session of credentials processing.

For the opener, in addition to Japan, reporters and camera crews came from all parts of the U.S. Swanson issued credentials to media from Alabama, Washington, D.C., New York, Los Angeles, Houston, Chicago, Miami, Salt Lake City, North Platte, Nebraska, Farmington, New Mexico, and Casper, Wyoming, to name a few. And then just about every daily paper and many of the little weekly papers in Colorado, not to mention all the radio and TV stations from across the state, wanted a piece of the action as well.

"If they've got a paper or a station then they deserve to be a part of history, is how I look at it," Swanson said.

But it was the heavy hitters from the Denver area who really reveled in wretched excess. The two Denver daily newspapers each had between 25 and 30 people with credentials in Mile High for the opener. Each of the three Denver network-affiliate TV stations had between 35 and 40 people there. The hoopla would die down following that first weekend, but only a little. Swanson issued nearly 190 full-season credentials.

The magnitude of the Rockies story forced local media outlets to spend a lot of cash and devote a big chunk of space and air-time to baseball. The two Denver dailies added local and national baseball writers, and expanded their sports sections to make room for the Rockies. The *Post* added a second sports section on Mondays, dedicated exclusively to baseball, and the *Rocky Mountain News* devoted so much space to baseball that its writers were able to go into exhaustive statistical and personal detail in their numerous daily stories. At times, it seemed as though the *News* provided daily updates on such trivia as which players had hangnails, or how many hours sleep each player got the previous night. I had to hand it to Jack Etkin and Tracy Ringolsby, the *News*'s two baseball beat writers. They were "crank monsters," newspaper lingo for reporters who churn out impressive volumes of copy each day.

Television news departments couldn't add minutes the way papers added pages, so the Rockies story forced them to do things differently. KCNC Channel 4 hired Rockies catcher Joe Girardi— one of the brightest and most articulate players on the club—to participate in a weekly Rockies show. KMGH Channel 7 signed on Eric Young, an outgoing and magnetic personality to do a weekly feature called "Young Gun."

"We won't be expanding the sports time on our news broadcasts, so this will take away from some other sports," said Mark Baker, executive sports producer for KCNC-TV, the NBC affiliate. "You'll probably see fewer video highlights from minor golf tournaments and things of that sort during the summer."

Facing the biggest changes were KOA Radio and KWGN-TV, the stations under contract to broadcast the Rockies games. At KOA, where all 162 games were to be aired, the sports staff was expanded with an announcer and a full-time producer. In addition, the sales staff grew, and programming was juggled dramatically, with sports taking precedence over everything else.

Because KOA broadcast the Denver Nuggets basketball, and Broncos and University of Colorado football as well, the station had to make some tough decisions, said sports director Larry Zimmer. A sort of contractual pecking order developed, with the Rockies bumping the Nuggets off the air whenever a conflict arose, but the Broncos, thanks to a no pre-emption clause in their contract, taking precedence over the Rockies.

The Denver media, bristling with microphones, armed with strobe flashes and neck-deep in video cameras, was ready to bring baseball into everyone's living room, whether they wanted it there or not.

What about the fans? Rockies executives were busy determining who their fans were, and how best to please them. Much of this work fell to Bernie Mullin, the Liverpool-born senior vice president for business operations. For Mullin, a better educated and more articulate man than your typical sports executive, baseball was not just a game. It was a marketing strategy. He had a Master's degree in marketing and a Ph.D. in business from the University of Kansas, and he planned to put both to good use with the Rockies.

Mullin got a kick out of talking about baseball market research. It was scary how much the marketers knew about their fans. But it was never enough. They wanted to know more, and they had ways of getting that information. For example, market research told Mullin that Friday was typically boys' night out at the old ballpark. So, he was ordering more up-tempo music over the loudspeakers on Fridays (Bruce Springsteen's "Glory Days" and "Born in the U.S.A." were especially popular), and more "hard-hitting" video clips on the Diamondvision scoreboard screen. Also, because Friday nights were the biggest for beer sales, the Rockies were going to make sure they had more security in the stands. Saturdays were big for "group dates," Mullin said, and Sundays were popular among families. The atmosphere at Mile High Stadium would be adjusted to fit the tastes of the particular crowd type.

All of this information, however, was based on general baseball research. The Rockies wanted their own data base of information on their fans. Mullin advised fans not to be surprised if one summer's evening, as they watched a game from their seats, a purple-jacketed employee happened along and asked if they'd mind filling out a survey. This being the era of the Powerbook, no pencil or paper would be required. Fans would answer the survey on a laptop computer, and the answers would be processed instantly.

"We will vary what we ask, but we will be taking surveys several games during each home stand," said Mullin. "One night we'll ask about the broadcasts: how do you like the announcers, the production, the in-game entertainment, and so forth. We'll ask about the music mix, what song they'd like to hear, those sorts of things. We might ask about the food, and we'll ask consistently about parking and access and ingress and egress questions."

One benefit of using lap-tops for surveys was that the team could respond quickly to complaints, unless they involved the quality of play on the field. "In the surveys is what we call the venom question—'Did anything happen tonight that would cause you not to come back?'" Mullin said. "People input their section, row and seat number, so if anything has happened to them in that game, we come right to them and fix the problem."

Mullin divided people into three categories—baseball fans, entertainment fans, and neither of the above. "The non-baseball fan, we don't really target. They'll come because they come with a baseball fan. So our marketing is to the fan." Trying to please both baseball fans and entertainment fans was challenging, because their interests often were diametrically opposed. Research showed that baseball fans disliked fuzzy mascots, the Diamondvision, and the loud music that had become a part of big-league baseball during the past 15 years. But those things were precisely what attracted the entertainment fans.

"The problem is, if you take the hard-core baseball fans and multiply them out by the number of times they're going to come, they are the majority of the attendance," Mullin said. "But most teams . . . need to get the entertainment fans as well. So you try and accommodate the two." Mullin shied away from saying specifically how the Rockies planned to do that, but promised "a somewhat conservative entertainment package outside the white lines. The goal is we would never interfere with the game on the field. Never. All of our features will be designed to enhance the game of baseball."

That meant that between innings, the big screen on the scoreboard would show baseball bloopers, great plays, highlights from games elsewhere and scores. But as the season went on, the Rockies veered ever closer to the tacky, with the obnoxious fan-o-meter to "measure" crowd noise level, and "home-run ball races."

By then, Mullin was on his way out, ousted in a slow-motion palace coup that had started months before. Mullin's greatest sin was that he had been hired by John Antonucci, the former Rockies chief executive who was dethroned in January 1993. Although

Mullin had a respectable baseball pedigree, he was regarded within the Rockies power structure as Antonucci's hire, and therefore Antonucci's man. He was too vital a cog to remove during the crucial days leading up to the start of the season. But as the inaugural year wound down, it became increasingly clear that he had no future in the organization. So at the end of September, he left to run Denver's new minor league hockey franchise.

Although Mullin undoubtedly had a brilliant marketing mind, one major screw-up laid at his doorstep may have hastened his downfall. It involved much-coveted tickets to the opening game in Denver. A San Diego-based computer ticketing company, wholly owned by the Rockies, threw a series of wild pitches at antsy fans, many of whom were still, two weeks before the game, wondering if and when they'd be getting tickets to the opener on April 9.

The situation was a true public relations nightmare for the Rockies. Here they were, trying to prove that they were a big-time outfit, and they were screwing up their first big opportunity. I could only imagine the screaming and yelling that must have been going on behind closed doors in the Rockies executive suites.

Massive computer foul-ups over a three-month period had left some people who thought they had tickets to the home opener with no tickets, and some with fewer tickets than they were told they'd get. Yet others who expected to have a block of tickets together learned very late in the game that their seats would be scattered all over the ballpark.

To make matters worse, there were screw-ups in computer-generated letters sent out in mid-March by Rocky Mountain Teleseat of San Diego. The letters were supposed to tell ticket holders where their opening homestand seats were located, but the computer in some cases had fans sitting in seats that weren't theirs. That had to be corrected in a second letter, which was worded confusingly. With opening day just 14 days away, only season ticket-holders had received tickets to the sold-out opener.

"Obviously, the people most impacted by this are our fans, and they mean everything to us," a nervous Mullin told me as I prepared a story on the subject for the *Post*. "We apologize that this whole process has been less than the standard that we hold ourselves to. It has not been acceptable." To a certain extent, Mullin was blowing smoke. He was more than happy to divulge the name of the computer company, but he didn't bother to add that the Rockies owned and operated it.

The Rockies decided late in 1992 to hold a lottery to determine who would get tickets to the home opener, with a limit of four per person. People who entered the lottery sent in money for the tickets they wanted. The Rockies cashed the checks. After all entries were received, the team found that about 20,000 tickets remained available. So a postcard was sent out to everyone who entered the lottery, informing them that more seats were available. This is where the first mistake occurred.

"Unfortunately, the language of the postcard was not good," Mullin said. "It said if you get your order in by such and such a date we will seat you together. That was a mistake. It should never have made that kind of guarantee." Some people ordered hundreds of additional tickets. Then, the computer company (or, if you wish, the Rockies) made the second, and biggest, mistake. They began processing all orders alphabetically, instead of chronologically. That meant a person near the top of the alphabet who ordered four tickets in the original lottery, and hundreds in the second wave, would get all the tickets ordered. A person near the bottom of the alphabet, who had been guaranteed four tickets, would get none.

"They ran out of seats before they got through all the people in the lottery, people who earlier had been guaranteed four seats," Mullin said. So the Rockies ordered the company to start anew, processing the orders chronologically. Unfortunately, some people who called in before the error was discovered, to ask where their seats would be and how many they would be getting, were told one thing, only to get a rude shock when the entire list was reworked.

In all, about 7,000 more tickets were ordered than seats were available. But the Rockies were adding those 4,000 temporary bleacher for the first game. So only about 3,000 ticket requests, from 900 different individuals, couldn't be honored. Those people were promised full refunds, but they were hopping mad.

Philip Viles, Jr., a Tulsa lawyer, sent in his money for four tickets in December "and we still haven't heard word one," he said on March 25. "I'm a big baseball fan, and I wanted to be part of history, but heck, Denver is 700 miles away. St. Louis is only 400 miles and Dallas 300, so we have other options."

That wasn't the kind of thing the Rockies wanted to hear. They were counting on a big regional draw. Lucky for them, this was by far the biggest mistake they made all year. In fact, it was damn near the only mistake they made.

Aside from that one blunder *(Other than that, Mrs. Lincoln, how did you like the play?),* the Rockies seemed to have their promotional house in order. But I thought I'd check in with a master, just to make sure they were doing things right. On a trip to Ft. Myers, Florida in February, I stopped in with my father to pay a visit to Mike Veeck. His dad, former White Sox owner and master-promoter, Bill Veeck, had been a friend of my father's. Mike had inherited his dad's flare for the dramatic and zany. In the spring of 1993, he was running the Ft. Myers Miracle—the Minnesota Twins Class A club—pulling some of the same crazy stunts his dad had done in Chicago, and some new ones as well. Bill Veeck, who died in 1986 at 71, was the club owner who once had a midget pinch-hit, had a clown coach first base, and installed a shower in old Comiskey Park's center field bleachers.

Mike, 41, was back in baseball after 10 years on the unofficial blacklist. When his father owned the Chicago White Sox between 1975 and 1981, Veeck, then a brash fellow in his mid-20s, ran the team's marketing and promotions operations.

He was branded a problem child after dreaming up Disco Demolition Night, July 12, 1979. The idea seemed funny at the time: have fans bring disco records to the game, collect them at the gate, place them in a huge bin, and blow them up in the outfield between games of a double-header.

But the event ended up sparking a mini-riot and a bonfire in the outfield. The White Sox had to forfeit the second game of the double-header, and it took weeks for the outfield to recover.

Not too long after that, Veeck punched team broadcaster Jimmy Piersall, further tarnishing his image. "He made some very unflattering comments about my mother," Veeck said, angered by the memory. "I would have killed him for what he called her, a four-letter word that never should be applied to anybody's blood."

Now, after a decade in the advertising business, he was back, and having a blast. His brashness was still evident, but he had, by his own admission, mellowed somewhat. This was due in part to a heart attack at age 35 that "really got my attention." He was a workaholic, but he spent what little free time he allotted himself pedaling his road bike like a lunatic along southwest Florida's congested highways. He didn't feel right unless he'd put in at least 70 miles every weekend day.

When Veeck thought of the opportunity presented by the Rockies' vast market—"They've got a territory the size of the Louisiana Purchase!"—he practically salivated. I asked him how he'd promote the team and he exploded into a rapid-fire monologue brimming with enthusiasm and off-center ideas.

"Give people sight gags. Give people things between innings to talk about," Veeck said. "Don't give them instructions from the scoreboard. Don't tell them when to stand up and cheer. Most people have been around long enough, they know when to stand up. You and I, I'm sure we're stupid, but we know how to stand up for the national anthem, right? So probably, when something wonderful happens, we know enough to cheer. So get rid of all the instructional things and the idea is (to use) between innings for little things, unannounced, to happen, to create conversation in the stands."

Veeck was especially fond of what he called "living billboards." In Fort Myers, he had a dog named Jericho, a golden retriever who brought new balls to the umpire, Gatorade to the players, and performed stunts on the field as well. Jericho was wildly popular and actually was a gate attraction unto himself.

It was a stunt that worked, and even better, it brought in money. Jericho's doghouse, which sat in foul territory in the park, had a large IAMS dog-food sign painted on it.

"IAMS pays, for Class A baseball, a vulgar amount of money for that," Veeck said. "People love it, proving that people will accept commercialism. People aren't standing around going 'You shouldn't get money for things.'"

Another living billboard Veeck installed in 1993 featured exercise bicycles for fans to ride in the grandstands, with the name of a local cycle shop on a sign behind the bikes. "This combines one of the worst things in the world, which is exercise, with one of the best, watching a ballgame," he said. Veeck also planned to install a pink-sand beach in the right field corner. "It's for people who want to spend the day at the beach and their spouse wants to see a ballgame," he explained. "Is it stupid? You bet it is. And everybody will sit in there and say, 'God, Veeck is such a moron.' But they'll laugh."

Even more vital to fan satisfaction than gimmicks, however, was "a touch of the personal." Veeck made a point of standing at the park's main gate before every game, inviting fans to comment on their likes and dislikes. Rockies management should do the same, he suggested. "If you have a beef, you can come right to the guy and get right in his face. There's no reason you can't do it at a major league park. Now you might not like to, but you should do it anyway."

Owners and management should also get out of their private boxes and into the stands. "You should walk down and sit your butt all around your ballpark. There shouldn't be an owner's box in baseball. There shouldn't be executive suites for the ballclubs. They should all be out in the stands. Just imagine: getting a splinter in your rear end in your own stands."

Above all, everyone involved, from ushers up to the team owner, needs to be solicitous of the fans, Veeck said. This is doubly true of the children. "If you come up to me and say, 'There's a kid in my seat,' I'll say, 'Is there a seat next to you, sir?' If you say, 'Yes, there is,' I'll say, 'Well sit there.' If you say, 'Well that doesn't please me,' I'll ask you, 'Are you asking me to move a kid?' If you say, 'Yeah,' I'll tell you, 'You probably don't want to be here. This probably is not your kind of ballpark.'"

There was a world of difference between baseball, Veeck-style, and the Disney approach to customer service preached by the Rockies. Letting a kid in Mile High Stadium have a seat that wasn't his, when the paying customer demanded access? Out of the question. Turn down the volume on the P.A. system and let the fans enjoy the natural sights and sounds of baseball? Forget about it. In terms of sending executives out into the crowd, I did see Jerry McMorris in his seat behind the Rockies dugout many times. But I sure never saw him or any other big-shots in the $1 Rockpile section or anywhere else far removed from their private box behind home plate.

But then, to paraphrase Zessin of Andy Frain, if McMorris had wanted to sit next to people who paid a dollar for their seats, he'd have paid a dollar, not the $95 million it cost him and his partners to bring the Rockies to life.

CHAPTER FOUR

"WELCOME HOME!"

I caught up with the Rockies again on April 5, as they rolled into New York for the first two regular-season games in their franchise history, against the New York Mets. This was *the* place to be if you were a well-heeled Coloradan. Anyone could go to the home opener later that week. But flying to New York to catch the first game, now that was something to brag about.

The Rockies players were just trying to get their adrenaline production under control long enough to play the game. Their clubhouse in Shea Stadium that morning was a scene of utter chaos as the team dressed for batting practice. There were twice as many people crammed in there as I'd ever seen in the Tucson clubhouse; this was despite the fact that the number of players had been cut in half. Each big-league club starts the season with 25 players on its roster. But in spring training, there are no such limitations. There had been 63 players in the Tucson clubhouse.

But the media more than made up for the relative dearth of players. Every step I took, I tripped over microphone wires, or got clunked in the head by a video camera. Everyone, it seemed, wanted to record the historic first dressing of the Rockies. All four Denver television stations were in the clubhouse, as were the New York stations, countless radio stations, various TV networks and scores of print reporters. A lot of media types were just hanging out, not doing anything productive that I could see. This was in direct defiance of a sternly worded directive mounted prominently on a clubhouse wall: The Mets understand that reporters have jobs to do (it implied), but since so many of you are low-life scum-sucking parasites, please do what you have to do and then get the hell out of the clubhouse, where you are not wanted. I never saw anything remotely like this warning in any other clubhouse. But then, New York has a unique, super-competitive media environment.

The players looked tense. Most of them had stony "stay-out-of-my-face" expressions as they undressed before the multitudes. A Denver TV station was following Eric Young around every second that day. I wondered how he felt as the crew filmed him slipping out of his civvies and into his Rockies warm-ups. I had pondered doing a few interviews of the "how-do-you-feel" variety, but I saw that ground was being covered ad nauseam, so I got out of there.

Shea Stadium was crawling with Coloradans that day. Several dozen had flown in on a Continental Airlines jet chartered by the team's ownership group. They threw parties and had parties thrown in their honor at the Grand Hyatt Hotel near Grand Central Station. This group was seated in a cluster of prime seats near the Rockies dugout. But they were by no means the only people who had made the 1,700-mile trek. Everywhere you looked in Shea that day, you saw someone in a Rockies hat. Barrie Sullivan was there, for one, sitting in the upper deck behind home plate with his wife, Sandy, and several friends. So was Patty Calhoun, editor of *Westword,* the irreverent Denver weekly alternative newspaper, and Lew Cady, a Denver ad man who became one of the Rockies' most fanatical followers.

For Coloradans lucky enough to have made the trip, these were exciting moments. There they were, down on the field—the Rockies, by God—wearing their regular-season road uniforms for the first time ever. Look! There's Dante Bichette! And Andres Galarraga! And that plump guy, why, it's Charlie Hayes! Three guys who had been around a few years and whose names even light-weight fans probably recognized. From the stands, it was hard to see the players during batting practice, so overwhelmed were they by the swarming media hordes. There were easily five reporters for every player. Still, every stolen glimpse was a thrill.

New York fans were caught up in the frenzy as well. Hey, this was the Rockies first game. Better buy a few dozen programs! They'll be worth a fortune some day! But the programs were impossible to find. The rumor had been flying around the Big Apple all weekend: big-time memorabilia collectors from around the country were going to descend on Shea Stadium and sweep up all the opening day programs. No one ever established that as fact, but it was true that something crazy was going on.

The Mets had printed 28,000 programs, almost twice the usual number. The cover featured the Rockies and Mets logos and the words "opening series." Ninety minutes before game time there wasn't a program available anywhere in the stadium. But it wasn't Colorado who bought the programs, at least not exclusively. "I'll tell you what happened," said John Morley, the dapper operations vice president of concessionaire Harry M. Stevens. "That all-American virtue, greed, took over. Plain and simple."

Just about everyone who entered the ballpark as the gates opened that day bought several programs, thinking to make a few bucks selling them later, Morley said. As result, many fans had nothing on which to keep score. "They were like lemmings going into the sea, these people," Morley said.

What Morley found ironic was that the programs had little monetary value. "I'm having another 40,000 printed, and I'll keep printing 'em until there's no more demand," he said. "I feel a little sorry for all those people who bought a dozen, but that's the way it's going to be." Morley's biggest customer for the programs was the Rockies, who ordered 3,000 programs to sell at the team's pricey Dugout stores around Colorado.

Depending on who you were, the opener at Shea Stadium represented the worst of times or the best of times. Seated within shouting distance of each other at the opener, Steve Ehrhart, the Rockies first general partner, and current team-owner, Jerry McMorris might as well have been a million miles apart.

For McMorris, of course, this was a day of crowning glory. He was widely credited with having rescued the franchise when, in mid-1992, financial scandal took down Mickey Monus, one of the team's principal owners. McMorris stepped forward and took charge just when it looked as though the franchise might sink before it ever had a chance to swim. So there sat Jerry, square-faced and prosperous-looking, a Rockies cap perched atop his big head and a huge, quarter-moon smile glued on his face. He was surrounded by family and friends adjacent to the Rockies dugout, cheerily signing autographs for an endless stream of Coloradans and New Yorkers.

"I'm having a great time," McMorris told me after I'd squeezed through the throng of admirers and caught his eye. "The people of New York have been wonderful to us—absolutely first class. The excitement level here is very, very high, higher than I had anticipated. What a thrill it is to look out there and see on the scoreboard 'Colorado vs. New York.' It makes me realize we really are in the big leagues."

A few aisles over, Ehrhart sat with friends in a box belonging to Mike Nicklous, one of the team's first potential investors, back in what Ehrhart now called "the darkest hours of August, 1990."

Back in 1990, when Ehrhart entered the fray, Colorado's chances of landing an expansion franchise appeared negligible at best. The five-county metro area had just approved a sales tax increase to build Coors Field, but no one had stepped forward and put together an ownership group.

Ehrhart, with a background in sports law and long-standing ties to professional sports leagues, cobbled together a partnership including McMorris, and Colorado businessmen Oren Benton and Charlie Monfort. While far from a stable or cohesive group, the people involved could bring millions of dollars to the table and at least carry the process forward. Thanks in large part to Ehrhart, Denver made the first cut and was included among the final six cities vying for a team.

A short time later, Ohioans Monus and Antonucci threw in a load of money, and a credible ownership group was formed. After Monus was toppled, Antonucci, CEO at the time, had much of his power stripped away as he was forced by money troubles to sell his stake in the team. Ehrhart, tarnished by his close ties to the Ohioans, was demoted to club liaison with the stadium district, in charge of overseeing the construction of Coors Field. Then, in January 1993, Antonucci was summarily dismissed by McMorris, and Ehrhart received the boot as well, almost as an afterthought.

So now opening day was here and Ehrhart was jobless and glum. Who could blame him? He was a man who had come within two months of realizing a fantasy—bringing a big-league baseball team to his hometown—only to have it all come crashing down around him. As the first game progressed, Ehrhart consented to an interview, but chose his words carefully when talking about the Rockies. He was simultaneously thinking about suing McMorris, and hoping to get back in his good graces. He didn't try to hide his anger, but I sensed he was holding back the stuff he really wanted to say, stuff that would have made great copy but would have made him look mean-spirited in print.

"I'm real proud for everyone in Colorado, because certainly this is a culmination of a great effort," he said as he watched the Mets' Dwight Gooden mow down Rockies hitters en route to a shut-out. "But it's a bittersweet feeling, no question about it."

Ehrhart said he and the Rockies continued to talk, but he didn't expect to be back with the team in any capacity. "I'm obviously very disappointed the situation is where it's at today. I'm proud, but this hurts. I think in time the right things will happen. Let me just leave it there."

Ehrhart said he planned to be in Mile High Stadium for the home opener April 9. But that was no thanks to the Rockies, who didn't offer him a seat. "I have some friends on the U.S. Olympic Committee. I'm grateful to them that they got me a ticket," he said, with a smile that didn't reach his eyes.

Visiting with Ehrhart and McMorris had been interesting, but they weren't the real reason I was in Shea that day. I had come to watch the game with some original Mets fans—people who had bought season tickets in 1962, and had stuck with the team through good times and bad ever since. They couldn't know on this brisk spring day brimming with good cheer that 1993 was going to be, beyond a doubt, the worst year in Mets history, poisoned by acrimony between players and the press. It was to be the year in which Mets outfielder, Vince Coleman, threw an explosive device into a crowd of autograph seekers outside Dodgers Stadium, seriously injuring a couple of them. And it was to be the year the hapless team lost a shocking 103 games, eight more than the Rockies.

I arranged to meet my chief contact at the main gate of the stadium at noon. When I got out there, I found cops in uniform hard at work keeping a growing and restless crowd from charging the still-shuttered gates of Shea.

But then along came 68-year-old Kal Liepper, smiling a crooked smile and calling each officer by name, and the cops parted like the Red Sea and let him through. That's what life was like when you were a native New Yorker with money and you'd held season tickets to the Mets since 1962. Liepper, a gnome-like man with a prominent nose and curly mop of fading red hair, commanded a dozen seats directly behind the visitors' dugout, which meant he and his party had a better view of the Rockies during the team's first game than anyone in the place, including McMorris who was to the side of the dugout.

"Listen, over the years I've found housing for a lot of the players, I've sold them condos in Florida, I even lived with Willie Mays for a while in Florida," Liepper told me as he grabbed my elbow and guided me to his box. He surveyed the crowd around the dugout and waved to other old-timers. "Until they passed these new rules a few years ago, I used to walk all over the field and into the clubhouse. These are my people. Now I can't do that anymore. They worry about drug dealers and gamblers and all that. Now, do I look like a drug dealer to you?"

Liepper ran a family floor-covering business his father started in the 1920s, and also had an interest in a southwest Florida construction company. As of opening day, he calculated he'd been to over 700 Mets games over the past 31 years, but he admitted seeing the Rockies first game was something special. "Sure, a sell-out, a new team, hey, this is exciting," he said, biting into a hotdog smothered in sauerkraut.

So, I asked him, "what stands out in your mind after all these years of watching the Mets?" Liepper shrugged out of his Burberry overcoat and stroked his chin. "Hmm. I still remember in the late Sixties when Gil Hodges was managing the club, how he walked out onto the field one day and took Cleon Jones by the arm and yanked him out of the ballgame because Cleon didn't chase down a base hit in the outfield. God, I still remember watching Hodges. He quietly walked all the way to left field and escorted Cleon off the field."

Alan Liepper, 37, the second of Kal's three sons, lumbered down the aisle and settled into a seat behind his father. He greeted the cop standing atop the dugout. "Hey, Richie, what's new?" he asked with a wave. He then greeted three elderly ushers by name, as well as two cops on the field. They all replied, "How ya doin' Mr. Liepper?" It was an impressive show of benevolent clout. "Is there anyone here you don't know?" I asked father and son.

Alan grinned. "Yeah, sure," he said. "Who I don't know is all the guys up there." He waved to the upper decks, the cheap seats. Then he took a long look at me. "Hey, you know we're not usually very nice to visitors in here." He was joking, but I sensed behind the ribbing the power he knew he possessed. With one crook of his little finger he could have me bounced out into the street on my ear, media credentials be damned.

But the old-time Mets fans seemed exceptionally magnanimous

toward Coloradans on opening day, as if they pitied them for the suffering to which they were about to be subjected. "The Rockies don't have that terrible a ballclub when you look at it," Liepper the elder said as the players were introduced. "I'll practically guarantee you they won't be as bad as the Mets were in 1962."

He was right. Of course, as it turned out, they weren't as bad as the 1993 Mets either. The 1962 Mets were the worst team in baseball history, the original lovable losers. They lost 120 of the 160 games they played. Liepper had blocked a lot of the painful details out of his mind. He remembered their first-ever game only faintly. Back in 1962, the Mets played in the old Polo Grounds. They lost the first game, that much Liepper remembered. But he'd conveniently forgotten the score and the opposing team.

So had Diana Cuca, a 55-year-old Brooklyn schoolteacher who had had season tickets since 1962 in the front row as directly behind home plate as you could get. "I suppose I should remember the score of that game," she said in thick Brooklynese. "I keep score and I keep all the scorecards, so I could look it up." (For the record, the Mets lost their first home game to the Pittsburgh Pirates 4-3. The date was April 13, 1962, and only 12,447 fans attended.)

On this fine day, Cuca was playing hooky from P.S. 46, where she had taught for 33 years. Sitting with her was Norman Forman, 76, her baseball buddy from way back. I could tell Cuca was a Shea veteran. Although the afternoon started out warm, she was dressed in a bulky black overcoat and red knit beret. She was prepared for the cold winds that blew in late in the afternoon.

"You know, of all the games I've been to here, all the excitement and everything, you know which was the most interesting?" she said. "I sat next to the supervising National League umpire, a guy named Al Varlick. He was pointing out to me where umpires should be positioned, when they were right, when they were wrong."

Forman, who like McMorris owned a trucking company, said he had two favorite games. "Of course the sixth game of the 1986 World Series, when the Mets were down by two with two outs in the 10th and won when Bill Buckner (of the Red Sox) let that ball go through his legs. But even better? Was when they won the 1969 World Series. That was only seven seasons after they came into being, so your Rockies fans should take heart. I'm not a very emotional person, but my sister has pictures of me crying when they won that series."

There was no crying this day. Cuca and Forman were almost condescending in their assessment of the Rockies as the 3-0 shutout loss wound down. "This has been a good game, considering," said Forman. "They're pretty competitive."

"They're not hitting," I complained.

Cuca turned and grinned. "That's what you have to expect with an expansion team, darling," she said.

Fans were not nearly so forgiving with their own team. The worst performers from 1992's over-paid, under-achieving Mets team were booed lustily during introductions. And they were slow to forgive the snafu that deprived most of them of programs. White-haired and stooped, brothers Bobby and Joe Donnelly had been ushers at New York baseball games since the 1950s. Bobby said he'd never seen anything like the rush on programs.

"I can't believe the team wasn't ready for this," he said, a trace of an Irish brogue detectable in his voice. "If this is any indication of what management has done to my team, then it's going to be a long season."

How right he was.

After a day off in New York, the Rockies played the Mets again April 7, losing 6-1, but scoring the team's first-ever run in the process, on Dante Bichette's home run into the Mets bullpen. After that game, the team boarded a bus to LaGuardia Airport and took a Continental Airlines charter flight to Denver. Many of the Rockies hadn't ever been to Denver, and hadn't found places to live. So the team offered them all a free week in a downtown hotel.

April 8 was a beautiful, balmy, early spring day in Denver. A perfect day for a parade, which was just what the team had in store. Never before had a winless team received a conquering heroes' welcome, as the Rockies did that day. But it was easy to understand why. Only those lucky fans with the time or money to journey to Tucson or New York had seen the team in the flesh. Denver's pent-up demand for baseball had the entire city throbbing. It was as if everything else ground to a halt that morning, and didn't really get going again until after the following day's home opener.

Thousands of people lined a mile-long expanse of 17th Street in the heart of downtown, awaiting the appearance of their anonymous heroes. And they truly were anonymous. Most of the players could have walked into a crowded restaurant and no one would have recognized them. As the players stepped off two chartered buses at the Union Station train terminal, the crowd applauded politely, but it was obvious most people had no clue who these guys were. To enlighten the fans a bit, organizers steered each player, with their family members, to open-topped convertibles. Each car had the player's name taped to the side. As the parade got under way from Union Station, I could hear the crowd erupt in cheers down the length of the street.

I decided to walk alongside David Nied's car, because he was arguably the most recognizable player at this early juncture. The experience made my heart race and my eyes mist over. I can only guess how he must have felt.

"Welcome home!"

Time after time, that greeting floated out of the crowd and reached Nied's ears as he rode in a green Jeep near the front of the parade with his fiancee, Malissa Murray. The first time he heard the greeting, a wide smile crossed his boyish, innocent face. Unlike most of his teammates, Nied planned to make Denver his year-round home, but surely he couldn't call it home yet. He didn't even know his way to the ballpark.

"Is that the Capitol?" Nied asked in his soft Texas accent as his Jeep turned off 17th Street onto Broadway and the sharp spire of City Hall came into view.

"This is just unbelievable, man," Nied said, grinning ear-to-ear as he crossed Larimer Street, and wave after wave of fans trotted alongside the Jeep to get his autograph. He signed everything shoved in front of him, from T-shirts to cereal boxes. He also accepted gifts of food—a bag of sunflower seeds and some cotton candy.

"It's just overwhelming. A little bit of draft day all over again, but even more people. I bet a lot of the guys will remember this and have some trouble sleeping tonight." As he spoke, a fan sprinted up and handed him another stick loaded with pink cotton candy. "Hungry, Dave?" he panted.

Andy Frain ushers hired to provide security for the players didn't know how to handle this unprecedented situation. Fans kept darting out of the crowd and jogging alongside Nied for autographs. The usher walking with Nied shrugged and let them through. "David, man, I drove three hours for this," pleaded Anna Dekshinkoe from the mountain town of Ward. When Nied signed for her, she looked ready to cry. "Oh thanks, man. You're the best!"

Other ushers weren't as tolerant. People trying to get autographs from Dante Bichette were kept at bay by a grumpy and frazzled usher who kept snarling "no autographs!" at anyone who dared approach the vehicle.

In a convertible half a length behind Nied, soon-to-be folk hero Andres Galarraga drank in the scene with a huge smile on his face. "I've never seen nothing like it," the Big Cat said. "It's beautiful, it's great. We're enjoying it, and it looks like the people are enjoying it."

Catcher Joe Girardi, relatively speaking a grizzled veteran with 3½ years of big-league experience under his belt, shook his head in disbelief. "I remember just one parade I've ever been in before this. It was Double A ball in Pittsfield, Massachusetts. I think 100 people showed up."

Following the parade, players were sped by chartered bus to a huge white tent outside Mile High Stadium, where team sponsors and large corporations feted them at a gourmet luncheon attended by 750 people. Most players were so busy signing autographs throughout the event that they hardly had time to eat much. But these people represented the Denver power elite. The players, in their jackets and ties, remained accommodating throughout, though

I noticed several of them casting their eyes longingly toward Don Baylor, awaiting the signal to head to the clubhouse so they could suit up for their first Denver practice.

Finally, it was off to the stadium for a workout, under the watchful eyes of at least 5,000 fans and 200 reporters. The first Rockies player ever to take the field at Mile High Stadium was pitcher Bryn Smith, who walked into left field at 2:19 p.m. to play catch with his 10-year-old son, Cody. Cody, Smith said, "was conceived in Denver" while Smith was a Bears pitcher in the early 1980s. Playing catch with Cody kept Smith calm. You'd never have known it by looking at him, but he was nervous. He was to be the starting pitcher the following day, and the prospect of pitching in front of 80,000 screaming fans was a bit unnerving, even for an old pro.

"One time when I was in the minors with the Bears, I pitched in front of about 62,000 people here on the Fourth of July. You've got to be careful in a situation like this. It has the potential to get kinda out of hand, on the inside I mean. I know a body's gonna go out there to pitch tomorrow, I'm just not sure yet who's gonna be inside it."

After the opener, in which he pitched seven shutout innings, I asked him who had been inside his body. "It was Bryn Smith, believe it or not," he said with a grin as he wrapped his arms around Cody.

CHAPTER FIVE

LIFE IN THE STADIUM

People who flocked to Mile High Stadium in 1993 to see baseball were more likely to witness a messy slug-fest than one of those dainty and intricate pitchers' duels that so delight die-hard fans. The baseball was often bad, and occasionally it was exciting. While most people had their eyes cast out toward the vast expanses of the Mile High Stadium playing field, where this comedy of hits, runs and errors was being staged, I spent much of my time poking around in the guts of the stadium, trying to get a sense of how the stagehands worked their mundane magic. I wandered through the press box, the organist's booth, the first-aid stations, the complaints booth, the security bunker, and of course, the clubhouse, asking stupid questions and getting some surprisingly intelligent answers.

It became clear early in the season, when the team was playing abysmal baseball and bringing in 60,000 fans per game, that the Rockies would draw extremely well throughout the year. The big crowds fed on themselves, making Mile High an exciting place to be. But the excitement, at least as far as I was concerned, spread far beyond the stands and the playing field. Every inch of the sta–

dium and everyone in it, or so it seemed, had a compelling story to tell.

There was so much to the Rockies first season that the fans didn't see. My assignment for *The Denver Post* was to spend the season poking around in the entrails of big-league baseball in search of the odd, the offbeat and the hidden. At first, gaining entree into the world of baseball was like acquiring a passport and jetting off to an exotic foreign land. The culture was that distinct and that different from anything I'd ever encountered. But just as the foreign traveler gradually adjusts to the cultural dissonance that disorients him during his first days abroad, so I grew accustomed to those aspects of baseball culture that at first seemed so strange and inexplicable. Because everything appeared so new at first, I was a keen observer in those early weeks. But my eye dimmed a bit as the season wore on, or perhaps the more honest way to put it is, I grew jaded.

Never, until now, had I hung around with sportswriters, studied them as a breed, or spent time in a press box. Nor had I examined how a multi-faceted "entertainment product" was staged. Back in Tucson, Bryn Smith talked about a summer when he spent a few days on tour with his musical heroes, the rock band Rush. "I learned a lot about baseball and performing on the baseball field by noticing the difference between backstage, what went on behind the scenes, and what goes on when you're on stage," Smith said. "I remember one of the guys saying you just can't describe the sensation when at the end of your fingertips there's all these kids, and if you play one note everyone goes nuts. And then once it's over, that's it. I really watched that and tried to handle it the same kind of way those guys would do it. It really helped me out a lot. You know there's a screaming 17,000 people out there, they want you, then you walk off the stage, sit down and have a coke or a beer or whatever, and it's over and you unwind. Very similar to a baseball game. It was a good learning experience for me."

For some reason what Smith said stuck with me throughout the season. Perhaps it made such an impression because I was experiencing some of what he had with Rush. I never looked at the production of baseball in quite the same way again after our conversation. Players used to call the major leagues "the big show," and that's how I started thinking of it—a show, with the props and scenery and lighting and soundtrack and stage managers as important as the actors up there on the stage.

I noticed right off that to the people involved in running the production, this was deadly serious business. Never had I seen so many earnest young people engaged in a single enterprise. They wore expensive business clothes, and scurried around with portable radios and cellular phones. The Rockies director of stadium operations, director of in-game entertainment, guest relations director, manager of promotions and publications director, were all in their late 20s or early 30s. They had about them an air of self-absorption and a focus I found truly remarkable. Their jobs, after all, simply involved making sure people had an enjoyable time watching a game. This meant devising suitable distractions from the action on the field. Hardly a matter of life and death.

Whenever big money is involved, I suppose, the enterprise is taken seriously. That's the American Way. But it got to the point where I wanted to grab some of these people by the shoulders and shake them, remind them that this was nothing but a game, the big show, so lighten up, relax, have fun. I can't count the number of times I asked permission to do something that to me sounded pretty reasonable—sit in the organist's booth during the game, watch the scoreboard operators work, ride on a team bus—only to be told by some rigid young executive with a horrified expression, that of course this wasn't possible. They didn't like criticism either. Anything I wrote for the *Post* that hinted all wasn't perfect elicited a rapid, defensive rebuttal.

After spending the four previous years writing about what to my mind really are serious issues—public housing, the homeless, social services, migrant farmworkers—I had a hard time getting used to how seriously everyone took this game. The more I pondered this, the more it troubled me. The issues I usually wrote about were of little concern to the average citizen. People didn't want to read about poor people and their problems. Sure, major league baseball provided marvelous entertainment. It was a great escape from the pressures of daily life. It gave a lot of people gainful employment. But baseball and other sports seemed to occupy a disproportionate amount of society's time and resources.

But after all, I was only another parasite feeding on the beast of baseball. So I learned to adjust. And first was to life in the press box. News reporters are used to having to pry their information from balky sources. I'd always been impressed by the sheer volume of information sportswriters were able to cram into their stories and notes columns. But a couple of days in the press box opened my eyes to the extent to which sportswriters had their work done for them as they sat there watching the game. A bevy of team media-relations people announced the scoring of every play over a public address system. The Rockies, and whatever visiting team happened to be in town, provided a daily ream of game notes chock-full of trivia and statistical effluvia that a lot of beat writers dumped almost verbatim into their stories.

That's not to belittle the job the Rockies beat writers did. Sportswriting sounds glamorous from a distance, but in many ways it's a thankless job. During the season, it's common for a baseball beat writer to go weeks at a stretch without a day off. The hours are long. Twelve-hour days are not uncommon, beginning with interviews in the clubhouse as players arrive four hours before game time, and ending with deadline writing into the wee hours of the morning.

Day after day they have to deal with ballplayers, many of whom are arrogant, unapproachable and rude. And worst of all is the travel. I attended roughly 25 percent of the Rockies road games in 1993, and just that small amount of traveling wore me down. Sure, the team stayed in nice hotels, usually in exciting parts of major cities. After a while, though, one city blurred into the next, and it was hard to take much interest in where I was. Some sportswriters chose to stay at airport hotels, bypassing city life altogether in favor of a quick exit to their next destination. To many, compiling Marriott Points (similar to frequent flier miles, but good towards free Hawaiian vacations) was more important than sleeping in the same hotel as the team, or being in the center of vibrant cities.

It also took me a while to adjust to the proliferation of freebies. The Rockies served up a whale of a multi-course meal prior to every game, in a spacious cafeteria behind the football press box. It was free to the media and other hangers-on with credentials. At first unaccustomed to this brave new world of sports ethics, I felt funny about taking the food. After awhile, I stopped thinking about it. The pressbox also is the best place in any city to acquire free tickets. Again, this is a strict no-no in the world of journalism, unless you happen to write sports. No one thought twice about asking traveling secretary, Peter Durso, a dour little chain-smoking guy, for complimentary tickets to any game. He always complied.

As a lifelong baseball fan who grew up watching games from the stands, I found the atmosphere in the press box stifling. Cheering, or otherwise expressing any emotion not dripping with cynicism during a game was strictly verboten. This struck me as hypocritical, especially since sportswriters from *The Denver Post,* the *Rocky Mountain News* and other daily papers didn't hesitate to take money from the Rockies, in exchange for articles they wrote exclusively for the team magazine. Yet those same writers felt that cheering somehow compromised their objectivity. Once or twice I heard someone bellow "Nice play!" or some such inoffensive remark. To which, without fail, someone would reply "Homer!" in a snarling tone. Homer is the sportswriter's derogatory term for someone who favors the home team.

Having said all that, I should add that there were delightful characters to be found in the press box, some of them doing the real, behind-the-scenes grunt work most people never heard about. Without a doubt, the most universally popular person in the press box was Frank Haraway, the 76-year-old official scorer of the Rockies, who worked as a *Denver Post* sportswriter from 1938 until 1982.

Haraway was hired by the Rockies in February of 1993. When the word got out, people called to congratulate him on his new job. He had to laugh at that. "It's not a new job," he'd tell them. "I've been doing this for 52 years. It's just the same job with a new team and a better label."

He figured he'd been the official scorer for over 4,200 games before the Rockies called. He started in 1941 when Denver had a team in the Class D Western League, a low-level, non-professional confederation of Colorado and Nebraska ballclubs. Until 1982, Haraway performed double-duty, scoring for the Denver Bears and writing sports stories for the *Post*. After 1982, he devoted his attention full-time to scoring.

By 1993, the sportswriter as official scorer was a thing of the past. The newer breed of editor worried about a possible conflict of interest. Never mind that those same editors turned a blind eye to blatant conflicts, like their writers freelancing for the fan magazines put out by the teams they covered. There wasn't much consistency in the policy, but consistency has never been a strong suit among newspaper editors.

"The leagues used to want sportswriters to be the official scorers, because they could always depend on them to be there for every game, and they were experienced at watching and analyzing games," Haraway said. "Whether they were all sober is another question. They weren't, I know that."

The cramped Mile High Stadium baseball press box was named in Haraway's honor. He was a fixture around the ballyard, making his way along the catwalk behind the luxury boxes and broadcast booths on crutches. He'd had calcified hips since he was a young boy, the result of a bout with tuberculosis of the hips. He needed the crutches to get around, but said the condition had never caused him any pain. "I spent about three years in bed and five years in a wheelchair before I graduated to crutches when I was 14," he said. "People ask isn't it hard for me, but I've always looked upon the crutches as a boon after all that time in bed and in a chair.

"I saw my first ball game in Merchants Park in 1928, when I

was 11 years old. I couldn't walk then; I had casts on my legs. They had a parking area behind the left field fence. Right at the foul line the fence was only about four-foot high, so they parked the car at the end of the foul line facing toward home plate. I remember sitting there for my first game, observing the hemorrhoids of the left fielder and third baseman. That was about all I could see."

But Haraway had developed a love for baseball even before that. During those long years when he was confined to bed, he occupied his time, in the summer at least, listening to ball games on the radio. Haraway knew he'd never be able to play sports, but he knew from a young age that he wanted to be around them. He attended college at the University of Denver, and dreamed of a career as a sportswriter for the *Post*.

His dream came true. *Post* sports editor C.L. "Poss" Parsons, a friend of Haraway's father, offered the lad a summer job in 1937, filling in for vacationing writers. Haraway toiled hard all summer covering all manner of minor sporting events. The next year, after graduating from the university, he worked up the nerve to go see Poss and ask for a job.

"Poss always chewed tobacco and he was the most accurate spitter I ever saw," Haraway said. "He could aim at a cuspidor across a room—8 to 10 feet away—and never miss. He was great. So I went in and told him I was in need of a job, and there he sat, I can still see him, with this big chaw in his mouth, and he let go with one of his little pellets of tobacco juice and he hit—ping!—right in the middle of the cuspidor, and he said, "Goddammit, Frankie, you know we don't ever have any jobs around here unless somebody dies or quits." But a few weeks later, someone did quit, and Haraway settled in at the *Post*, covering a little of everything.

He always loved his second career as an official scorer at least as much as sportswriting. He didn't find many differences between scoring for the minors and his new assignment for the big-league club, except that in the majors everyone was so obsessed with statistics. "There is so much more attention and importance attached to it, that every call you make is under much more intense scrutiny.

But I didn't have any incidents this year at all. Oh, once in a while I'd hear some grumbling about one of my calls in the press box, or word would come up from the clubhouse now and then that some guy was irritated with a call I made. But the players have been swell about it.

"Of course there are always times some player or other won't agree with you, because on plays that are borderline, each player wants it scored so it'll favor him. A pitcher wants an error scored because it helps his E.R.A., and the batter wants it scored a hit because it boosts his average."

Haraway still remembered with great pleasure the more controversial plays he'd been involved in, especially one involving Pete LaCock in 1974. It was late in the season, and LaCock, first baseman for the Wichita team (he was to go on to have a middling career with the Chicago Cubs), had a good shot at winning the American Association batting title. During a game in Denver, he hit a ball that the left fielder misplayed. Haraway scored an error, which counted as an out on LaCock's stat sheet, reducing his batting average by a fraction of a point.

"When he saw the scoreboard flash up an error, he just about took off; he was flapping his arms out at second base and glaring up toward me in the press box," Haraway said. When the inning ended, LaCock took his position at first base. That inning, he mishandled a low throw and Haraway charged him with an error.

"The umpire at first base told me later that LaCock told him, "When this inning is over I'm going to hit that cocksucker right between the eyes with the baseball." Sure enough, he caught the ball over at first base for the third out, then he trotted over to the pitcher's mound and fired one at me up there in the press box. It hit the overhang just above the press box and just to the right of me. The Governor of Colorado at the time, John Vanderhoof, he was sitting to my right and it came closer to him than to me."

LaCock received a one-game suspension.

Haraway remembered another scoring call that earned him some notoriety, again related to a race for the batting crown.

"There was a player named Howie Bedell, and he was playing with Louisville in 1961. There was a play I scored as an error on a ball he hit, back in July if I remember correctly. He gestured a little down there, but I didn't think anything of it. Now, a couple of months later, it's the end of the season, and Denver and Louisville were in the playoffs. I went to Louisville for the first game, to cover it for the *Post*. And first thing I saw there was a column by the lead columnist for the *Louisville Courier-Journal*, Dean Eagle. Now, I had just gotten married. And I saw the headline on this column that said "Honeymooning Denver Scribe Costs Bedell Batting Title." Turned out Howie had lost the title by a fraction of a point to Don Wert of the Bears. Bedell told Eagle that if he'd gotten a hit on that play back in Denver, he'd have been the batting champ instead of Wert. And I thought, Jesus, here's a guy goes back to a play scored in July and picks out that one play and says he got screwed out of the batting title. That's carrying it pretty far. But then, I guess those are the lumps you take in this business."

Haraway may have been the official scorer, but there were other folks up in the press box who were scoring with equally serious intent. There were three guys who took turns tracking every pitch for Sports Team Analysis and Tracking Systems Inc. (STATS), a Lincolnwood, Illinois business that provided an unending array of baseball statistics to a dozen big-league teams, newspapers, television networks, and even fans with access to a computer and modem.

To the casual observer of major league baseball, keeping score during a game might seem like folly. Why would anyone want to sit with a scorecard perched on his or her knees and a pencil in hand, tracking the game in a mysterious code that has to be written into spaces so small the writing is rarely decipherable later? After all, there's so much to see and do at a baseball game—food to eat, beer to drink, people to watch. Why focus attention on a scorecard?

Well, anyone who thinks garden-variety, amateur scorekeeping is overly meticulous and a waste of time ought to try scoring with the big boys from STATS. In 1993, STATS paid baseball enthusiasts

$20 per game and got them free season passes. This occurred in every big-league park. In exchange, the statisticians tracked every pitch of every game played in the big leagues. Each game was scored for STATS by three people—one in the press box and a couple watching or listening at home. Scorers for STATS kept track of each pitch simultaneously on computers and on paper scorecards. Not only did they note each pitch, they marked down where every ball was hit, using a 26-section grid defined by the letters of the alphabet. They had to estimate how far the ball was hit, and how hard. For example, Colorado Rockies catcher Joe Girardi's 9th-inning single one April Saturday was described in newspapers as a line drive to center field. On the STATS scorecard, it was shown as a K150H, meaning it was hit to the K area (just to the left-field side of dead center), about 150 feet from the plate, and hard. All the information was sent by modem each half-inning to the STATS monster computer in Lincolnwood.

When I first heard about STATS scorers, I assumed they'd be a bunch of dweebs and statistics nerds who chose to spend their free time scoring in such a manner. I was wrong. One April Saturday afternoon, I decided to keep score along with STATS, using the organization's elaborate score sheets, which were utterly unlike anything else I'd ever used for scoring. The STATS man in the press box that day was Mark Hughes, 37, the Sierra Club Legal Defense Fund's lead lawyer in the Rocky Mountain region. The two other STATS men assigned to the Rockies were Jim Warnock, a history professor who used to pass the time before the game reading dense academic treatises, and Carmen Corica, an enormous economics student who could have doubled as a stand-up comedian. Most of his jokes were at his own expense, and involved his weight.

Hughes, well known for battling corporate polluters, said he found the high-pressure scoring ordeal relaxing. "I like doing this because I have to concentrate so I hard I can't think about anything else," he said during a rain delay, the only chance he had to talk in more than 30-second snippets. "It's kind of relaxing in that way. I can't sit here thinking about what some judge is going to do to me on Monday."

Relaxing? Hardly. Imagine sitting glued to your seat for three hours, so committed to witnessing every pitch that you can't get up to go to the bathroom. "Well, I've never heard them say we can't go to the bathroom," Hughes said. "But we're supposed to get every pitch, so if we go, we have to make it quick."

To show how relaxing STATS scoring could be, Hughes invited me to score along with him. It seemed easy enough at first, simply jotting down the starting lineups for the Rockies and the Florida Marlins. But then all the ease went out of it. The 57-page STATS instruction manual listed 17 different codes to describe each pitch. There was *B* for a ball, *S* for a swinging strike, *T* for a taken strike, *M* for a ball called because the pitcher went to his mouth while on the mound. And it got increasingly more arcane.

Thank goodness baseball moves at a leisurely pace, because it took a while to figure out how to mark each pitch. But that wasn't the worst of it. The act of following every pitch during a game was hard work. I found myself daydreaming on occasion, an irreversible error in the line of duty. It was all too easy to start staring at the scoreboard, or looking at those black clouds rolling in from the north, and suddenly the count was two balls and a strike and I hadn't the foggiest notion how to score those pitches.

"Uh, Mark, excuse me . . ." I said on several dozen occasions.

Hughes, an easy-going sort, was happy to oblige and answer my inane questions, even though doing so required him to yank off his earphones (he listened to the radio broadcast of the game to help in scoring) and fall behind a pitch or two himself.

Three hours later, as the game ended in a taut, 2-1 Marlins victory, I had a completed scorecard, with every pitch accounted for. I knew, for example, (as if I cared to) that the Marlins pitcher threw over to first base four times in the third inning when Alex Cole was on with a single, trying (unsuccessfully) to keep him from stealing.

I threw my scorecard away a couple of weeks later, but at the time I felt pretty proud of it. Until, that is, I called STATS in

Lincolnwood and talked to worker Jules Aquino. "Oh, a 2-1 game is a piece of cake," he said, laughing. "Next time, try scoring one of those 14-12 barn-burners, with millions of pitching changes and pinch hitters and defensive switches. Now that's a challenge."

I enjoyed the STATS guys, so I made my permanent press box perch the seat directly to the left of them. To my left was a glass partition, on the other side of which was a luxury box for the use of Denver Mayor Wellington Webb, his staff, friends, and political supporters. I rarely saw Webb in the box, but his aide, Jim Martinez, attended almost every game, entertaining friends and chomping on an unlit cigar. Beyond the mayor's box was a small cubicle occupied by organist Chuck Shockney. Ballpark organists have a subliminal effect on fans in most stadiums, stirring them to make noise when the home team is at bat, playing subtly derogatory tunes when the visitors are hitting. So I thought it would be interesting to see how Shockney, a novice at the ballpark business, approached his work. It took me a while to convince those businesslike, yuppie Rockies executives to allow me some time with Shockney, but they finally agreed to let me sit with him for an inning or two, "as long as you don't disturb his concentration," said in-game entertainment director, Jennifer Berger.

It would be safe to say that Shockney wasn't the most popular entertainer in the stadium among the fans. Many called the music he played during Rockies games corny or schmaltzy or old-fashioned. But Shockney, an affable guy proud not to have a "hip" bone in his body, didn't object to the derogatory labels. He liked the music, and in any case, he was just following orders. "They've told me they want mostly old stuff," said Shockney, a portly man of 48. He seemed happiest when playing tunes like "K-K-Katy," "Hail, Hail, The Gang's All Here," "Ain't She Sweet" and "The Band Played On." He loved the tunes, he said, as he swayed to the rhythm and sang along in a strong tenor.

"Coors Field will be a pretty traditional ballpark, a throwback, and they want traditional baseball music, not stuff you hear on the radio every day," Shockney said as he turned on the organ an hour before an early-season night game. And then, as if making a slightly naughty confession, he said, "I mean, I go home and listen to my rock tapes and other more contemporary stuff, but that's not why I'm here."

Stacked on top of the $15,000 Rodgers organ in Shockney's glass-walled cubicle were such sheet-music classics as "Those Roaring Twenties," "The Greatest Songs of 1890-1920" and the shockingly modern "Wonderful Years: 1950-1961." His new job was a dream come true, even if it did mean adding dozens of hours onto a work week already overloaded by a full-time job selling church organs, and a part-time stint as music director at Bear Creek Evangelical Presbyterian Church. "I've loved baseball all my life," he said, gazing down at the field from his perch directly behind first base. "I grew up near Kokomo, Indiana, rooting for the Reds and the Cubs. I guess I'm a Rockies fan now."

Shockney started playing piano back in Kokomo at age six, and took up the organ when he was 10. In the early 1970s, he moved to Denver and landed a job selling church organs. He lived now in the suburb of Littleton with his wife, Cheri, and daughters Elizabeth, 14, and Mary Ann, 9. The job came his way in unconventional fashion, during those panicky final days as the Rockies brass tried to get ready for opening day. Shockney had heard in December 1992 that the Rockies were seeking an organist, so he put in a call to the team offices. He didn't hear back until 10 days before the April 9 home opener.

"They asked me if I could come out and audition right away," he said. "They'd auditioned something like 200 people, but they said they wanted to hear me." Shockney couldn't oblige. He'd been hospitalized for more than a week with a staph infection in his leg, "and I was still hooked up to an IV." He assumed that was the end of it. But then, a few days later, they called again. Shockney auditioned for them, and team officials liked his perky, fluent style, and his deft touch with hands and feet.

"On Tuesday night, three days before the home opener, they

called, said I was the unanimous choice." They also asked if he could help them procure an organ. Wells Music, where Shockney worked, was happy to help. An organ was shipped to the stadium, hooked up to the public-address system and readied for that frenzied Friday. "I was a little nervous that day," Shockney confessed. "We didn't have time for a meeting or get-together to say who was doing what, so I just played it by ear."

As was the Rockies' way, the job was fraught with rules, and required more concentration than Shockney expected. "It gets pretty intense at times. I have to really watch the game to make sure I'm doing the right thing." It was a league rule, he was warned, never to play a note when a hitter was in the batter's box. It didn't matter if he was in the middle of a musical phrase; the moment a toe went into the batter's box, the music had to stop dead. He also was told to stay silent while the visiting team was at-bat, unless a Rockies fielder made an outstanding play. He was, in other words, a musical propagandist. "Sometimes you have just a few seconds. You can lose a chance to get a lick in if you're not watching."

His bosses also required that he accentuate the positive. That meant not playing "Three Blind Mice" when the umpires gathered at home plate before the game, no "Na, Na, Hey, Hey, (Kiss Him Goodbye)" when a visiting pitcher got shelled and removed from the game. Shockney's time was programmed to the second by Berger, his boss. When he arrived at work a couple of hours before game time, he'd find a three-page game "communication schedule" on team letterhead sitting on the organ bench. It detailed when he was to play. He didn't get that many chances. The booth next to his was where the big Diamondvision screen was programmed, the scoreboard was operated, and the taped music selected and played. More often than not between innings, an ear-splitting Coca-Cola or Coors commercial would flash across the board and come blasting out of the speakers. Or a baseball-bloopers video would be shown, accompanied by loud rock music. During those interludes, Shockney would sit patiently, arms crossed over his ample girth, tapping his foot and staring out at the field.

Although he liked the job, Shockney seemed worn down by the long hours. He had to arrive a couple of hours before game time, and stay at least 90 minutes after the game was over. "I'm supposed to play until after everybody's gone, including the grounds crew. I play for them and the people cleaning the bleachers."

After a few weeks in the hermetically–sealed press box, I was ready to get out and mingle with the real people. I couldn't think of a better place to get a different perspective on the crowd than from the security bunker tucked into the concourse behind home plate, where cops, Andy Frain ushers, city officials, a team representative, and paramedics worked together to keep those huge crowds under control. No question about it, these were control freaks. They prided themselves on spotting potential problems fast and nipping them in the bud. A couple of games in there, I thought, and I'd have a good idea of what kind of shenanigans take place among a crowd of 60,000-plus.

My first thought on pulling up a metal folding chair in the chilly bunker was that Mile High Stadium was a lousy place to pick your nose. Likely as not, an electronic eye was watching you. Few people knew it, but two remote-operated cameras mounted on the underside of the stadium's second deck constantly monitored the crowd. The cameras were controlled by a Big-Brotherish Digatron console that sat in the command post. The cameras were mounted on swiveling, mechanically controlled brackets, and could zoom in on any of the 76,000 seats in the place. Usually, the console was operated by Margaret Geddes, an aide to Denver's stadium operations manager, Gary Jones, or Andy Frain supervisor, Steve Berger. The Digatron could videotape any incidents as well, for use in court when necessary. They let me play with the thing at will, which was fun at first. Soon, however, I started feeling like a voyeur. Those cameras had powerful zoom lenses.

But the Digatron was just one feature of the command post, which served as the stadium operations nerve center during Colorado Rockies and Denver Broncos home games. The stuffy, cramped bunker was a beehive of activity from two hours before the first pitch until the last fan left. In the spring, narrow, sliding windows that faced out toward the field were left closed, because the crowds were so loud people in the bunker couldn't hear calls over their radios. But in the summer, it got much too hot in there, and the windows had to be opened. Working amid all that noise guaranteed a headache by the end of the game. Fortunately, people weren't allowed to smoke inside the bunker, or it would have been unbearable.

The command post was stuffed with information for coping with a wide range of emergencies. Tornado about to hit the stadium? Bomb threat phoned in? Massive power outage? There were detailed lists of evacuation procedures for each type of problem. Incidents of a less serious nature, ranging from gang fights to bird droppings on seats, were handled from inside the command post as well. The variety of incidents was amusing, so I kept a log of everything that transpired around me during a game against the San Francisco Giants on Wednesday evening, May 12.

6:10 p.m.—An Andy Frain usher gets smashed on the ankle by a batting-practice line drive. Treated by paramedics, he stays on the job.

7:00 p.m.—Steve Berger, a hulking Andy Frain Services supervisor with graying hair and a white beard, is seated at the Digatron, scanning the crowd, looking for pot smokers, boozers or other miscreants. He spots a man in one of the luxury suites between home and first base sitting in the open window of his box.

"If he's had a few beers, it wouldn't take much for him to fall into the lower deck," Berger says, dispatching an usher to move the guy. He keeps the camera trained on the man until the usher taps him on the shoulder and the fan takes a seat.

7:10 p.m.—Patrons in section 109, row 36, complain that something is dripping on them from the rafters. Rockies assistant stadium operations manager, Todd Zeo, mutters into his walkie-talkie and a team employee scurries down. Several fans are moved to dry seats.

7:12 p.m.—Margaret Geddes, scanning the stadium with the Digatron, spots something on the warning track behind Rockies right fielder, Dante Bichette, during the top of the first inning. She zooms in the camera and sees it's a tennis ball. An usher is informed by radio and dashes on the field between pitches to retrieve it.

7:30 p.m.—Ushers at a gate behind the east stands report that three men crashed through the gate carrying liquor and have disappeared into the crowd. They had surrendered their tickets to the usher first, so Berger zooms the Digatron on their assigned seats. But they're smart enough not to sit in them, so they don't get caught.

7:50 p.m.—Berger, surveying the stands with binoculars, notices an usher watching the game instead of the crowd. He dispatches a supervisor to reprimand him. That's a sure way to get fired fast by the Andy Frains. "For me, this is rest and relaxation. I love it." Berger says. "I sell real estate for a living. Now, that's work."

8:05 p.m.—Zeo looks up from his binoculars. "What inning is it?" he queries. Someone informs him it's the bottom of the fourth. The game is nearly half over, and it's only an hour old. Most Rockies games to date have featured the opposing team having a field day against Colorado pitchers, and have lasted an average of three hours. "No one say anything about the speed of this game so far. Don't say it, just don't say it," Zeo warns.

8:21 p.m.—A pregnant woman seated down the right-field line faints. A paramedic rushes to her side, but she needs no treatment.

8:34 p.m.—A drunk is passed-out near a television truck just outside the stadium gates. The police are dispatched to haul him away to the detox center.

8:37 p.m.—A drunken man is throwing up on the concourse behind Section 103 along the right-field line. Paramedics, ushers and janitors hurry over to deal with him.

8:39 p.m.—Kids are throwing debris off the upper deck. An usher is sent to reprimand, and if necessary, eject them.

8:54 p.m.—A fan is hit in the head by a foul ball and is taken to a hospital for observation. "We call it minor; I'm sure he wouldn't," paramedic Ann Shimkus says.

8:55 p.m.—Drunk men in a luxury box are pitching trash on customers in the seats below them. They are ejected.

8:58 p.m.—Eight young men celebrating a birthday in the east stands are ejected for drunkenness and smoking marijuana. Police officer, Bob Tabares, stays in touch with his men in the stands to make sure they have the ejections under control. The eight rowdies try a half-dozen times to sneak back into the stadium during the next hour. They're thwarted each time.

9:00 p.m.—The lights in the men's and women's rooms behind the south-stand bleachers go out. Margaret Geddes sends someone to fix the problem—a tripped circuit-breaker.

9:13 p.m.—A drunken man is ejected from the south stands.

9:14 p.m.—A Denver detox van is sent to pick up a man passed out on the grass outside the stadium.

9:15 p.m.—A drunken man is ejected from the east stands upper deck.

9:16 p.m.—A drunken man is ejected for urinating off the back of the south stands into the parking lot far below.

9:30 p.m.—A brawl erupts on the field between the Rockies and the San Francisco Giants. Berger quickly sends a few ushers onto the field to keep fans from joining in. "Do not, repeat do not, get involved in anything between the players," he says.

9:35 p.m.—Brawl instigator, Barry Bonds of the Giants, is ejected and walks off the field toward the clubhouse to a chorus of jeers. Berger and Tabares dispatch ushers and cops to make sure no one throws anything at him or jumps from the stands.

The night is over. Everyone agrees it was a slow one.

"Last night we had trouble in the south stands because the Rockies gave away 10,000 community seats out there and somehow the Crips and the Bloods got a hold of a bunch of them," Berger says. "One gang at a time, now we can handle that. But both on the same time? I mean, come on."

This comment, which appeared in the *Post* a few days later, got Berger in trouble with Rockies stadium operations chief, Kevin Carlon. Although he apologized as ordered, he was, at heart, unrepentant.

One day I discovered the "cycling paramedics." While watching a couple of games from the bunker, I noticed paramedics darting in and out, dressed in cycling gear. They were part of a team that patrolled the stands on bikes. An avid cyclist, I decided I had to participate in that. Late in the summer, I finally got my chance to ride with Denver's chief paramedic, Jeff Forster, during a game between the Rockies and the even-lowlier New York Mets.

I caught up with Forster 10 minutes before game time on a balmy August Sunday afternoon. Just as we shook hands, a call came crackling over Forster's radio: a pregnant woman seated in the stadium's top level down the left-field line was having labor pains. Forster, a sturdy 37-year-old with the thick thighs of a serious cyclist, was lounging in the paramedics station in the lower level of the east stands when the call came in. He had three choices. He could walk and run down two levels, out the gates, down the street and back into the main section of the stadium, then up five stories-worth of ramps to where the woman waited. That would take at least five exhausting minutes. Or, he could hop aboard one of the paramedics' golf carts, and weave slowly through the throngs of people still streaming into the ballpark. That might take even longer.

Forster chose the third and by far the fastest option. He hopped on his custom-made, $1,300 hybrid bicycle, screamed down the ramps, miraculously avoiding the clot of fans, pedaled out the gates, back into the stadium and up the steep ramps in a sprint. He was at the woman's side in about 90 seconds, winded but ready to work. I like to think I'm pretty good on my mountain bike, but this business of riding through crowds was a little different than jumping stumps on the Colorado Trail. I tried to follow Forster, but found myself bailing out on the first down-ramp when I came perilously close to slamming into a nice suburban family.

Meanwhile, Forster attended to the woman as a golf cart, driven by paramedic Tim Gulbranson, made its slow way up the ramps. The patient appeared to be fine, and in no imminent danger of giving birth. When the cart finally arrived five minutes after Forster, the two paramedics helped load the woman on. Gulbranson drove her down to the first aid station off the main concourse, where Dr. Rich Wolfe, a Denver General Hospital emergency physician, waited to take care of her.

"We were the first paramedic team in the country to use bikes when we started this for the Denver Grand Prix back in 1991," Forster, a kamikaze-style mountain biker in his spare time, said after he caught his breath. "When I suggested it, I got a lot of raised eyebrows and skepticism from administrators. But it's been phenomenal at big events." At Rockies games during the first season, paramedics on bikes saved lives on at least three occasions, when they arrived quickly and restarted the hearts of fans who had gone into cardiac arrest. All three survived—"saves" in the medics' parlance.

Forster had gotten 12 of the city's 76 paramedics certified to work on his department's 16 bikes. Bike detail was voluntary, and paramedics who took stadium shifts got overtime wages. They rode bikes custom-made to Forster's specifications by Robert Stone, a New Jersey bike designer and manufacturer. The bikes were lighter than true mountain bikes, but plenty rugged enough to hop curbs and ride down flights of concrete stairs.

"We need cycling to be one of their passions if they're going to do this," Forster said. "Most of us are pretty serious mountain bikers. We can go from the 500 (top) level in the right field corner down to ground level, out and back to the 500 level in the east stands in under two minutes."

Maybe they could, but it wasn't something mere mortals entered into lightly. Everytime I hopped on my bike and tried to follow Forster, some pesky fan would get in my way and I'd have to hop off fast, my ego wounded but my body intact. Forster, meanwhile, would have snaked through the crowd and disappeared over the horizon. He rarely touched his brakes, choosing instead to shout "paramedic!" and hope that people would get out of his way. Kids invariably stopped in their tracks, mouths agape. "Awesome!" shouted one boy as he watched Forster speed out of sight down a ramp. As he exited the stadium at one point in the afternoon, Forster coasted down a flight of 10 steps as if they weren't there. "It's easy," he coaxed me with a shrug. "Just relax and loosen your grip on your handle bars." No thanks. I walked my bike down the stairs.

That particular Sunday was a slow day for Forster. We answered a half-dozen calls and he treated another nine people who dropped by the first-aid station behind the left-field stands. Most needed bandages and pain relievers. Two people requested eye drops, which he didn't carry, another wanted sunscreen, which he didn't have, either. In one of the aid stations, the paramedics had compiled a stupid-request log sheet, which consisted of serious but absurd requests they'd received from the baseball-going public. The list was tacked to the back of the station door: Diapers. Safety pin for broken zipper. Cough drops. Emergency arthroscopy. Something for feminine hygiene. Salt. A douche. Matches to light a joint. Crutch repair. Chapstick.

What paramedics did carry on their bikes or in fanny packs was sufficient to handle a wide array of medical emergencies. Foster had a recusitator bag, 1,000 ccs of saline solution for starting up an IV, a variety of bandages, indo-tracheal equipment (tubes to jam into the lungs to help with breathing), a stethoscope, a blood-pressure cuff, and a 50-percent dextrose solution for diabetics.

Although the day was slow, Forster did have a couple of interesting cases. At 1:21 p.m., during the bottom of the first inning, he was called to check on a boy who had been hit behind the ear by a home run ball, off the bat of Rockies catcher, Joe Girardi. The boy's father had already secured some ice and the boy was holding the dripping plastic bag against a red lump behind his left ear. The ball had deflected off someone else's hand and hit the boy. Forster quickly determined that the injury was minor, but counseled the youth's father to keep a careful watch on him the rest of the day. Paramedics were used to seeing fans injured by batted balls. Next to heat stroke, it was the most common affliction in the stadium. Most of the injuries, however, occurred in the pricey seats on the infield, where foul balls often came screaming into the stands. It was relatively rare to see someone hurt by a home run, because there was so much more time to react to the incoming ball.

In the bottom of the seventh inning, however, the second home run casualty of the day arrived at Forster's aid station in the left-field stands. Sean Lucy, a nine-year-old from Boulder, had tried to snare Freddie Benavides' home run in his glove. But he misjudged the ball and it slammed into his chest, inches above his right nipple. He had a perfectly round, red welt where the ball had hit. Forster checked him over carefully while Lucy's father looked on. The boy seemed fine, alert and cheerful. "Hey, am I gonna be in the newspaper?" he asked me. But Forster was being cautious. "Watch him tonight for uncontrollable coughing or difficulty breathing," he advised the lad's father. "A blow like that can pop a hole in a lung, or bruise it."

After the Lucys returned to their seats, Forster said Sean had been lucky. "A blow like that a few inches more toward the center of his chest could easily have killed him," he said.

Riding a bike around a stadium and treating people might sound like fun, but to Denver paramedics, it was basically grunt work, routine stuff for the most part. "We're all adrenaline junkies," said Rich Wolfe, the physician on duty in the stadium that day. "We get addicted to the great cases—you know, hypertensives who need to have their chests cracked right then and there, the cardiac arrests in the stands, stuff like that. It's hard to get emotionally involved otherwise."

But if you really wanted to see people with their emotions whipped up, the best seat in the house didn't even have a view of the playing field. It was behind the counter at the Rockies Guest Relations booth on the concourse behind home plate. This was where disgruntled fans came to vent their spleen. And since all Rockies employees were supposed to utilize the "Disney approach to customer service," the guest relations workers, in silly, straw cowboy hats and purple blazers, had to stand there and take it with smiles on their faces. I spent one full game in the booth, and I left ready to wring someone's neck.

It started even before the game began. The first complaint came from a big guy in a yellow cap. He was steaming, and guest relations worker Juan Gonzales, wearing a pained smile, was doing his best to calm him down.

"Somebody screwed up, and I'm irritated as hell!" the guy bellowed, sticking his flushed face through the open window of the booth. "Apparently, someone told me a lie, and I'm not gonna put up with it." Gonzales, who had the unenviable task of staffing the guest relations booth day-in and day-out, was scrambling. The big guy was angry because he wanted to sit with his parents, both of whom used wheelchairs and were seated in a special section. Someone had told him over the phone that he and his wife could sit in the section as well, but now Andy Frain ushers were saying that wasn't possible.

This particular annoyed fan was not alone on this night. A steady stream of people stopped by the guest relations window to air a variety of gripes, from rude ushers to ticket foul-ups to lousy food. Throughout my evening there, I asked every worker in the booth to describe the most bizarre situation they'd been in to date. "The strangest thing yet?" asked guest relations director Bob Butler. "There was a guy who tried to bring his pet rat into the Rockpile. Some of the other people there got kinda upset, so we told him he'd have to leave. So then he asked if he could bring the rat in if he bought it a ticket." The answer was no.

"The strangest one I've seen?" Gonzales said, mulling it over. "Oh, here's one: I had some guy come in here complaining about that airplane that flies over the stadium pulling advertising banners. He wanted us to call the Federal Aviation Administration, because he was worried about the plane crashing into the stadium."

Butler, who graduated from the University of Denver in May of 1993, was lucky enough to walk right into the guest relations job. He was the perfect specimen of the Rockies hyper-serious young execs. He wore expensive suits, and was highly visible in the stadium, with his shock of white-blonde hair and Dudley Do-Right chin. He seemed never to be in one place for more than a few seconds. He scurried around endlessly like a trainee trying to impress the boss, lugging three portable radios to maintain contact with his 65 purple-jacketed guest relations employees.

I tried to interview Butler, but it was tough. I asked questions and he fed me pablum that sounded straight out of some "dealing with the media" chapter of an undergraduate business management textbook. "The role of the guest relations staff is 100 percent guest satisfaction, regardless of the situation," he said, as if by rote. "If someone has a problem, a representative is to remain at that person's side until the problem is solved, regardless of how long that takes. This is a new team, and we're trying to establish new traditions. We want a Disneyland-type atmosphere. People drive from hours away to see a Rockies game. We want to show them the best time we can, and deal with all problems as quickly and efficiently as possible."

Some problems were easier to solve than others. The big guy in the yellow cap who wanted to sit with his parents was accommodated because the wheelchair section happened to be half-empty that night. The man was still fuming as he was taken to his seat, but he got the result he wanted. Meanwhile, Gonzales and co-worker, Doug Ruhl, were trying to put out another brush fire, this one involving a woman who had driven 1,100 miles from Evansville, Indiana, to take 19 people to the game in honor of her parents' 50th wedding anniversary. Someone had promised her over the phone that a motorized cart would meet her mother, who suffers from a heart condition, at the stadium gate and transport her to her seat high in the upper deck. But that cart belonged to the paramedics, and wasn't available for routine transportation.

"If she gets palpitations and has to leave after we drove 1,100 miles . . ." the woman said, her voice filled with menace. A representative was dispatched to take the elderly mother to her seat via elevator and wheelchair. "I want someone to keep an eye on them and make sure everything's OK," Ruhl said into his radio. He also arranged to have some complimentary water bottles brought to the members of the anniversary party.

People found some ingenious ways to upgrade their seats. In the early innings of that night's game, a woman approached the window looking pale and shaken. "I can't sit in my seats. They're in the upper deck and I'm scared of heights," she said. Ticket office employee, Francie Fowler, who worked out of the guest relations office, tapped her computer keyboard and issued three lower-deck seats to the woman, her daughter and son-in-law. The woman paid $18 for the upgrade. It wasn't cheap, but it got them seats down there among the season-ticket holders, seats that otherwise weren't available to the general public.

The biggest problems that night occurred after the game. The Rockies had planned to put on a laser show following the game, then changed the promotional schedule in early April. But all tickets sold before the change still said "laser show" on their face, and no one had thought to put the word out that the show wasn't happening.

"This is just fraud, that's all it is," said one of the many customers who flocked to the office after the game to vent their anger on the hapless Ruhl and Gonzales. "Yeah," another man chimed in, "I sat here until almost 11:00 p.m. with my 5-year-old, pinching him to keep him awake so he could see the show, and now you're telling me there isn't one?"

Ruhl and Gonzales took down people's names and addresses and promised them they would be compensated, most likely with discount ticket coupons.

After dealing with those gripes for 45 minutes, it was time to close the shutters and go home. For Ruhl and Gonzales, the rancor was just another night at the ballgame. As for me, I left the booth and went out for a couple of cold beers to soothe my throbbing head. Here's hoping they did the same.

I had made my way through the bowels of the stadium, and had seen the stage hands performing their grunt work. It was almost time to focus in on the supposedly glamorous part of the game—the clubhouse, domain of the players, those monied young men the fans paid to see perform. But first, I wanted to spend some time with Tom Lujan, the Mile High Stadium groundskeeper. A compact, reserved man, Lujan shied away from the press. He had been vilified by Rockies manager Don Baylor and several players for the uneven playing surface they found at Mile High in the early part of the season.

When I called Lujan to make an appointment, he balked. Every time he'd read his name in the papers that summer, it was attached to a string of expletives. Every other day, it seemed to him, someone in the Rockies organization was leveling another blast at him. He thought they were a bunch of jerks and prima donnas. During the opening homestand, Lujan's boss, Denver Mayor Wellington Webb, rushed to his defense, saying he didn't see how the splotchy grass had much to do with the three-run homers Rockies pitchers kept serving up to the opposition. That silenced the Rockies, but not for long.

Until I called him in late June, Lujan hadn't seen his name in print for weeks. That was just fine with him. Perhaps that's why he failed to show up the first two times we set up a meeting. He probably was hoping I'd just go away. Lujan, 37, and a Denver native, was a 17-year veteran of the Mile High grounds crew. He had a father's pride in his field, which he pampered 12 months a year.

"I've grown up on this field, learned everything I know here," he said on a radiant summer afternoon. He paced across the broad expanse of center field, a wad of Red Man chewing tobacco stuffed in his cheek. I'm no expert, but the outfield looked gorgeous to me as I stood there, surrounded by acres of close-cropped grass. The only visible flaws were pesky clumps of Poa-annua grass that kept the Prescription Athletic Turf (PAT) from presenting a perfect, deep green-hue to fans. "We'll resod the entire surface before next season so it looks perfect," Lujan promised.

It's not that there was anything inherently wrong with the Poa, a high-quality bluegrass. Balls didn't take strange hops off it, and it didn't grow differently from the other turf. "It's a purely aesthetic thing," Lujan said. It was aesthetics that drove him to his Waterloo, an ill-conceived attempt in January to kill clumps of Poa grass with a herbicide called Round-up. The Round-up worked its magic, and everything would have been fine had bad early spring weather not interfered.

"I came back in here the first week of March and reseeded the areas where the Poa had been, using a pre-germinated rye-grass mixture," Lujan said. "Then I top-dressed it with sod and a Dakota peat mixture. This is widely done all across the country. But between our altitude and the wet spring, we didn't get the temperature we needed to continue the germination process. About 50 percent of it grew in, but 50 percent didn't." As a result, the 80,227 fans who streamed into Mile High Stadium on opening day saw an outfield that looked like Max Yasgur's farm after Woodstock. Well, it wasn't quite that bad. But it was full of what, from the upper decks, appeared to be craters, and bare patches where the dirt looked to have been dyed green in a feeble attempt to cover up the defects.

Eventually the PAT grew in, and Lujan hadn't heard any complaints about the turf for months. But that didn't mean the complaints had stopped. Rockies infielders spent a lot of time bitching and moaning about the infield dirt, which several described as the worst in baseball. They said the dirt was so hard that the ball took funny bounces, a nice excuse for the errors being made on an almost daily basis at second base and shortstop.

So team officials brought in some of their own experts to examine the dirt. "They thought the clay content was too low," Lujan said, scooping up a handful of the coarse, tan-colored earth. "When cleats pushed into the dirt, it was breaking up into hard little clumps, creating a potential site for a bad hop." The real problem, Lujan said, wasn't the dirt itself, but the fact that his crews weren't wetting the dirt down enough. "If it's watered correctly the clods of dirt can be crumbled with the toe of your shoe, no problem," Lujan said. "But that wasn't happening."

So, while the Rockies were on a 10-day road trip, Lujan met with Rockies general manager, Bob Gebhard, and stadium operations director, Kevin Carlon, to work out a solution. The solution they agreed upon was trucked into the stadium a couple of days later—175 tons of new dirt, 70 percent clay, 30 percent sandy loam. When the Rockies returned to Denver, they were greeted by a new, presumably improved infield. The grounds crew spent four long days removing the old dirt, and replacing it with the new, slightly darker mixture. The risk presented by the new dirt was that the infield wouldn't be able to handle as long or hard a rainfall as the old infield could with its lower clay content.

Lujan knew he didn't have to worry much about how weather affected the outfield. The turf and its simple, effective drainage system could handle up to seven inches of rain an hour and still be playable. The turf was laid over a 16-inch base of sand with a plastic-lined reservoir underneath. Drains in the outfield could be closed to hold in moisture, or opened to remove moisture rapidly. Lujan liked to keep the grass short to help drainage. When the Rockies were home, Lujan and his crew mowed the grass every day, cutting the outfield to 1½ inches and the infield to 1¾ inches. Mowing was slightly less frequent when the team was on the road. Daily field work for Lujan and his crew also included raking and watering the infield dirt, and rebuilding the pitching mound and batter's box areas, both of which were 100 percent clay.

Once the baseball season ended in late September, Lujan set to work getting the stadium ready for football. First, he had to sod over the infield dirt. Then he had to toil to keep the grass as healthy as possible during the Broncos season. One sport at a time he felt he could handle.

But there was one hellish 10-day stretch in August when Lujan, and the entire Mile High Stadium operations team, had to convert the stadium from a baseball field to a huge, outdoor cathedral for the visit of Pope John Paul II, then to a football field, back to a baseball field, to a football field again, and finally, back to a baseball configuration.

To accommodate the huge welcoming ceremony for the Pope, contractors built a Woodstock-sized stage in what had been right field. City workers then laid a covering of special quarter-inch felt called Geotek over the outfield grass. This allowed the grass to breathe and, Lujan hoped, survive the onslaught. Three layers of half-inch plywood were placed on top of the Geotek, and on top of that went several thousand folding chairs.

That was only the beginning. City workers removed the pitcher's mound with a forklift, took down the left-field fence and the foul screen behind home plate, and removed the huge, iron foul poles.

Pope John Paul arrived Thursday night and was greeted by 90,000 fervent believers. The sound that rose from the crowd when he entered the stadium in his cartoonish "Popemobile" surpassed the roar of Rockies fans when Eric Young's opening-day home run cleared the fence. Throughout the day Friday and until noon Saturday, huge religious education classes were held in the stadium. Finally, as the last of the faithful departed, city crews went to work at top speed. To them, this Pope stuff was just another event. The Broncos were playing Monday night, and there was work to be done. Down came the stage in record time. Up went the folding chairs, the plywood, and the Geotek. Next, the 13-story, 9-million-pound East Stands were moved in 145 feet on clusters of water bearings used to lift the stands and float them. Lines marking 10-yard increments were painted on the field. Special asphalt-like walk-ways were laid along the football sidelines.

As soon as the Broncos game ended Monday, the crews were back at work. The Rockies were playing the Philadelphia Phillies the following three evenings. It took a crew of 25 people 15 hours to get Mile High Stadium ready again for baseball. The stands were floated back out. The fences were reinstalled, along with the foul poles. The foul screen went back in. The asphalt walkways were removed. The football lines were erased and baseball lines laid back down. A forklift reinstalled the pitcher's mound.

But the work wasn't finished. As soon as the Rockies and Phillies left the field Thursday night at 10:00 p.m., two more all-nighters began. The Broncos were playing again on Friday night, followed by a Rockies double-header Saturday afternoon. "These guys will make a lot of money in overtime, if they live through it," their boss, Gary Jones, said with a weary laugh.

No one was happier than Lujan that come the spring of 1995, he wouldn't have to go through this type of ordeal again. With Coors Field slated to open that year, Mile High Stadium would become a football-only stadium for the first time in its 45-year history.

Lujan had no idea whether he'd be the groundskeeper at Coors Field as well. Nor was he sure he wanted the job. But the Rockies made it clear they wanted their own groundskeeper. As far as they were concerned, Lujan was a football groundskeeper, and that just wasn't good enough for them.

CHAPTER SIX

LIFE IN THE CLUBHOUSE: NO WRITERZ ALLOWD

Whenever I told friends who were baseball fans that I was helping cover the Colorado Rockies in their inaugural season, I got the same immediate reaction. "Wow, cool!" they'd say. "You get to go into the clubhouse and everything? Get to know the players?" Well, yes and no. Yes, I spent a lot of time in the Rockies' clubhouse, before and after many of their 81 home games. Yes, I interviewed most of the players. But I never got over feeling acutely uncomfortable being in the clubhouse.

From the first time I ventured inside that inner-most of inner sanctums during spring training in Tucson until the last day of the season, October 3 in Atlanta, I felt awkward and out of place in there among the players. Maybe it had something to do with my lifelong relationship to the game and its players as a fan. To the best of my recollection, the closest I'd ever come to a player before 1993 was when I was 14, waiting outside the Comiskey Park players' parking lot for autographs. White Sox catcher, Brian Downing, came screeching out of the lot in his Camaro and ran over the tip of my shoe.

So the first few times I entered the Rockies clubhouse, I felt, if not exactly awestruck, then at least a bit intimidated. I kept forgetting that I was 10 years older than most of the players, and not some teenager looking for autographs.

The term "clubhouse" described the atmosphere perfectly. Every time I walked in I felt like I'd crashed a party. I wasn't a part of the club and no one felt at all obliged to make me feel welcome or at ease. Quite the contrary. Ballplayers have an uncanny ability to look right through you unless you thrust yourself in their path and humbly request a moment or two of their time. In the clubhouse, I often found them eating, reading mail, signing box after box of baseballs, or getting dressed. Some of them always were willing to grant me a few minutes' audience. Others seemed to feel a writer's submissive request for a brief interview was an affront. I never encountered the slightest hint of menace or hostility. Yet it was made clear, somehow, that I was off my turf, and if I didn't have a specific piece of pressing business to attend to, I felt pressure to clear out. No girlz or writerz allowd.

On its surface, the Rockies clubhouse at Mile High Stadium was just a slightly fancified version of a YMCA locker room. The players had walk-in cubicles in which to hang their clothes and stash bits of memorabilia, photos of their families, or whatever they chose. Off the purple-carpeted locker room was a dining area, a TV permanently tuned to ESPN, a trainer's room, a whirlpool room, a video room, and a shower and toilet area. Before games, and after if the Rockies had won, music blared from a huge boom-box provided by the team. Alex Cole, the first player the Rockies dumped at the end of the season, seemed to be the DJ, and he favored bass-heavy rap and funk.

When games were lost, the clubhouse was silent as a morgue. The tension was palpable after a loss, and intrusions by writers were especially unwelcome.

The lord and master of the clubhouse was Rockies equipment man, Dan McGinn, whom everyone knew as Chico. Players got along with him, or so it appeared, but most everyone else found

Chico an insufferable, self-important tyrant. He was only 26, but had spent nearly a decade in big-league clubhouses—first as a Minnesota Twins batboy, and later their assistant clubhouse manager. He was ill-mannered, a puffed-up macho man who had adopted some of the swagger and none of the charm of the pro athlete. He took great pleasure in chasing reporters out of the clubhouse, and never failed to answer a question as monosyllabically as possible. He did everything in his power to add to the discomfort writers like me felt in the clubhouse.

At first, I attributed my discomfort to inexperience. I'd never done anything like this before. Undoubtedly there was an elaborate set of unwritten rules I wasn't privy to, and I was going to have to feel my way gradually. There was food and drink lying around, but I dared not touch it. I saw a couple of writers cadge pieces of bubble gum or a handful of sunflower seeds from huge bins of the stuff in the clubhouse, but I was certain I'd have my credentials yanked off my neck by Chico the first time I tried that. I didn't have a clue how to behave.

But as I started talking to professional sportswriters, I discovered I was not alone. One day, as I leaned against a wall in the clubhouse in Tucson, trying to figure out what to do next, Bob Kravitz, an affable sports columnist for the *Rocky Mountain News,* saw that I looked out of my element and strolled over. "It doesn't matter how long you do this for, you never really feel comfortable in a clubhouse. It's like a fraternity, and you haven't been rushed."

Some of the discomfort had to do with the unequal relationship between writers and athletes. You need them to do your job as a writer. They, in fact, need you just as badly as their liaison to their fans, but few of them seem to realize it. Athletes are young, rich and gifted celebrities. Ballplayers seem to think their fame is solely a result of their heroics on the playing field. This is true, but only to a certain point. What they don't seem to realize is that without the mass media, they wouldn't get much exposure, or those fat endorsement contracts that double and triple the incomes of the luckiest among them.

As the season progressed, I grew increasingly fascinated by the relationship between players and writers. None of the writers I talked to liked players as a breed. They had a laundry list of unflattering adjectives to describe them: spoiled, pampered, arrogant, egotistical, rude, ignorant. "Baseball players are the worst of all the pro athletes," one writer told me. "I don't know why that is exactly. Maybe it's because so few of them have been to college, compared to other sports. That's not to say that football players get great educations, but something of that academic atmosphere does seem to rub off on them. All their lives, baseball players have been told they're something special, and a lot of them have never gotten out there into the bigger world for a dose of humility." Whatever the reason, writers thought baseball players were the most conceited group of pro athletes. Of course, some were better-liked than others. Local writers found Dante Bichette, the Rockies right fielder, always available for his own brand of zany, spaced-out, surfer-boy quote. Bryn Smith, while he was with the team, was accessible, as was Eric Young.

Compounding the problem, a couple of local writers told me, was the fact that, collectively, the Rockies weren't a very bright bunch. "This is the story we can't write, but the Rockies are, without question, the stupidest bunch of athletes I've ever covered," one beat writer told me. "That's one reason they were available in the expansion draft. You need to be able to think at least a little to play this game, and some of these guys can't do that." The lack of mental candlepower added to some players' arrogance, the writer told me.

There were obvious exceptions. Joe Girardi, the catcher, got his industrial engineering degree from Northwestern University in 1986. He was articulate, affable and most always accessible. Eric Young had an undergraduate business degree from Rutgers. He got his degree in eight semesters while playing on the school's football and baseball teams. As a general rule, these guys made for the best interview subjects. But there were other players who, while nice enough, couldn't utter a coherent sentence if their lives depended on it.

In terms of arrogance, the most notorious major league baseball player was also arguably the best in the business—Barry Bonds of the San Francisco Giants. A local writer approached Bonds near the Mile High Stadium batting cage one evening, during the Giants first trip to Denver. Before the writer could utter a word, Bonds snapped: "Move, man. You're standing in my light." When told that story, one ex-Rockies executive who knew Bonds laughed and shook his head. "Fucking Barry. He's an amazing talent, but his brain's in his dick."

None of this comes as a big surprise. We've read about well-monied athletes and their arrogance for years. From my observations over the course of one season, much of what sportswriters wrote about baseball players is true. But at times, I had to question the writers' motives. How could sportswriters—rumpled, cynical, overweight and underpaid as a breed—not resent these sleek, rich young men with their BMWs, cellular phones and Armani suits?

In the clubhouse one day during spring training, someone on the Rockies walked up to Jim Armstrong of the *Post,* a beefy guy who was decked out in a bright new pair of running shoes. "Doesn't look like you'll use those much," he cracked. Armstrong, a good-natured sort, smiled. "Hell, man, these aren't running shoes. They're eating shoes!"

So, late in the season, I decided to try an experiment. I would wander around the Rockies clubhouse and ask the ballplayers what they thought about sportswriters. I had no idea what to expect. For the most part, when I had tried to interview players on topics not directly related to the game, they hadn't had much to say worth printing. I didn't know whether this topic would engage them or if they'd shy away from it as something sure to stir controversy.

The first player I approached was Alex Cole, a fleet outfielder with a penchant for making terrible plays at the worst possible moment. Cole always struck me as especially standoffish toward writers. Great, I thought. If he's got a chip on his shoulder, maybe he'll talk.

"Alex," I said as I approached his cubicle. "I'm with the *Denver Post . . .*" He started to wave me away like a bothersome gnat.

". . . but I'm not a sportswriter. I'm interested in doing a story on what ballplayers think of sportswriters." Cole's face lit up and he pointed to a padded folding chair at his side. "Pull up a chair, my man," he said with a grin.

"I don't talk to our reporters," he said as he pulled on his black warm-up jersey. "Right from the start, they just didn't cut us any slack. They got on Charlie (Hayes) especially bad, and that wasn't fair. People say 'hey, they didn't get on you, so what's your problem?' But they got on my teammates, and that's just as bad. They been on Charlie all year for no reason. He goes out there day in and day out and busts his ass. He plays hurt, and not just little things either. I just don't know why they feel like they got to do that. I guess they think people here want to hear negative stuff. This is our first year playing together. Hell, we'll make some mistakes here and there. Of course, they never say much about how we have to play on field conditions that are worse than almost anyplace else. They just write the shit. And then they wonder why people don't want to talk to them."

I hadn't heard about other guys who wouldn't talk. I asked Cole if there were others. "Well, I don't know, really. There are guys who suck up to the media. But this is my fourth year in the big leagues and I just don't feel like I have to suck up to them. I'd rather not do it. My philosophy is that the best press is no press, good game or bad."

Some sportswriters can dish out criticism but get thin-skinned when the tables are turned. When Cole's quotes about refusing to talk to reporters appeared in a story I wrote, several writers approached me with barbed comments. "Next time you should talk to some of us," said Jack Etkin, the *Rocky Mountain News* beat writer. "Cole hasn't refused to talk to us. We just rarely have the need to talk to him, except when he fucks up." *Post* sports editor, Mike Connelly, took me to task for writing what he thought was an unbalanced story, giving the players free shots at his writers. That was the precise point of the exercise, but I let the criticism slide.

I asked Cole if he could understand why tension between writers and players had boiled over in the New York Mets clubhouse over the course of the 1993 season. Writers had been threatened by players, and pitcher Bret Saberhagen sprayed bleach on a group of reporters. "Hell, yeah, I can understand the anger and frustration. Sometimes they come in and ask the stupidest questions and people just get fed up with it. They're always trying to make something out of nothing. Maybe I'd cut them a break if they'd cut some of the guys on the team a break."

Two stalls over from Cole, reserve outfield Daryl Boston sat chain-smoking Salems. Boston, a 6-3, 210-pounder with a stern countenance, appeared intimidating. But in fact he was one of the friendlier guys in the clubhouse, quick to smile and willing to talk. He'd been on the Mets the year before, when tensions started mounting between the swarming New York media and the hapless, overpaid team. So I asked him about it.

"What's happened there with the guys and the press doesn't surprise me at all. They got reporters there just hanging around looking for dirt. I mean, they hide behind walls and listen in on conversations. They print all sorts of stuff that's supposed to be off the record. They may tell you to your face that they won't print it, but it'll come out later, when it suits them. Like in a book. In New York, if it ain't dirt, it ain't going in the paper."

And what were Boston's impressions of the Denver media? "The press here is similar to New York, with the inaugural season and everything. Just the constant attention every day. Seems like there's 10, 20 reporters around all the time. It doesn't bother me too much. But someone like Andres Galarraga, everybody wants a piece of him. I see his face sometimes when another group of reporters goes over to talk to him. But 'Cat' (Galarraga's nickname) is such a good guy he don't know when to say no."

Boston said he dealt with reporters by ignoring what they wrote. "I don't read the papers anymore, just the boxscores in *USA Today*. That way you don't get mad when they write something bad, or get a big head when they start paying attention to you."

Boston's stall was next to that of Charlie Hayes, the third baseman who was having a great year on the field but a rocky year in the press. Writers started getting on Hayes early in the season for being overweight. They rode him as well for his scowling demeanor, his abruptness with fans, and his occasional lack of hustle on the field. Much of the criticism was justified. In San Diego one May evening, I was sitting in the Rockies dugout with a couple of other writers during batting practice. Hayes was standing on the dugout steps, adjusting his batting gloves. Two young boys leaned out over the dugout, pleading. "Mr. Hayes! Mr. Hayes! Can we please have your autograph?" Hayes didn't look up. "What day is it?" he mumbled. "Tuesday," the boys replied in unison. Hayes shook his head. "Naw, I never sign autographs on Tuesday," he said. "Come see me tomorrow." And he walked away.

Justified or not, all the printed criticism clearly rankled Charlie. At one point in the season, he boycotted reporters for a few days after *Post* sports columnist, Mark Kiszla, wrote a column about Hayes and his bad image. The column was well done, subtle and not unsympathetic to Hayes' plight. Charlie took it wrong, though, and clammed up for a time. But that was much earlier in the season, and based on what Cole had said about Hayes and the media, I thought Charlie might have some interesting things to say. I was wrong.

"All they do is try to sell papers," he said, standing up and walking away from me. Then, over his shoulder, he added, "I don't pay too much attention to it. I don't read the papers, man. I can't read. You know that. I don't know nothing about no reporters. Honest."

Next, I sought out Bruce Hurst, a recent arrival whose 14 big-league seasons included a World Series appearance with the Boston Red Sox in 1986, and a stint with the San Diego Padres. Hurst is a tall, round-shouldered guy with an easy smile and a relaxed manner. Dealing with the Boston media is no piece of cake, so I turned on my tape recorder and asked Hurst to expound on it. "I've always felt like there should be a line drawn between the person and the player," he said. "I'll get along with writers who for the most part don't cross that line, if they don't start taking personal shots at a guy in the press. If I pitch bad and you write that I pitched bad, fine. There's always a few writers that are going to be real cute, real sarcastic. It's their style. Earlier in my career, that hurt some. It bothered me. Now it's just somewhat annoying and you don't really pay attention. After so many years, you've been called everything, been labeled so many things. You just kinda don't put much stock in it. I guess the biggest problem with the media is that people read things the way one person interprets it. The truth sometimes gets lost in the shuffle.

"In Boston, they can be hard on you, no question. But I'd rather be there, in a place where the media is very competitive, than a San Diego, where there is just one paper and they dominate the information market."

I asked Hurst if he'd seen examples of writers bearing personal grudges against particular players. "Sure. I saw it happen in Boston. One of the high-profile writers there wrote that one of our pitchers was "as useless as a bag of doorknobs." The pitcher took exception to it, and confronted the writer. They had words, there was a lot of finger pointing and yelling. The writer, for the rest of the year, it didn't matter what that pitcher did, how well he performed, he just got blitzed. The pen is mightier than the sword, no question about it."

And what was his take on the Mets situation? "Sometimes it's just such a helpless feeling when you're a player and they cross the line and write all about your personal life. It's a helpless feeling because you have no recourse. They'll always get the last word. Always. Your only recourse is to try to be diplomatic and sometimes that really makes no difference. So guys can feel helpless. In New York, maybe the media crossed the line one too many times and guys didn't know what to do, and stupid things happened as a consequence."

I asked Hurst to elaborate on his imaginary line between the professional and the personal. "Well, there is a difference between Bruce Hurst the pitcher and Bruce Hurst the person. If they write something bad about Bruce Hurst the pitcher, then they're probably right more times than not—I probably was a bad pitcher that day. But if they cross the line and say I'm doing this as a person or I'm doing this and that off the field, or when they write that a guy's going through a divorce and that's why he's not playing well, I have a problem with that. I'm sure we could all go into our personal lives and there are plenty of skeletons in everyone's closet. You can color a person any which way you choose. But remember: this is just a game, a spectator sport, and that's all I want to read about when I pick up the paper to read about football or basketball. I don't want to read about who's going through a divorce. I'd rather just know what he is doing on the field."

Kent Bottenfield, a young pitcher the Rockies picked up midway through the season, took an approach diametrically opposed to Hurst's. "I'd rather the public know more about me as a person than as a ballplayer, so I don't mind that kind of question or story at all," he said. "Sometimes, at social occasions, people try to talk to me about baseball, and I really try to steer the conversation to other topics. I have other interests, I can speak intelligently, I think, about other subjects."

As Bottenfield saw it, the problems between athletes and reporters had deeper, societal origins. Simply put, people took sports too seriously. "A lot is expected of us as athletes. But we have bad days on the job like everyone else. I've seen the New York media just rip people brutally, and it's not fair. If a player won't talk, they get ripped. Baseball isn't anything like the presidency. What we do on the field isn't going to affect the nation, and yet sometimes the things we do or say are treated that way in the press."

Bottenfield was right. The local media poured resources into covering baseball that dwarfed the money and attention they gave to any other type of news. It never ceased to amaze me how many writers, broadcast reporters, cameramen and freelance radio types descended on the clubhouse following each game. It had all the trappings of a ritual dance, and it was interesting to observe. Although I rarely wrote a daily, breaking baseball story, I liked to join the swarm and go into the clubhouse after games just to see how the ritual played out.

As soon as the last out was recorded, reporters would leap from their seats, notebooks and tape recorders in hand, and hurry along the catwalk from the press box to a private elevator that dropped to the clubhouse entrances under the north stands of Mile High Stadium. Major league baseball rules allow a 10-minute "cooling off period" after each game, and regardless of the type of game it was, reporters were barred from the clubhouse by PR director, Mike Swanson, until those 10 minutes had elapsed. We stood around in a dark, dank space under the stands, 50 feet from the clubhouse door. A small, carpeted platform had been placed there for the opening homestand, but it hadn't been used since then. If a game ended early enough—before the 10 0'clock news—manager Don Baylor would emerge from the clubhouse still in uniform to do a quick post-game post-mortem for the cameras. Despite his commanding presence, Baylor was soft spoken, and people had to crowd close to hear him.

Baylor never failed to impress me with his frankness, even when it verged on being tactless. If a player had a bad game, he wouldn't hesitate to say it for the cameras and tape recorders. He didn't hide his feelings about players who frustrated him. One September evening, after Alex Cole misplayed a fly ball and turned it into an inside-the-park home run, Baylor just shook his head. "I didn't see the replay, did it hit his glove?" Everyone shook their heads. "No, it hit him in the shoulder," someone said. Baylor shook his head again. "Jesus," was all he said. Cole didn't play again for almost a week.

After the cameras were gone, Baylor would hold court for the writers. He'd be seated behind a cheap office-supply-store desk in his tiny office in the clubhouse, wearing a white, grey and black long-sleeve undershirt, leaning back in his swivel chair with his hands locked behind his head. He'd done nothing to personalize the place; there were no photos of his family, no inspirational sayings, no posters. He seemed to like it that way. He'd answer questions for

10 or 15 minutes in a relaxed manner, praising those who'd played well and making a few tart comments about those who hadn't.

When the Baylor session ended, the reporters would fan out into the clubhouse seeking interviews with heroes and goats. Players who wanted to avoid the media could hide in the trainer's room or the dining area, both of which were off limits to reporters. Post-game interviews represented pack journalism at its worst. If one guy went over to talk to a particular player, many of the rest would follow. This was especially true of the video cameras. They all had to be in the same place at the same time.

One day in late September, light-hitting shortstop Freddie Benavides smashed a three-run homer in the eighth inning to propel the Rockies to a 6-5 victory over the eventual National League Champion, Philadelphia Phillies. The big hit broke a nine-game Rockies home losing streak, and the clubhouse was a raucous place. Benavides, who wasn't used to the spotlight, sat in a chair by his stall sipping a Diet Coke, an avocado-green towel wrapped around his waist and bags of ice on his knees. He was hemmed in on all sides by cameras, tape recorders and mikes, and he looked alarmed. "When I hit it, I knew I hit it real hard," he said. "But I don't have much experience hitting them out, so I didn't know it was out 'til it went over the fence."

"And how did it feel, Freddie?" came the inevitable, inane question from somewhere deep in the pack. The proper answer would have been, "How do you think it felt, moron?" but Benavides was an obliging sort. "Great. It's always a great feeling to help win a game like that."

Players, even those as green as Benavides, had learned somewhere along the line how to deal with the media. There's a scene in the baseball movie *Bull Durham* where the grizzled catcher, played by Kevin Costner, is coaching the raw rookie, played by Tim Robbins, on how to deal with reporters. He teaches him all the hackneyed cliches that ballplayers never fail to trot out during interviews. "Well, I'm just happy to be here and I'll do everything I can to help this club win." I found that scene to be remarkably true to life. When writers walked over to a player, it was as if the player switched to autopilot, and the cliche program in his brain kicked in. Eventually, I learned that if I just sat and chatted for a few minutes, phrased the same question a few different ways, sooner or later I'd get a more straightforward answer.

There were some subjects, however, that few people wanted to address. Chief among them was tobacco in the clubhouse. When it came to ballplayers and chewing tobacco, the Rockies, and probably other ballclubs as well, took hypocrisy to a new level. On June 15, 1993, major league baseball clubs imposed a ban on smokeless tobacco use by their minor league affiliates. The stuff was forbidden in clubhouses, dugouts or on the field. But thanks to the strength of the players' union, the Major League Baseball Players Association, the ban didn't extend to the majors. Quite the contrary in fact.

In a storage room off the Rockies clubhouse, cases of a half-dozen brands of leaf and dip chewing tobacco dominated a row of metal shelves. When I started asking what I thought were innocuous questions about who supplied the stuff, people clammed up fast.

"I'm not going to talk about that," snapped Chico, the dictatorial clubhouse manager. "It would be cutting my own throat. They ban smoking, they ban everything, and now you want me to talk about giving these guys tobacco? I don't think it's something that needs to be talked about." So, having struck out with Chico, I climbed the corporate ladder to general manager, Bob Gebhard. Geb, as he was widely known, usually was good for a quick quote. Although he sometimes danced around issues, at other times he could be surprisingly frank. As someone who was fighting a never-ending battle to kick the cigarette habit, I thought Geb might be pretty frank about the issue of tobacco in the clubhouse. But he got edgy with me too.

"Some things aren't necessarily public knowledge," he said, adding that he had no idea who supplied the "chew"—leaf tobacco chewed in large wads—and "dip"—snuff used in small quantities between the lower lip and gum. "I know we do not buy it for the players. In the past, companies sent free samples of different products to teams. That's probably what's happening here, but I honestly don't know."

So I called the National League offices in New York, and spoke with Katy Feeney, one of their public relations operatives. She told me the league prohibited teams from "having chewing tobacco sitting around in bins for players to grab for free," but said it was unclear whether it was permissible for teams to keep it on hand for players who asked for it. "How could we prevent tobacco companies from sending free samples?" she asked.

Although several people insisted major manufacturers of smokeless tobacco did send free sample to ballclubs, Alan Hillburg, spokesman for the Smokeless Tobacco Council, said companies definitely steered clear of that practice. "But that's not to say local distributors don't do it," he said, leaving himself a clever out.

Well, my curiosity had now been aroused. There's nothing like having people blow smoke in your face, so to speak, to make you want to get some straight answers. After several interviews in which I agreed to protect my sources' identities, (though I don't know why they were so hesitant to talk about something so essentially unimportant on the record) I learned that the system in the Rockies clubhouse probably worked something like this: Chico either got free samples of the stuff from distributors or bought it in large quantities out of his own pocket. If that was the case, players either paid him for it as they used it, or factored the service into the tip ballplayers traditionally give clubhouse managers at the end of the season.

Either way, being a tobacco connection kept Chico busy, because over half the Rockies players chewed or dipped. Coaches, some team executives, and even some of the beat writers also indulged in the unsightly habit. Major league baseball runs programs during spring training each year to teach players about the inherent risks in using smokeless tobacco, but its use has continued to increase year after year. Dr. Greg Connolly, a dentist who ran the Massachusetts Health Department's Tobacco Control Program, has been lecturing big-league ballplayers since 1986 on the dangers of chewing and dipping. He told me an estimated 12 million people in the United States, one-quarter of them children and teens, use smokeless tobacco regularly.

"Nolan Ryan told me that when he first came up, in the late 1960s, about a third of the guys smoked, and only one or two guys on any given club chewed," Connolly said. "No one dipped snuff. Teams had their own favorite brands of cigarettes, more often than not the brand that sponsored the team, had its advertising in the stadium, and so forth." During the 1980s, Ryan told Connolly, smoking among players declined dramatically, as did the use of chew, but dip became increasingly popular. Ryan attributed the change to free samples of dip coming into clubhouses. Some clubs imposed an outright ban on accepting free samples, Connolly said, most notably the Philadelphia Phillies, whose trainer, Jeff Cooper, was an ally of Connolly's.

During spring training in 1993, Connolly went on the usual training camp lecture circuit, but this time he brought with him 28-year-old Rick Bender, who suffered from mouth cancer, and who had lost a significant portion of his lower jaw during eight hours of surgery. Connolly said Bender was an eloquent speaker, and succeeded in shocking some players straight, at least temporarily. "I knew he was effective after we went and talked to the Phillies," Connolly recalled. "My yardstick was Lenny Dykstra, who goes through four pouches of chew a day. After listening to Rick, he lasted through the sixth inning before he popped some into his mouth."

To Connolly, the great villain in all this is U.S. Tobacco, manufacturer of SKOAL and Copenhagen, the two most popular brands of dip. "They were a dying company until they started marketing these products to kids in the early 1980s," he said. "Now what we've got is an epidemic of dip use among high school and college athletes." Connolly wrote a scathing commentary about the marketing campaign in the March 1992 issue of the *American Journal of Public Health*.

"In countless neighborhood grocery stores, gas stations and truck stops across the country, these products are displayed at check-out counters alongside the candy and cough drops," Connolly wrote. "There is even a shredded chewing gum called Big League Chew that prepares very young mouths for the future chewing of tobacco. The introduction in 1983 of SKOAL Bandits, an easy-to-use tea bag of snuff, with the slogan "Take a pouch instead of a puff" has made it extremely convenient for teenagers to take up the habit. The "Bandit" is a low-nicotine teaching tool that allows novices to slowly develop tolerance to the toxic effects of the alkaloid. As one industry brochure says: "Like your first beer, SKOAL Bandits can be a taste that takes time to acquire and get the most out of." Once a "taste" is acquired new dippers gradually move to the more potent and addictive brands of snuff, such as SKOAL and Copenhagen."

The problem with all this, said Connolly, is that dip is more than addictive. Mouth cancer, gum recession and chronic mouth lesions have been linked to prolonged use of smokeless tobacco. Dip is the worst, he said, because it contains far more nicotine than leaf tobacco. According to the National Cancer Institute, smokeless tobacco contains 28 cancer-causing substances. Federal health officials have linked smokeless tobacco to nearly 75 percent of the 30,000 new cases of oral cancer diagnosed in the U.S. in 1992.

"It's the stupidest thing in the world for a team like the Rockies to have tobacco in the clubhouse for players," Connolly said. "If you use this stuff for 30 years, your chances are pretty good of developing mouth cancer."

As you might expect, Hillburg of the Smokeless Tobacco Council pooh-poohed Connolly's warnings as the hysterical rantings of a fringe lunatic. One thing research has shown consistently, Hillburg said, is that youngsters who start using smokeless tobacco don't do so because they've seen ballplayers doing it. "Five studies since 1986, all conducted by critics of smokeless tobacco, show kids using smokeless tobacco had nothing to do with professional athletes and everything to do with peers or parents introducing them to it," he said.

Connolly conducted a survey in the late 1980s and found that 34 percent of big-league players regularly used smokeless tobacco. Dip was far more prevalent than chew. A third of the steady users reported they had regular problems with their gums, or had sores or white spots in their mouths.

One regular dipper on the Rockies was relief pitcher, Darren Holmes, the star of a shaky bullpen. Holmes had been quoted early in the season saying he was going to quit dipping, so I asked him how he felt about smokeless tobacco. "It was the biggest mistake I ever made in my life to start in with this stuff," Holmes said as he dressed for a game. "It's bad. It's bad for you. It's a terrible habit and nothing good can come from it." Holmes, who was 27 during the inaugural season, said he started chewing leaf tobacco 20 years earlier as a boy growing up on a North Carolina farm. Eventually, he graduated to dip. He did in fact quit as promised early in the season, but started back up again. "I didn't really miss it when I quit, but I started eating everything in sight. In two weeks I gained 10 pounds, so I started up again. I'll quit in the off-season, when I can afford to gain weight."

Holmes said one of his main motivations for quitting was fear of providing a negative role model for kids. "I'm a Christian, and I believe it's something that hinders me, so I don't want to pass that on to other people. I've had little kids come up to me and show me their tin of SKOAL. I don't want them looking up to me and saying, 'Well, Darren Holmes does it, so it must be OK for me to do it.'"

The minor league ban imposed in mid-1993 kicked up a hell of a ruckus. The Phoenix Firebirds, the San Francisco Giants Triple A team, retaliated against baseball by refusing to sign autographs or do interviews for a few weeks. If that sounds nonsensical, it is, but the players seemed to think it was an effective form of protest to punish kids and writers. Even late in the season, minor league players were still bitching and moaning. "The problem was they announced the ban June 2, effective June 15," said Chris Costello, spokesman for the Colorado Springs Sky Sox, the Rockies Triple A Club. "It gave guys a two-week window to kick a habit."

But Costello had found a bright spot nonetheless: Dugout floors in the minor leagues were no longer nauseating swamps of brown spit mixed with sunflower seeds. "Let's put it this way: Our clean-up crew is a lot happier these days."

When my story on tobacco appeared in *The Denver Post* in early September, I hoped it would have some impact, perhaps forcing the Rockies to clean up their act and get the free tobacco out of the clubhouse, or at least to look into how it got there. No such luck. Nothing changed. So much for the power of the press.

Baseball is a game of mysterious rituals and strange secrets. I found it surprisingly difficult to get people to discuss some of these things. The issue of tobacco was one everyone tried to ignore, for obvious reasons: it was embarrassing. But I couldn't figure out why people in the know were so balky about discussing mud.

Without question, Lena Blackburne's Rubbing Mud was one of the game's most obscure secrets. For no particularly good reason, the powers-that-be in the national pastime didn't want to say much about it. Trying to learn about the mud, which is rubbed into every baseball ever used in a game, was a lot like trying to pry the secrets of nuclear weapons technology out of a government scientist. It was in fact used to "de-gloss" factory-fresh baseballs, so that pitchers could get a good grip. The American League had used Lena Black-burne mud exclusively since 1938, and the National League hopped on the bandwagon in 1955. No one seemed to know why only Blackburne mud was used.

"It's just a soft, cold-cream-like mud," said Katy Feeney, a spokeswoman for the National League. "It's dug, sifted and stored by one guy. It comes from Pennsauken Creek off the Delaware River in New Jersey." But the exact location was a closely guarded secret. Ah-ha, I thought when I learned of its general location. They must dig the stuff up next to some factory discharge pipe. Time to investigate how many former big-league pitchers have contracted horrible skin disorders on their hands, or maybe even some rare form of cancer. But no, that would be too logical.

The sole purveyor of the fine, silty clay was a man named Burns Bintliff, who may or may not live in west-central Florida. I tried to track him down, but he wasn't listed in the phone book, and the only Bintliff in the region said he thought Burns was his uncle, but he wasn't sure. "I think he's my dad's brother," said Gary Bintliff when I got him on the phone. "He's hard to find. I get a lot of calls about him. In fact, I should probably try to get the number myself so I don't have to pester my dad about it."

Feeney was willing to share her limited knowledge about the mud, but said Bintliff absolutely, positively wouldn't give interviews. She even balked at contacting him to see if he'd make an exception for an enterprising reporter in an expansion city. If in fact she made the contact, Bintliff never called back.

According to a 1991 *Los Angeles Times* article, Bintliff got into the mud business through family connections. He was the son-in-law of a man named John Haas. Haas was a boyhood friend of Russell Aubrey (Lena) Blackburne, a coach with the Philadelphia Athletics in the 1930s. Blackburne discovered the mother lode of perfect mud near his New Jersey home. Legend had it that Haas and Blackburne harvested the mud once each year but, of course, no one knew exactly when that was. Bintliff had carried on the tradition. After harvesting, the mud was packed in white plastic quart containers with screw-on lids.

One quart was shipped to each major league team during spring training. Often, that one quart would last the entire season. Occasionally, Marty Stelnaker said, a team had to order a second quart, but that was rare. Umpires used to rub all the balls to be used in a game, but in the big leagues, that time-consuming chore had been passed on to clubhouse attendants. For the Rockies, the mud man was Marty Stelnaker, who looked after the umpiring crews while they were in Denver. Stelnaker, far more articulate and affable than most of the clubhouse people, was eager to show me the mud, and how the rubbing ritual was performed.

Several hours before each home game, Stelnaker gathered six dozen brand-new Rawlings baseballs, which used to be assembled in

Haiti, but in 1993 at least, came from Costa Rica. Ballplayers called the unrubbed, bright-white balls pearls. Stelnaker took the pearls to a back storage room off the clubhouse. There, he reached high up on a shelf and pulled down the mud container from its hiding place. "This stuff is kind of a sought-after commodity," he confided. "If I leave it lying around out in the open, it tends to disappear."

Stelnaker pulled up a couple of chairs alongside a huge, industrial-sized washer and dryer. He unscrewed the lid on the container and showed me the mud—a deep, dark secret revealed. It was not a defining moment in my life. It looked like plain old, everyday mud—dark as night and gooey. When it was rubbed on a pearl, it gave the ball a slightly brownish cast. Stelnaker had to nurture that mud, making sure there was water in the container to keep it from drying into an impenetrable mass.

"It takes me maybe 25 minutes to rub up six dozen balls," he said as he pulled a pearl from its cardboard carton. "There's not much to it, really." Ah, but what's a baseball ritual without a little saliva? He cupped his palm and spit into it. Then he scooped two fingers into the container and brought forth a small quantity of the mud. He mixed it with his spit, then spread the mixture on a pearl. The next step was the most important. "Now I cup it in my hands, apply pressure and rotate the ball 360 degrees to get an even spread and to bring up the hide a little. Once I've done that, I rotate the ball 45 degrees, and do it again. Here, you try it." He tossed me a pearl. I spit into my right palm, and reached my left hand into the container. The mud was cold and slimy and very finely textured. I mixed it with my spit, then spread it around the ball. "Really press down," Stelnaker coached. "You want the horsehide to come up, that's what gives the pitcher a grip." It was hard work. When we finished the task, we washed our hands with a stiff scrub brush at a laundry sink. "This stuff is hard to get off," he remarked.

Pitchers valued the mud, or at least what it did for them, even though most didn't know much about the stuff. Bruce Ruffin, a Rockies left-hander who wandered by while we were rubbing up the balls, said he couldn't pitch with a pearl. "It'd be too slick. This stuff helps you get a grip. Especially if your hand is moist, the mud really helps you grip the ball. If you pitch in Atlanta or somewhere humid, you sweat plenty and can grip the ball great. Here, the heat is so dry, you sweat and it dries off real fast. I've had to start chewing gum while I pitch so I can lick my fingers to keep them moist."

And what did Ruffin know about the mud? "I know it comes from the Mississippi, right?" he asked. Wrong.

"Oh, well. Then I guess I don't know much about it."

"Join the club," I said.

If the clubhouse was the place where baseball's secrets were kept, then the trainer's room was the nerve center of the clubhouse. No one was more important to the on-field performance of a major league baseball team than its trainer. In Denver, that role belonged to Dave Cilladi, a wispy, 31-year-old Wally Cox look-alike who had more than his share of work during the team's inaugural season. Normally, the trainer's room was strictly off-limits to the press. It was the place players could go sulk if they wanted to avoid reporters, or have their aches and pains attended to without dozens of pairs of eyes looking on. But one day Cilladi granted me an audience in his lair, several hours before a night game, at a time when few players were around.

Cilladi may have been the Rockies most valuable player in 1993, when you consider the seriousness of injuries suffered by some of the team's most important players. David Nied, the great pitching hope of the future, partially tore a ligament in his elbow in early June, and first baseman (and National League batting champ), Andres Galarraga, suffered two serious leg injuries, one to a hamstring, the other to a knee. But Cilladi, in concert with doctors under contract to the team, got them both back into action in relatively short order.

Yes, Cilladi was a key player, but he never got any cheers from the crowd. In fact, his appearance on the field, usually at a dead sprint, always caused the fans to let out a collective groan. That's because he appeared only when a player was in trouble. But Cilladi's most important work took place off the field, far from where fans could see him.

From his windowless office, Cilladi ministered to the chronic aches and pains that inevitably plagued ballplayers over the course of a 162-game season. It wasn't the torn hamstrings, injured elbows and blown-out shoulders that could wear a team down, according to Cilladi. It was the little things.

"These guys play hurt. They have to. No one in the stands realizes what it feels like to get hit by a 90-mile-per-hour fastball. A guy gets hit in the arm and runs to first base. You very seldom see a player even touch it. It might be the second inning. Now they're gonna have to play seven more innings with an arm that's probably swollen and tender as hell. It bruises, it stiffens up, and they play right through it. Then they come in after the game for treatment, and a lot of the time, I can see the imprint from the thread marks on the baseball on the bruises."

Icing the bruise after the game reduces the pain and swelling a bit. But when the player comes back to the park the next day, the arm might be so stiff he can't lift it over his head. So it's more ice, and then out to the field. "The fan who comes to the park that next day has no idea what happened the day before," Cilladi said. "This guy keeps playing and playing. His arm's going to keep hurting for three or four days. Now on top of that, the same player might turn an ankle running the bases, and no one ever knows that because he keeps playing. They have to play every day, and they have to play with a lot of pain, because that's the nature of the sport. They get paid to play. They know that. They want to play. That's where you really see the competitiveness of the professional athlete. Hurt or not, they want to play."

During the course of a season, every player suffers from a number of lingering maladies. The most common, typically, are low-grade pains in the elbow and shoulder. "Because everyone has to throw, that's the most common pain, for all positions. Arms go through peaks and valleys. There will be a period of time when the team plays in hot weather and everything feels good. Then a player may have to make a throw from deep in the outfield or deep from shortstop and ugh! The arm starts hurting. So now they're back in a valley where their arm hurts for four or five days. We treat it a little bit, try to help the pain, ease it a little bit. Then all of a sudden it gets better, until the same thing happens again. Ice is the saving grace here. Ice helps some of the soreness, and helps them recover for the next day."

Cilladi backed into his career as an athletic trainer. "Growing up, I was always involved in sports. I was a high school wrestler and went to Kent State University on a wrestling scholarship. I knew I was never going to be a professional athlete, and the more I thought about it, the more I realized that I was never going to make any money if I ended up as a high school wrestling coach. So I decided that I'd better give up athletics and do something I could have some fun in and still be around sports, but that would take me a lot farther than just being a coach or some sort of amateur athlete."

Athletic training seemed like the way to go. So he transferred to Penn State University, and earned a bachelor's degree in health education in 1984. In 1985, he was hired by the Chicago Cubs as a trainer for the Class A Peoria Chiefs. The next year, he was promoted to the big club, where he served as assistant trainer until signing on with the Rockies for the 1993 season. Before going to work for the Cubs, Cilladi had never worked in baseball. At Penn State, he worked primarily with the powerhouse football team, and occasionally with the basketball squad.

Baseball, he quickly learned, posed a unique set of challenges to a trainer. "First of all, a football team at the college level has over 100 players, and at the pro level 48. On a baseball team you have 25. And for the most part, all 25 players have to be prepared to play every single day. On a football team, if you have an injury, you have more guys to fall back on." The 162-game schedule makes life tough as well. In other sports, athletes with injuries get time to recover. Baseball trainers have to get their athletes ready to play the day after they suffer a minor injury.

For that reason, conditioning for baseball is unique. During spring training and over the course of the season, most players get in shape and stay in shape by doing little else than playing the game. Some players get involved in distance running for endurance, but Cilladi said he never stresses aerobics as an essential part of baseball conditioning. "Everything we do has to be for a purpose. If they're gonna go out and run all this distance, it does not serve a purpose in baseball. We have them go out and run sprints, but of only maybe 90 or 120 feet, because that's how they're gonna run the bases.

"We have to condition them to do what we call angular running. They're not gonna run in a straight line too often. From first to second base is pretty straight, but if they go from first to third or second to home, it's running at an angle. And sprinting all out isn't something we stress too much. If you watch a game, look and see how many times a player runs at 100 percent. Not too often. It's controlled running. Yeah, they'll go from home plate to first base 100 percent sometimes. And defensively, they'll go 100 percent to break for a ball. But once they're close to it, they'll slow down. When they're running from first to second base, they have to look for the ball, so they may not be going 100 percent that whole distance. So in short, we try to condition the athlete to play the actual game. Everything we do conditioning-wise you can take straight out of a baseball game." Running bases, throwing the ball and swinging the bat are the main features of a Cilladi baseball conditioning program.

During the off-season, many ballplayers do weight training to build strength. But when the season starts, only the most dedicated fitness buffs stick with a weight-training regimen. "The whole idea is for them to be strong to play the baseball game. We don't want to wear them out in the weight room so they can't go out and play."

Cilladi served as team nutritionist and dietician as well. "If in the off-season a player calls us and says he's worried about gaining weight, we'll send them stuff on how they should eat, what they should stay away from, and what time of day they should eat. The problem with baseball is if the game ends at 10:00 or 10:30 p.m., they don't eat until 11:00 or 11:30. Then they go home, go to bed.

Ideally, we try to make sure the meal we serve them in here after the game is nutritional, not too heavy for them. If they're going to eat something heavy, we suggest they stay up a little bit where they get a chance to digest some before going to bed."

Cilladi always suggested that his players eat their biggest meal of the day four hours before game time. For a night game starting at 7:05, that meant having a big lunch in the mid-afternoon. Ballplayers tend to sleep in until about 11:00, so many eat breakfast when most people eat lunch, then they have a late lunch.

In his years with the Cubs and his first season in Colorado, Cilladi saw a lot of players return from the off-season with some funny ideas about fitness regimens. "What happens is these players meet with people in the off-season who have new ideas, things that they think are going to work. There are programs out there, for instance, that are incorporated with karate. You'll see a guy doing balancing acts on walls with one leg, sort of like The Karate Kid. I had a pitcher that would put five gallon buckets on the floor and then do push-ups off the buckets, which I thought was a little strange. But most often what you see is players coming in with a whole line of sports drinks and pills and powders and candy bars. They think this is what's going to make them a winning pitcher. And they take them for two or three weeks, every day, religiously, and it's a lot of money they spend on this stuff. Then they find out nothing happens. So then they try something else and that doesn't work, so they go onto the next thing."

Ask any boy in America if he'd like to be a batboy for a major league baseball team and he'd almost certainly answer with a resounding "Yes!" The job has a glamorous image. After all, batboys get to hobnob with the players, and watch games from the unequaled vantage point of the dugout or on-deck circle. But there's another way to look at the job as well. How would a typical boy respond if someone were to sidle up to him and say, "Hey, kid, want a job that involves shining 30 pairs of shoes a day, washing loads of filthy laundry until after midnight and scrubbing toilets, all for $4.25 an hour?"

Doesn't sound so glamorous, does it? But that's what the job actually entails. It's drudge work for slave wages, but the five Denver-area teens who were selected as inaugural season batboys would have fought to the death to keep their jobs anyway.

"I told my dad, before I even went in for the interview, I said, 'I don't care, they don't have to pay me a thing and I'll still do it,'" said David Adams, 16, a Regis High School student and one of three batboys who worked out of the home-team clubhouse.

But Jon Sites, a 17-year-old Overland High School student, took a more pragmatic approach. "I love this. I wouldn't trade it for anything. But no way I'd do it for free. I need the money."

So, how did these kids land such plum jobs? It took luck, good grades, connections or a combination of the three. Applicants had to be at least 16, have a *B* or better grade average, and be available to work all 81 home games.

Adams and Sites got their jobs the hard way—by writing letters to Rockies general manager, Bob Gebhard, then going through interviews with Chico, who was a batboy with the Minnesota Twins a decade before. "I read somewhere that there were 500 applicants, 15 people got interviewed, and five got the job," Adams said one afternoon, seated in front of catcher Joe Girardi's locker. "I saw that and I said, 'How I ever got my letter through against 500 people and got the call, I'll never know.'"

Two other batboys, Dustin Gallegos, 16, of Horizon High School, and Sven Offerson, 17, a Faith Christian Academy student, worked as batboys for the minor-league Denver Zephyrs in 1992. "Knowing people and having experience definitely helped," Gallegos said. The fifth batboy, Rob Alvarado, a 16-year-old Cherry Creek High School student, was the son of Linda Alvarado, a limited partner in the Rockies ownership group. Alvarado worked in the visiting clubhouse, and his boss, Keith Schulz, said he was hired because of his qualifications, not his lineage. But even Alvarado didn't buy that line.

A Rockies batboy's workday was long and arduous. For a night game, the five arrived at Mile High Stadium as early as possible—

1:00 p.m. if there was no school and by 3:00 on school days. "Before the game we cater to the players' needs. Whatever they need, we get it," Gallegos said. "If they want a Coke, and they don't feel like getting up and getting it, they ask us for it, and there's no hesitation. We go and get it. If they're missing something, we look for it until we find it."

During each game, one batboy worked the dugout, retrieving bats and helmets and running errands. Another sat in the bullpen, chasing down foul balls and protecting the bullpen catcher from line drives while he warmed up relief pitchers. The third home-team batboy worked the clubhouse, washing batting-practice laundry and getting the post-game meal set out.

"The laundry seems like it never ends," Sites said.

Once the game was over, the real grind began. First came the shoe polishing. After each game, the batboys polished the shoes of every player and coach, with the exception of outfielder Jerald Clark. "He gets mad if we do his shoes," Sites said. "He likes to do his own." By the time they finished with the shoes, the players were long gone. Then it was time to wash game uniforms and clean the clubhouse. "It goes quickly when you've got the music going and you're laughing and talking," Gallegos said. "People say 'Oh, man, you've got do all that?' But it's fun. I've only known these guys (the other batboys) for maybe two months, and I can already say that we know each other pretty well."

I asked the three home clubhouse batboys what they considered the worst part of their jobs. All three said there was nothing bad about being a batboy, except working until after midnight. And the best thing? "Just being around the players," said Sites, a chubby, freckled redhead.

"Yeah," Adams agreed. "And the fact that I can go out there and say—well, all of us can say—we were part of the inaugural year of the Colorado Rockies. Nobody else can say that."

"Yeah," Sites said. "We're the answer to a trivia question!"

"The best thing for me," Gallegos said, "is being in the dugout. You're standing right there next to Don Zimmer and the skipper, and you hear them talking about, like, 'well, should we get Tatum up for a pinch hitter or Castellano?' You're right there. It's like we're part of the team.

"You can laugh about it, but I'm sure that picture of the inaugural season team will go into the Hall of Fame. I'll be the first Horizon High School student to be in the Hall of Fame. I just can't stress enough what an opportunity this is. It's a really great thing."

The batboys said despite the long hours and the major distraction the job created, the quality of their schoolwork didn't slip. But they admitted life got easier once school let out for summer. "I kind of expected my grades to suffer, because to tell the truth, I had a lot of trouble with homework," Adams said. "I was just too tired or spaced out or whatever. We never get out of here until about 12:30, and I was having to get up an hour early, at like 6:30, to get my homework done. But then I took my exams and I did very well."

Batboys were assigned for the season to either the home or visiting clubhouse by Chico. The three batboys who worked the Rockies clubhouse said they wouldn't have traded their jobs to work the visitor's side. "Over there, they've got each team for maybe eight days all year," Gallegos said. "They really can't get to know them. Here, every day we come in and it's the same guys. We can come up and say, 'Hey, what's up, Joe?' (to Girardi) And he knows your name." Some Rockies players tipped the batboys, others gave them equipment. Girardi, they said, gave them shoes he got through his contract with Nike. And Charlie Hayes gave Adams a pair of $120 Oakley sunglasses early in the summer.

But over on the visitors' side, Alvarado and Offerson said their jobs were the plum assignments. They liked meeting the visiting stars. Most, they said, had been courteous, and they tipped generously as they left. "And if there's somebody you really don't like, he's gone in four days," Alvarado said.

They agreed that the rambunctious Phillies were the most fun to be around, and that the San Francisco Giants were the nicest bunch of guys. Even the notoriously arrogant Barry Bonds, the $43 million superstar?

Offerson and Alvarado shot each other a quick glance. "Ummmm . . ." they both said, and started to laugh. They couldn't say what they were thinking, because Bonds and the Giants had another trip into Denver later that summer.

"Well, Will Clark was great," Alvarado said.

"Yeah, he was a good guy," Offerson echoed.

CHAPTER SEVEN

LIFE ON THE ROAD I: CAUTIONARY TALES

Big-league baseball players get paid handsomely for playing a game that many people claim they'd play for free. It's a glamorous life, filled with riches, fame and adulation. There's nothing like being young, gifted and rich, after all.

But playing baseball is a job, and baseball's season is brutally long. Players report for spring training in late February, and by the time they go home for the winter in October, they've played in 162 games, spent the equivalent of four months or more on the road, and logged tens of thousands of air miles. Ballplayers lead a gypsy's life. Few of them put down roots in the cities where they play, which means they're actually away from home for all but about 3½ months of the year. Married players with children spend the winter at home, but once spring training starts, many of them don't see their families much until the summer—when their wives and kids come to live with them during that part of the season that doesn't overlap with school time. But ballplayers spend a lot of time on their own.

I thought going on some road trips with the Rockies would

give me insight into what it's like to be a millionaire migrant worker. So I tagged along, as an official member of the traveling press corps, on three Rockies trips: one to San Diego and Los Angeles in May, one to Chicago and Miami in July, and the final trip of the year, to San Francisco and Atlanta in late September and early October. I stayed in the team hotels, went out to the park four hours before game time, arriving at about the same time as the team bus, and wandered the strange cities alone in my spare time. These trips also gave me the opportunity to explore the culture of baseball in other cities. In each of the cities we visited, I found some interesting cautionary tales for the Rockies, as they strove to build an organization, and a Denver baseball culture, that would thrive over the next century. I found exemplary (at least by my standards) baseball operations in Los Angeles and Chicago, places that had refused to let the entertainment aspects of the "total baseball package," as the marketing people called it, overwhelm the beauty of the game itself. I found troubled organizations in San Francisco and San Diego, where fan apathy threatened the future of baseball, and where, in San Diego at least, parsimonious owners added to the apathy as they stripped a fine team down to almost nothing. In Miami, I found another expansion club trying to build an identity in a part of the country that had almost nothing in common with Denver.

There's a lot to tell about all these places. But first, a few observations on team travel. Despite the grind of 81 road games a season, it's hard to pity ballplayers too much, for when they travel, it's in a manner entirely different from that to which you or I are accustomed. On the day the Rockies were scheduled to leave on a road trip, players would show up at Mile High Stadium with suitcases packed and ready to go. Packing was about the only thing they had to do for themselves. They'd park their luxury or sports cars in a fenced, guarded lot adjacent to the clubhouse. Their bags would be taken from their cars and loaded onto an air-conditioned bus. After the game, the players would shower and change into their traveling clothes. Manager Don Baylor required all players and coaches to wear jackets, ties, and dress slacks on "getaway days." Then they'd climb aboard the bus for the 20-minute drive to Stapleton Airport.

At the airport, a Continental Airlines chartered jet would be awaiting them, fueled and ready to go. The bus would drive the team out onto the tarmac. Players never had to go through a security check, walk down a long concourse hallway, deal with ticket agents or mothers with yowling infants, or get mobbed by autograph seekers. Each would walk up the steps onto the plane, grab an entire row of seats, and relax during the flight. When they arrived at their destination, they'd repeat the process in reverse. A bus would be awaiting them on the airport tarmac. They'd board the bus and ride it to a luxury hotel, where traveling-secretary Peter Durso would hand them room keys. Their bags, which they hadn't seen since handing them over at the stadium in Denver, would be delivered to their rooms.

Not a bad life, all in all, but still, so much travel did get tiresome. And after awhile, it didn't matter how nice the hotel was. "When you travel as much as we do, what's the difference between an Intercontinental and a Motel 6?" said veteran pitcher, Bruce Hurst. "They both have a bed and a shower."

Durso, the man in charge of all these arrangements, had one of the more interesting, and lesser-known, jobs in the organization. Imagine trying to juggle six knives at once with people tugging at your sleeve. That's what Durso's job was like. Perhaps that explained why he often seemed in a sour mood, scurrying through the clubhouse, shoulders hunched, cigarette dangling from his lips, looking much older than his 42 years.

Officially, Durso was the Rockies traveling secretary, a job he had held previously with the Chicago Cubs for seven years and the Montreal Expos for six. But that humble title didn't begin to describe the wide variety of tasks he performed. Sure, he booked hotels and charter flights for the team, but he also dispensed meal money, got game tickets for players' friends and families as well as for shameless media moochers, arranged for rental cars for players on the road, looked after the needs of reporters and broadcasters traveling with the team, and acted as a readily accessible restaurant and entertainment guide to each of the 13 road cities.

"It used to be you'd come into one of these cities, play the games and leave," Durso told me in rapid-fire New Yorkese as we relaxed in his smoke-filled, non-smoking suite at the Sheraton Harbor Island Hotel in San Diego. "But more recently, for whatever reason, you go into one of these cities and you set up shop, with an entourage of players, staff, media, players' families. Before you know it, you've got yourself quite a package in a hotel, like 65 to 70 rooms. Here, for instance, we have a traveling party of 50 people or so. There are the 25 players, the manager, the coaches, staff (two trainers, the equipment man, and Mike Swanson, the PR person), broadcasters, production people, a buncha reporters, and then you get into family members—wives, children, parents who either came along on the trip or who live in this area."

I found it hard to keep up with Durso, a compact man who never stopped moving and talked at a Gatling gun clip. But the middle of a long road trip was one of the few times he felt he could relax a bit. He'd made all the arrangements necessary for that trip, the stack of bills and correspondence he dealt with at home didn't trouble him on the road, and he got a few minutes now and then to unwind.

But only a few. Just when things seemed to be running smoothly in San Diego, the team made some roster changes and Durso had to hop-to. When pitcher Mark Knudson and outfielder Gerald Young were demoted to Colorado Springs in May, for example, the team had just arrived in San Diego, and players were settling into the lovely resort hotel overlooking San Diego Harbor.

Generally, when a player got the bad news that he was being sent down, the last thing the team wanted was to leave him hanging around feeling morose. "I got right on the phone first thing and made flight arrangements for them to head out early the next morning," said Durso, letting loose a stream of smoke from one in an endless series of Winstons. "Next, I had to get Darren Holmes and Lance Painter here from Colorado Springs. Then I had follow-up conversations with Young and Knudson, to make sure everything went smooth. We had to get their equipment out of the ballpark here, which we did. Then I had to call Los Angeles (the team's next stop after San Diego), make changes to the hotel rooms. It's not brain surgery, but it's all part of the production."

Getting it done fast was the key. If two players were being shipped out and two more were coming in, Durso wanted the two new arrivals in town on time for the next game, or else the team ended up short two players. "We're not planning a tour here, and we're not a tour group. This is a business trip," Durso said. "Speed is always of the essence. That's the key."

Booking hotels was something of an art form, though the fact that the Rockies were an expansion club made this job easier for Durso. In established clubs, a lot of veteran players had written into their contracts the right to a single room on the road. Barry Bonds was famous for getting a suite written into his fabled $43 million contract with the San Francisco Giants. But the Rockies' young players didn't have the clout to get that perk, for the most part. So players were paired up in hotels, unless they wanted to pay the difference between a double room and a single out of their own pockets. Some players wanted the single room, others didn't care, and yet others wanted single rooms in some cities and doubles in others. Durso kept track of all that, as well as who liked to room with whom. He also saw to it that players traveling with their families were segregated from the single guys, that the media was placed in a different part of the hotel than the players, and that Baylor and his coaches weren't on the same floors as the players.

He chose hotels for the team by keeping in touch with other traveling secretaries and referring back to his notes from past years. "It's a combination of a couple of things. In San Diego, as an example, I've stayed at three or four locations, and I've found this one to be the best. It's kind of a personal thing. I'd never put them in a bad hotel, obviously. It's got to be a good hotel in a good location, not too far from the ballpark. A place where we hopefully can spend many years. And security for the players. The hotel staff should know that stuff. It's pretty basic. If they don't, we move. From the security aspect, if you've got people hanging around in the lobby bothering the players, that's no good. These players aren't prima donnas, but they really don't want to be bothered. I've been in hotels where you come off the elevator and there's 200 people in the lobby with stuff to be signed. You can't have that. And the phone calls have got to be screened. And you can't have people wandering the halls, knocking on doors. We've had situations where other guests in the hotel are knocking on doors or following players to their rooms. So that means security is no good, and we have to move the next year. And none of us like moving around."

Durso also acted as team sugar daddy. At the start of each road trip, he handed each player an envelope containing their per-diem meal money—$60.50 per day in 1993. For the 13-game, four city trip that included San Diego, each player got $877 up front. Some used it for food, others for shopping, others to pay for a single room, or for in-room movies, clubhouse dues and other miscellaneous expenses.

That was the impersonal, details-oriented portion of the job, but there was another side to it as well. Durso grew up around baseball players and liked spending time around them. His father was Joseph Durso, a venerable *New York Times* sportswriter, who covered the Mets and Yankees for 30 years before switching to the horse-racing beat in the late 1980s.

"Half this job at least is the player relations aspect," he said. I'm really the liaison between the management of this club and the players. I'm the day-to-day point of contact for the players." When the team was at home, Durso arrived at the clubhouse two to three hours before game time. He'd sit there at a folding table in the center of the clubhouse, smoking cigarettes and jotting things down in a notebook. Players routinely wandered by and asked him to book plane flights and hotels for family and friends coming to town. They also made ticket requests through him. He seemed to have an easy and natural bantering relationship with players. I'd see him at his table or pacing through the clubhouse, ever-present cigarette in hand, expletives tripping off his tongue in a manner that would do a player proud.

Getting along with the players may have come naturally to Durso, but it was an essential part of the job as well. A traveling secretary on good terms with the players was cut more slack on those inevitable days when things went wrong. "It's not what you know, it's what you don't know in this job. There's always something out there that's going to go wrong. You've got to be on your toes. I've had planes break down, we've had mechanical problems with buses, hotels aren't always up to snuff. But baseball players are good travelers—hell, they've go to be—and they tend to understand.

"But I never forget the really bad days." Like the one in late September, 1986. "I was with the Cubs then, and we were in Montreal, heading to New York. The Mets (who would go on to win the World Series that year) were probably 20 games in first. We were playing, and the game was flying along, and I thought, this is great. We were gonna be in New York by midnight. But then the airline had a problem. The pilot who was going to fly our plane was supposed to take a commercial flight to Chicago to pick up the plane and ferry it up to Montreal. But he missed the flight. I finally got him to show up, but it was 5:00 a.m. and it was at the other Montreal airport (Mirabelle, much farther outside the city). Flying out of that airport meant we couldn't clear customs in Montreal, so we wound up having to fly into Kennedy instead of LaGuardia and clear customs there. That created a huge logistical mess. Family members were waiting for players at the wrong airport, trucks we had rented to haul the equipment to the stadium were waiting at the wrong airport, the chartered buses were at the wrong airport. And remember, the guys had been up all night, sleeping as they could in airport chairs, shit like that. We finally got out of Kennedy at 7:45 a.m. got to our hotel at 9:00. We played the Mets that night at 7:30, and they kicked the living shit out of us and they clinched their division. It was a miserable, miserable trip."

Sure, it sounded miserable; it sounded a lot like trips frequent travelers on commercial airlines suffer through at least once a year. But then, if you're paying for a charter, you expect something better.

I asked Durso if he'd ever had to handle any strange requests from players. He snorted. "Warren Cromartie (of the Montreal Expos) had a big, crown amazon bird. He wanted to leave spring training with the darn thing. The only problem was we were stopping in Memphis for an exhibition game, then heading up to Pittsburgh for the season opener. And after all that, he had to get the darn thing through customs in Montreal. So how did Warren handle that one? He wound up walking through customs with the thing on his shoulder and the guy asked him if he had anything to declare and he just said no and walked on through. And the customs guy didn't even flinch."

I left Durso after an hour's chat and drove out to Jack Murphy Stadium, an unattractive, multi-purpose stadium with orange and brown seats. The stadium is enclosed, so you get no sense of the beauty of the surroundings, other than the gentle ocean breezes that waft through in the evening. Jack Murphy Stadium in May was not a happy place. Fans were wearing bags over their heads already, and holding aloft signs with messages like "Save our team—sell it." What had happened to the San Diego Padres baseball team over the last three years should have made even the increasingly smug Colorado Rockies executives get humble fast. It provided me with my first cautionary tale.

At that point in the season, the Rockies were just beginning to get a firm grip on how astronomical their attendance figures could be. They had drawn 1,226,393 fans to Mile High Stadium in just 21 games. But one look at the Padres provided a haunting glimpse of how quickly things could go sour.

"You feel for the people in this organization, you really do," Rockies general manager Bob Gebhard said 30 minutes before the second game of a four-game series. He was standing in the Rockies dugout at the time, and there were fewer fans in the seats than used to attend a mid-week Denver Zephyrs game. "You look around and wonder what has happened to the fan interest here, and why. They've gotten some adverse publicity on what they've had to do with the payroll. They were so close to having a winner, and now they've had to unload some of their good people."

And how. After the 1992 season, the Padres traded outfielder Darrin Jackson, pitchers Craig Lefferts, Randy Myers and Jim DeShaies, and shortstop Tony Fernandez. They also left catcher, Benito Santiago, unprotected in the expansion draft, and the Florida Marlins grabbed him. No wonder fans in May were fuming. I can only imagine what the atmosphere must have been like at season's end. Between May and July, the Padres unloaded most of their remaining veteran stars—Gary Sheffield, Fred McGriff, and pitchers Greg Harris and Bruce Hurst, both of whom were dealt to the Rockies. In the end, the Padres finished in last place in the National League Western Division, four games behind the Rockies.

Even in May, before the destruction was complete, fans had voted on the changes with their wallets. During the 1992 off-season, the team's season-ticket base plunged about 30 percent, from over 16,000 full and partial packages to just over 11,000. Attendance started declining after the 1990 season when the team drew just over two million fans. In 1992, the Padres drew 1.7 million, and that dipped to 1.4 million in 1993. All this occurred in a market considerably larger than Denver's. San Diego's population stood at 1.1 million in 1993, and San Diego County, the team's true market, has a population of 2.6 million.

I wandered through the stands at Jack Murphy Stadium asking fans—the loyal few that remained—what they thought about the team. I got an angry earful. "The only thing I see is that the owners don't want to spend the big bucks to get quality players, so they're going with young players and the team is losing," said Don Crosby, a long-time fan. Crosby's view was representative, if a bit more diplomatically stated than most.

A group of 15 Southern California businessmen bought the 25-year-old expansion franchise from the Kroc family of McDonald's fame in 1990. Dubbed "the fab 15" by a less than adoring local media, the ownership group immediately moved to cut the team's ample payroll, slashing it from $28 million to $21 million in the off-season. But it wasn't just losing the players that hurt, fans said. It was how they were lost and what the team got in return. "The perception out there is that the team got a lot less than it gave up in all those trades," said Buster Olney, the Padres beat writer for the *San Diego Union-Tribune*. "We've had tons of letters in our paper ripping the shit out of the owners."

What really turned off the fans was a letter sent out in the off-season to season-ticket-holders by managing partner Tom Werner. The letter grudgingly acknowledged that some of the ownership group's moves had been unpopular. It then went on to name four star players that Werner pledged would form the team's future nucleus and would not be traded. Of those players—Sheffield, McGriff, Jackson and Tony Gwynn—only Gwynn remained following the great purge of '93. A popular T-shirt among San Diego fans in 1993 featured a reproduction of Werner's letter enlarged across the front.

I sought out a representative of the ownership group to see how management was weathering the storm. The official line: the trades were unavoidable. It would have been financial suicide to let the team's payroll get too bloated. And Bill Adams, the Padres senior vice president for business operations, argued that declining attendance had more to do with California's rocky economy and uncertainty about the future of major league baseball than with anything the owners had done. "This is a military town, and we have three bases on the closure list. That has us very, very concerned," Adams said. As a result, the Padres in 1993 offered a number of deep discount programs on tickets. "We're trying to find ways to bring people here," Adams said. "But that's more an economy thing than an apology that we let a few players go."

Adams said the local print media had thrown a lot of gasoline on this particular fire. "The media absolutely buried us with our fans in the off season. And frankly, it's a bit of a mystery to us how it got to this point."

The answer was simple, Olney replied. "If you made a list of 10 things a team should never do public relations-wise, they hit all 10. How can you not report that?" As an example, he cited the goofy promotion the Padres staged in conjunction with a local rock radio station the first night the Rockies were in town. The Padres spent somewhere in the neighborhood of $25,000 to spray man-made snow on a section of bleachers in right-center field. They then held a snowball fight for the fans before the game. "25,000 bucks on snow," Olney said, shaking his head. "That's the cash-strapped San Diego Padres for you."

So what could the Rockies learn from the Padres disaster? There were a few important lessons here. First of all, not to get swelled heads after the triumphs of 1993. Huge attendance numbers in Denver had nothing to do with the quality of the team, and little to do with the Disneyland atmosphere the team strove to create. I chalked it up to the honeymoon syndrome. But a few years down the road, the Rockies will have to make sure the fans—and the media—are satisfied, not only with the team and the ancillary stadium entertainment, but with the ballpark and the owners.

Being on the road with the Rockies gave me the chance to spend more time with sportswriters and broadcasters than I ever got in Denver. In San Diego, I sought out Charlie Jones, the Rockies' silver-haired TV play-by-play man. In some ways, I thought as I tracked Jones down, Denver still was a cow-town. The city seemed impressed with itself for having landed Jones, a national football play-by-play guy, to do the Rockies broadcasts. Although they did a first-rate job, no one seemed particularly interested in radio broadcasters Wayne Hagin or Jeff Kingery, or in Duane Kuiper, Jones' color man and a former big-league infielder. So I thought it would be interesting to chat with Jones, listen to his life story and hear what he thought his role was in bringing baseball to the uninformed masses of the mountain west.

Jones, a 62-year-old native of Fort Smith, Arkansas, was an engaging fellow. We took a seat in the Rockies dugout on a glorious spring afternoon in San Diego and chatted as the Rockies took batting practice. I noted that his honeyed, utterly distinctive voice was the same in casual conversation as over the airwaves. It sounded like it had a smile buried inside it. He'd had that voice since he was 15. As soon as his voice had changed, Jones knew those golden pipes were going to take him places. But at the time his only ambition was for a radio career in the nearby metropolis of Tulsa, Oklahoma.

Instead, Jones leapfrogged to Dallas, and from there, it was on to stardom. As we talked, he was in the 28th year of a career as a national football and baseball broadcaster with NBC. Although he was hoping to stay with the Rockies for the rest of his professional life, he had previous commitments under his contract with NBC. There were several occasions in 1993 when the Rockies had to find a substitute for Jones.

Right off the bat, Jones said, he found doing play-by-play as an employee of a ballclub to be an entirely different type of challenge, especially for an expansion team. But it also presented him with what he considered a great opportunity to be a trailblazer. "How tough would it be to have to come in and follow a legend like (Chicago Cubs broadcaster) Harry Caray, or (Los Angeles Dodgers broadcaster) Vin Scully? I would like to set that same kind of high standard. I want to make this the last job I ever have—be here 10 or 15 years. And I want to make the kind of mark that will make it tough on the guy who follows me."

He planned to make his mark by doing a lot of homework, schmoozing with the players, and bringing a distillation of his knowledge and the yarns he heard into the livingrooms of Rockies fans. By the end of the season, Jones and Kuiper were getting decidedly mixed reviews. In fact, when the San Francisco Giants started wooing Kuiper, the Rockies did nothing to hold onto him. Some critics thought Jones sounded totally disengaged. They didn't want him to be a "homer," but they wanted some emotion in his voice. It was true, he did sound listless at times, and he did miss some calls. But then there were times when his enthusiasm bubbled over a little too much, and he sounded like the homer he swore he'd never be.

Still, what Jones liked best about being a local TV guy was the chance to get to know the players personally, to move beyond the superficial "great game, Charlie, what was on your mind as you hit that three-run homer?" interviews that were the staple of the national broadcasters's work. "The difference between this and a national telecast is that here I've really worked hard to bring the local flavor to people," he said, ducking an errant throw that ricocheted off the dugout wall behind him. "And when you travel with the team (broadcasters rode the team charter buses and jets), spend some time with the players when you're not interviewing them, you get a sense of the type of persons they are, and how they feel and how they react to jokes; if they're pranksters or if they're very serious, whether they smile a lot or if they don't.

"It's more fun to travel with a ballclub and cover a ballclub. It really is. You get to know people, they get to know you, they're more comfortable with you. There's less the sense of being an outsider looking in. The players don't walk away from you, try to avoid you, that type of feeling. It's not like you're the enemy. The local fan is very interested in details about their players, so in turn we try to bring that personality to the viewer at home. And there's no question that I now know more about Dante Bichette in right field (for the Rockies) than I know about Tony Gwynn in right field (for the Padres). I collect stories about the players to share with the viewers. After all, we're in the storytelling business. We kid Dante, for example, about the way he dresses. He's dressing a lot better on the flights nowadays. You know, we wear coats and ties on the flights, on getaway days. The first two or three trips, Dante had some weird outfits. And we kidded him so much he's really shaped up.

"Then there are the more poignant moments. I remember in spring training one of the great statements I heard was from Dante when he got married. He said 'I could not live without her.' And I said this may be one of the most romantic statements I have ever heard. And we used it on the air and he heard about it, and he said 'did you really use that on the air?' and I said yeah, I just thought it was absolutely fabulous. I think he was touched."

Jones said he thought of his local baseball telecast as "entertainment/journalism, not journalism/entertainment." His goal was to strike an even balance between reporting and entertaining. By contrast, when doing a nationally televised game, Jones said, he put more emphasis on reporting than entertaining. Local baseball broadcasts presented an unusual ethical challenge to the announcers as well. Although at least some of what they did was supposed to be broadcast journalism—objective reporting of the games—it was hard to forget that the people they were reporting on also were paying their salaries.

Throughout professional sports, announcers are hired by and retained at the discretion of the team they cover. But Jones said he didn't think about that awkward situation. "I don't believe in being a homer," Jones said. "I think we should be what I call locally objective. We need to cover the ballclub and we need to cover it from a journalistic standpoint. I don't believe in saying "we" when I refer to the team, because I don't think "we" win. I don't have anything to do with it. The Rockies win. I don't think you should have that kind of involvement. At the same time, you have to point out stupid mistakes and boneheaded plays when you see them. Because if it's a bonehead play and you don't call it, the viewing public is smart, and they're going to say 'oh, come on, give me a break.'"

Some sportswriters spent a lot of time on the road fantasizing about marital infidelity and drunken binges, but most of them worked too hard to live out their dreams. It wasn't unusual for a few writers to gather in the hotel bar after filing their stories, for a couple of beers and some terse conversation. Occasionally, writers and coaches or players would run into each other in the bar and have a couple of drinks together, but that kind of fraternizing wasn't common. One night in San Diego, Bob Kravitz of the *Rocky Mountain News* and I headed down to the hotel bar for a beer. It was late and we both were tired after watching the Rockies lose to the Padres 7–

3, despite two home runs by Daryl Boston. It was the Rockies' last night in town. They had a game the following afternoon. Immediately afterwards, they were to board buses for the three-hour trip up Interstate 5 to Los Angeles.

Kravitz and I were hunched over our beers, munching on beer nuts, when Rockies pitching coach, Larry Bearnarth, pulled up an adjoining stool. "Uh-oh," Kravitz whispered to me. Bearnarth, a hulking 52-year-old known universally as "Bear," had a reputation for being able to hold an extraordinary amount of liquor when he felt like it. And after a game in which his pitching corps had taken their customary beating, he probably felt like having a few.

Bear started out quiet, gulping down a couple of vodka-based concoctions called sea breezes. Kravitz bought him a third and then he bought us a couple of beers and started talking. "I stink. The pitching coach stinks," he said. "I'll tell you, fellas, this losing business gets pretty old, especially losing this way, time after time." Bear wasn't your typical pitching coach. He had graduated from St. John's University in 1962 with a degree in English literature. He'd gone on to have a 10-year career as a pro pitcher, including stints with the expansion New York Mets in their second season, and with the fledgling Milwaukee Brewers in the early 1970s.

Every time I decided to get up and go to bed that night, Bear bought me another beer. After several, I asked him, "So, do you ever use your English lit. degree when dealing with pitchers?"

Bear, deep in his cups, snorted. "You kidding me?"

"You mean you don't walk out to the mound when a pitcher's in trouble and say, 'As Jane Austen would say, throw some fucking strikes?'" Bear almost spit out his drink, and after that, his mood seemed to lighten. Late in the evening, Daryl Boston wandered into the bar with two women on his arms. Both wore very short shorts and black stockings. He looked to be in a celebratory mood following his two-homer game. He proceeded to slug down six double Absolut vodkas in short order, but he was a big guy, well over 200 pounds, and his demeanor didn't change.

Bear looked over at Boston and shook his head. "The guy's a

classic underachiever," he said, echoing a remark I'd hear about Boston from various people throughout the season. "He should have games like tonight's four, five times a year. He's a hell of a talent. Instead, you see him in here drinking and chasing pussy, and watch, he'll strike out four times tomorrow."

Our party broke up a few minutes later. The next afternoon, Kravitz and I, our heads pounding, looked at each other and smiled the first time Boston stepped to the plate. He took two strikes. Here comes the strike-out Bear prophesized, I thought. Boom! Boston smashed the next pitch over the right field wall for a home run, and did a slow trot around the bases. I wondered if his head felt like mine. Across the press box, I heard Kravitz laughing.

I came into L.A. with this snide story all mapped out in my head. I'd been to L.A. a couple of times in my college days, but I didn't know the city and my impressions of it were all Woody Allen-fed stereotypes. I expected Dodgers Stadium in Chavez Ravine to be a bastion of the terminally hip, with people snacking on sushi instead of hot dogs and talking on their cellular phones instead of watching the game. I was going to write all about it, have some fun with it. Instead, I came away impressed with the entire operation. Chavez Ravine is one great place to watch baseball.

Los Angeles may have been a city choking on traffic and smog, and split by racial tensions to rival the Balkans, but baseball fans there already knew what I was just discovering; that Dodgers Stadium was a place where all that could be forgotten, at least for a couple of hours. The Dodgers knew how to provide their fans with a pure baseball experience, untainted by all the MTV-driven drivel that had overwhelmed the game in so many other places. I hoped Rockies management paid close attention to how the Dodgers ran their show, because baseball in Mile High Stadium more closely resembled the carnival atmosphere of abominations like Comiskey Park in Chicago than the palaces of baseball purity like this one, and Wrigley Field in Chicago. Bernie Mullin, the Rockies senior vice president for business operations, once told me that he would never allow the team to sully baseball by running "dot races" and other such distractions on the scoreboard. "That's just inappropriate," he had sniffed. But by the end of the season, Mullin was gone, and sure enough, "home-run–ball races" and the "Fan-o-meter" were dominant features of the Mile High entertainment package.

No such kow-towing to the lowest common denominator was evident at Dodgers Stadium, a 56,000-seat park that sits in the steep-walled Chavez Ravine. You'd never know the stadium was just two miles from downtown, nestled as it was amid palm-covered hills that hid the urbanness of the surroundings. The Dodgers had made a conscious effort to extend that tranquility into the park. Aside from small Coca-Cola signs on the scoreboards, there was no advertising visible from the stands. Although the requisite Diamondvision screen stared down from above the left-field pavilion, it didn't show video commercials or blare loud music. In fact, the only music I heard in three days at Dodgers Stadium came from an organ that sounded like it was straight out of a roller rink.

"Keeping the stadium a clean, non-commercial environment has been a philosophy of the organization for a long time," Paul Kalil, the team's director of advertising and special events, told me. "We try to keep the atmosphere here low key. We want to maintain Dodger Stadium's reputation as a pristine castle."

I did find some of the well-known stereotypes about Dodgers fans to be based on fact. They seemed so concerned about the endless Southern California traffic tie-ups, for example, that many didn't bother arriving until the game was well underway. And large throngs began heading for the exits during the seventh inning. Not that all that neurosis made a whit of difference. The traffic always lay in wait, regardless of the hour. But many of my other stereotypes fell by the wayside. Sure, there were plenty of Hollywood producer types in the box seats, in their pressed jeans, silk jackets and tasseled loafers. But most of the fans looked like regular folks. They ate Dodger Dogs and drank beer and did The Wave. I didn't see a raw fish or bottle of Chardonnay anywhere.

Fans respected the stadium's cleanliness and relaxed atmosphere.

The crowd's idea of rowdiness seemed to be batting beach balls around until they were confiscated by security guards. But that was about the only time ushers and security guards were conspicuous. Unlike Mile High Stadium, where ushers from Andy Frain Services watched each aisle like hawks and kept people out of seats that weren't theirs, the straw-boater-capped Dodger ushers took a laissez-faire approach to their duties. They were easy to find if a fan wanted them, but they stayed out of the way. It was a pleasant change of pace after the regimentation at Mile High.

"This is about the safest place you can be in this city," Kalil said. "It should be as relaxing as sitting in your living room." One of the first things I noticed about the Dodger crowd was how racially and ethnically diverse it was, unlike Denver and most other big-league parks, where crowds were predominantly white. Part of that was due to L.A.'s huge Hispanic, Asian, and black communities. But the Dodgers also made a point of wooing fans from all corners of the Los Angeles area. No other team I studied took a similar approach except the Florida Marlins, who aggressively courted Latin American tourists.

"Our fans mirror the ethnic composition of the city," Kalil said. "It has to be that way. The ethnic populations are growing at the fastest pace here. If we want to keep our fan base, we have to be aggressive about getting into those communities." The team did that by sending players into low-income neighborhoods to hold clinics, by keeping ticket prices moderate (the most expensive seat was $11, the cheapest $6), advertising in small foreign-language publications, and by holding special-event nights honoring the cultural heritage of various groups.

"We're having nine or ten different cultural events this year," Kalil said. Among those scheduled were Hispanic families night, Jackie Robinson night (in honor of the first black big-league ballplayer), Chinese families night, Thai night, and German night.

The week before the Rockies came to town, the Dodgers achieved what they believed to be a major-league first, by broadcasting their game live in four different languages—English, Spanish, Korean and Mandarin—throughout their viewing area. "We'll be doing a lot more of that kind of thing in the future," Kalil said. "I don't know what other teams do, but being part of the communities has to be a natural thing in this city."

And in a city where racial tensions were running high, the ballpark seemed to be a place where all that could be forgotten. "This isn't always the most relaxing city to live in, but we want people to come enjoy the game, the atmosphere inside the stadium, without bombarding them with all sorts of external stuff," Kalil said. "I guess the bottom line is you want people to come here to bond. We hear a lot of stories about kids who used to come here with their grandparents and now they bring their kids here, because the atmosphere hasn't changed since the park opened 32 years ago. That's what baseball is all about."

The signs were not encouraging, but one could hope that the Rockies would see the light and emulate the Dodgers Stadium atmosphere in Coors Field. How about a park with no lighted advertising and no loud music, where the video board isn't the center of attention? Dream on.

How fitting that my next road trip, in early July right after the all-star break, would take me first to Wrigley Field, that perfect little ballyard on Chicago's North Side. Again, I entered Wrigley for the first time looking to write a snide story, but for different reasons this time. I'm a native Chicagoan, raised on the South Side as a White Sox fan. Don't ask me why, but Chicago is one of those cities where no true baseball fan can root, root root for both home teams. Anyone who called himself a Sox fan had to, by definition, hate the Cubs and the team's legions of suburban, white-bread fans. I'll say it now and get it over with, because even as a mature adult it comes hard: Wrigley Field is the best ballpark in the world, edging out Boston's lovely Fenway Park for the honor. I rarely went to Wrigley as a kid, preferring instead the rough-and-tumble White Sox crowd and the old Comiskey Park, as big and drafty as it was.

So it had been years since I'd set foot in Wrigley Field. I'd never seen the old gal with her lights, which were installed in 1988. But I decided to cast aside my old prejudices and look at Wrigley as a living museum piece, a place where the Rockies, who were to move into a modern, old-time ballyard called Coors Field in 1995, might have a few of the Dodgers Stadium lessons reinforced.

You could describe Wrigley Field, with its ivied brick walls and views of Lake Michigan, by whatever clichéd adjective you wished—quaint, charming, pastoral or lovely. All did it justice. But to get the true feel of the 80-year-old ballpark, you had to crawl inside the guts of its manually operated scoreboard, which loomed three stories high above the center-field bleachers. That old scoreboard had remained unchanged in appearance since my childhood, or the childhood of my father, for that matter. It was quaintly outmoded. But there was nothing remotely quaint about the dark, dingy, steel-floored confines, where temperatures on a summer's day routinely topped 100 degrees.

To enter the scoreboard's innards, which looked like something out of the movie *Bladerunner,* three members of the Wrigley Field grounds crew climbed a steel ladder from the bleachers each day about 20 minutes before game time. The first one up carried keys to the sheet-metal trap door clenched in his teeth. When he was within reach of the padlock on the sheet-metal door, he opened it, then shoved the squeaking hinge open and in they went. When I climbed up after them, hand over hand, they seemed glad for the company.

Down on the first level, Darryl Wilson was responsible for sliding sheet-metal plates bearing each team's hit totals into the appropriate square windows. The plates were three feet square, sharp-edged and heavy. "I've never come close to dropping one, and let's hope I never do, because it would seriously fuck somebody up down there in the bleachers," he said. Wilson also had to post the score inning–by–inning for the game in progress. One level above him on a narrow catwalk, Brian Helmus scurried to and fro keeping inning-by-inning track of scores for all other big-league games in progress. He had a sports ticker plugged into an extension cord that connected to God-only-knows what power source up there. At times he had to move fast to keep the scores current.

"Does it get hot?" Wilson asked rhetorically before an afternoon Cubs-Rockies tilt. "Oh, man. It gets so hot sometimes you can barely touch anything in here. But I love this job. Look at the view." From his little window in the scoreboard, Wilson had a perfect view of the entire field. But as he spoke, he was looking straight down at fans in the bleachers, many of whom were scantily clad. "The women in the bleachers are awesome, dude, awesome!" he said. "And we can look right down their blouses from up here. To be honest, I don't think a lot of them mind. We got the wildest fans out here, the wildest. But just in case, I wear sunglasses, even at night, so they can't see where I'm looking."

The Wrigley Field scoreboard was installed in 1937, and little about it had changed since then. A narrow strip of electronic board was installed below the main scoreboard in the mid-1980s, but there was no video screen, no flashy lights. And, most notably, there wasn't a single billboard or advertisement on the board or anywhere else in the ballpark. Cubs management was proud of the scoreboard and other manifestations of the park's stubborn refusal to enter the modern era. Maybe a little too proud. Smug, even. "That little message board is our only concession to the electronic era," sniffed Wanda Taylor, a team spokeswoman. Well, there was one other concession, she acknowledged when pressed. The Cubs installed lights at Wrigley in 1988 over the vociferous objections of their fans and the surrounding neighborhood. Lights weren't installed because the team wanted night games, Taylor insisted. Management loved the tradition of day-only baseball. "But we were getting passed over for the All-Star Game, and the league and networks were unhappy about having us in post-season play because they want to televise those games in prime time. So we really had to do it."

A lot of baseball purists were unhappy about the lights. Undoubtedly, some of the snootiest have boycotted the park since 1988, ignoring the fact that the Cubs installed architecturally lovely lights, and that the old field looks wonderful at night. Reverence for Wrigley Field extended far beyond Chicago's boundaries, and was something the team had to take into account whenever it contemplated changes to the park. After all, as George Bush learned, it wasn't wise to incur the wrath of George Will, one of thousands of celebrity Cubs fans from around the nation.

"There's a bit of old-time religion involved here," said Tom Cooper, the team's stadium operations manager. "We have almost a Mecca for baseball fans." For any given game, Cooper said, 25 percent of the fans came from outside the six-state area around Illinois. The Cubs themselves, a mediocre team with a national cable-TV following, no doubt drew some of those fans. But Cooper thought Wrigley was at least as big a draw as the team. "We have made a commitment to keeping Wrigley Field an old-time park," he said. "Over the years we've added concession stands, bathrooms, and 67 mezzanine skyboxes (in 1989). But we're about built out. There's not much more we can do."

Wrigley's best-known feature, of course, was the ivy that covered its brick outfield walls. Keeping the ivy in shape was a challenge that fell to Roger O'Connor, the Cubs groundskeeper, a roly-poly Irishman with the gift of gab.

"It's constant work keeping it looking this good," he said, pointing to the walls from his perch in the Cubs tobacco-stained dugout. "We have to trim it every road trip, and Chicago's climate—all the humidity—makes the ivy prone to leaf spot. It's a mixture of Japanese Ivy, Boston Ivy, and Bittersweet, though not too much Bittersweet because it tends to grow wild. We feed it with fertilizer with a lot of micro-nutrients—copper, phosphorous, iron—mixed in to make it grow more leaves. It really takes a pounding every game. It needs a lot of TLC."

Keeping the old ballyard shipshape required constant vigilance on many fronts. Cooper said the Tribune Company, which owned the Cubs, spent about $2 million per year on routine maintenance and capital expenditures. "Fortunately, this park is so old that it's overbuilt," Cooper said. "I mean, it's like a battleship. Eighty years ago they didn't have expertise on load bearing, so they just loaded on the steel. It'll hold up forever, with proper care." It will have to; Cubs fans and baseball purists wouldn't ever allow the park to be demolished.

As far as management was concerned, Wrigley Field's biggest drawback was a lack of storage space. "It can be a major inconvenience, especially for concessionaires. They have to unload deliveries every day, because there's just no place to stockpile stuff," Cooper said. There was also a serious parking shortage, which forced fans to cruise neighborhood streets, to the endless irritation of residents. But all the minor pains were well worth bearing, Cooper said. "I don't think you can watch baseball in a better atmosphere than Wrigley Field. I've been here 10 years, and still, every time I walk up those steps and look at the field . . . well, it's a neat feeling."

In the purity of the baseball experience it provided, Wrigley was similar to Dodgers Stadium. But unlike Dodgers Stadium, Wrigley embraced its urban surroundings. Wrigley was squeezed onto one square city block. Old Chicago brownstones that surrounded the park rose above Wrigley's low brick walls. It truly was a neighborhood ballyard. Oh, man, I thought to myself as I sniffed the lake breeze and watched sailboats gliding across the surface of Lake Michigan from my press-box perch. I could grow to like this place. It was time to go mingle with the fans, see if I could revive those lifelong hatreds. As a student of baseball cultures, I also wanted to see if those legendary bleachers had an atmosphere markedly different from the cheap seats at Mile High Stadium.

Out in the bleachers, as luck would have it, I met a guy named Marvin Blum, who articulated my feelings perfectly. As far as Blum, a lifelong Cubs fan of 69, was concerned, many of the trendy legends surrounding Wrigley Field and the Cubs shattered upon close inspection.

A portly, retired produce wholesaler, Blum had been a bleacher regular for 50 years, and since retiring in 1990, he had attended all but two Chicago Cubs home games. He sat shirtless in the center-field bleachers every game, up in the back row where he could rest his fleshy back against the railing. "All this stuff you hear about Bleacher Bums, it's just not true, at least not anymore," Blum lamented in a nasal, South-Side accent as he watched the Cubs tattoo the Rockies on a mild Saturday afternoon. The Bleacher Bums were renowned rowdies during the 1960s. They'd taunt opposing outfielders mercilessly from their perch atop the left-field wall. They were a rough bunch, and their legend lived on only in the imaginations of the wannabes who now inhabited those seats.

"Yeah, you used to have more of the hard-core here," Blum said, puffing on a cheap cigar. "Now it's, well, I hate to use the word, but it's yuppified." He turned quickly to the fan next to him, a young man in Madras shorts and loafers without socks. "No offense, kid," he chortled.

Blum still loved sitting in the bleachers, but he was openly contemptuous of many of his fellow fans. "For a lot of these people, it's a cult thing. They're not interested in baseball, they just want to be here. It's like a meat market and they're out here shopping. Of course, I'm the first to admit I'm a dirty old man myself. I wouldn't lie to you."

Blum, who called himself "a critical Cubs fan," also had little use for the "lovable losers" label the Cubs had worn so comfortably for decades. "To hell with this underdog stuff," he said, his voice rising indignantly. "A lot of these people, to them, mediocrity is a big deal. I've got no use for that."

Amid the yuppies and frat boys in the bleachers, however, there were a few others like Blum, and he knew them all. "See that lady over there?" he asked, pointing to an elderly woman in a pink cap. "She's 92 years old and she comes to almost every game."

Carmella Hartigan acknowledged this was true. "What else am I going to do at my age?" she asked. "Where else could I want to be?"

No disrespect intended, but there were places I preferred. As much as I'd always hated the Cubs, I'd always wanted to watch a game from a rooftop perch across Sheffield Avenue. Nowhere else in the big leagues could you get an unobstructed, bleacher-quality view of a game from a private rooftop, a view better than that af-forded by thousands of the seats at Mile High Stadium. These rooftops perhaps best represented the true seat of baseball culture on Chicago's North Side. It was so unique to Wrigley Field—this sense that the ballpark belonged to the neighborhood. Wrigley wasn't like a flying saucer that had landed in the middle of a city block. It was an organic part of the community; so much so that a lucky few got to watch Cubs games from their rooftops. Maybe, I thought, the Rockies would be visionary enough to create a similar atmosphere in and around Coors Field.

So I wandered out the park gates and across Sheffield Avenue. Within five minutes, I had a lifelong illusion shattered. Those won-derful free seats weren't free after all. It's just that it wasn't the Cubs pocketing the money.

Nine buildings on Sheffield and Waveland Avenues had rooftop seating. By 1993, eight of them were owned by groups of investors who rented out the roofs at a steep price for private parties. The Cubs, of course, didn't like the idea of someone else profiting while the team paid Ryne Sandberg, the team's splendid second baseman, $7 million a year, so they had threatened to erect a screen to block the view. But the investor groups were willing to gamble that it was all a bluff, and so far their gamble had paid off. The money kept pouring in for groups like Conroy Productions, which owned three of the buildings on Sheffield. For instance, the day I paid my visit to a Sheffield Avenue roof, 40 high-school friends of Tom Moran from suburban Elmhurst were drinking beer and eating hamburgers as the game went on across the street. Few of them were paying any attention to the game. "I haven't seen one pitch," said an effusive fellow named Jeff Keller, who looked to be into the double digits in beer consumption. "It's the atmosphere I'm here for."

The day's entertainment cost Moran, who owned a thriving temporary service, $3,000. "I do this every year. It's a ball game and all you can eat and drink. It's a great party, a lot better than going in there." He made a contemptuous gesture toward Wrigley Field. And what about the poor souls who happened to live in the brown-

stones? Didn't they feel put upon by the non-stop partying atop
their homes? Of course not. No one just happened by chance to
live across the street from Wrigley Field.

Rob Nunn, a 24-year-old Navy pilot and Colorado State University graduate whose friends called him Top Nunn, said living at
3645 N. Sheffield was the dream of a lifetime. He and two friends
split the $1,200 monthly rent for a ground-floor, three bedroom
place. Unlimited access to the roof was part of the deal. "I've lived
in some great party spots—Vail, near Red Rocks, in Boulder—and
this is the best party atmosphere I've ever seen," the Persian Gulf
War veteran enthused while quaffing a cold Bud. "I'll tell you,
being in Operation Desert Storm was a thrill, but I like this kind of
excitement better, to be honest. You can't be getting shot at and
drink beer. I'm stationed at the base in Glenview now, but I've got
to go back to Pensacola this fall. It breaks my heart, damn it. You
just can't touch Wrigley Field. It's mystical."

But not everyone was so enthusiastic. "What they're doing is il-
legal, and they're going to wind up ruining it for those of us who
want to keep it among friends," said Jim Tracy, who managed
Murphy's Tavern on the corner of Sheffield and Waveland Avenues.
Tavern-owner Jim Murphy, a gruff ex-cop whose vocabulary consisted mainly of grunts, was the first to put bleachers on his roof in
the early 1970s. He had staunchly refused to commercialize his
roof, which was open only to tenants and their friends. "All you
hear now is bitches and complaints from the Cubs," he groused.
"It's only a matter of time before they put a stop to it. Then the
greedy ones will be sorry."

From the Wrigley Field idyll to the ballpark-as-shopping-mall,
all in one day. That's the dislocating experience I had when I flew
from Chicago to Miami for the second half of my second road trip
with the Rockies. It only made sense to pay a visit to the home of
the Rockies' sister expansion team during this, the inaugural season.
The Marlins received rave reviews in the early going for hiring
savvy baseball pros to run their operation. These guys, conventional

wisdom had it, would put a competitive team on the field in short order, and, thanks to their farsighted expansion draft picks, the big club would be backed by a deep farm system. The baseball cognoscenti rated the Marlins' expansion draft picks as far better than those of the Rockies. People had actually heard of some of the players the Rockies chose, while the Marlins set their sights on hot prospects buried deep within the minor-league systems of established teams. Sure enough, the Marlins started the season hot, and, until the all-star break, seemed destined to become the best expansion team in history. Of course, they fell on their collective faces late in the season, and the Rockies wound up finishing ahead of them in the standings by three games.

I wasn't all that interested in the team-building strategies of the two franchises. But I was curious about the development of Miami's baseball culture. Denver was fast turning into a city where baseball was a big social event, and Mile High Stadium was a place to go party with friends. People weren't baseball sophisticates, but they recognized that the ballpark was a good place to have fun. But what about Miami? Pen and notebook in hand, I wandered the stands of Joe Robbie Stadium to find out for myself.

My first impressions were entirely negative. Some people in Denver may have felt—correctly, I might add—that Mile High Stadium wasn't well suited to baseball. But at least the Colorado Rockies didn't play in a shopping mall as their expansion brethren Florida Marlins did. In fact, I thought as I wandered the carpeted, air-conditioned concourses, Denver fans could take some comfort in knowing that while the Rockies were stepping forward into the past with Coors Field, the Marlins would play for the foreseeable future in a stadium that painted an ugly picture of the future of baseball.

I hadn't really known what to expect as I began my wanderings through JRS, as the locals called their mallpark. Considering that Denver and Miami, two cities long starved for big-league baseball, were in the middle of their inaugural seasons, I had thought that the experience of watching a game in one expansion city would be much like the other. But the differences between stadiums, fans and overall ambiance were at once stark and illuminating. Fans in Miami as a whole seemed to know their baseball better than Denver fans. Granted, that wasn't saying much. But why was it so? A few random interviews and I'd answered that question: Many Marlins fans were transplants. Most everyone in the stands, it seemed, was from New York, New Jersey or Latin America.

"We're all transplants here," said a middle-aged man from New Jersey who didn't want to give his name, as he watched the two teams battle on a muggy Monday night. "I grew up in Yankee Stadium, and I love it there, but all things considered, I'd rather be watching baseball in Miami than the Bronx." I sensed a certain East Coast edge to the Miami crowd. Orestedes Destrade, the Marlin first baseman who was supposed to be the team's big slugger, was in the midst of a horrendous slump. The fans were booing him mercilessly. Whenever his name was announced, the crowd sounded like it was straight out of Philadelphia. Rockies fans, who jeered some of their bumbling pitchers early in the year, never booed them this enthusiastically.

"Yeah, that kind of surprised me when I heard it last night," commented Rockies coach Don Zimmer on the reaction to Destrade. Zimmer, who managed top-flight teams in Boston and Chicago that never quite lived up to their potential, was something of a connoisseur of booing. "Destrade makes a lot of money, and that gets publicized these days, so the fans were really letting him hear about it. What these people don't realize is that even though he had a couple of great seasons in Japan, he's a rookie in the big leagues. But they aren't cuttin' him any slack, are they?"

The clearest difference between the two expansion experiences, however, was in the stadiums. While both lacked charm, they did so in entirely different ways. Joe Robbie Stadium, the 6-year-old, $115-million, privately financed behemoth, had no pretensions to being an old-time, Wrigley-style ballyard. It seemed too perfect to be true. Access to everything—bathrooms, concessions, seats—was easy. Concourses were wide and well scrubbed. The crowd was orderly. Every seat, even those in the distant upper deck, afforded a fine view of the action. There was even a huge video arcade behind the left field stands in case the kiddies got bored.

But the stadium had none of the grit of history rubbed into its concrete soul. The fact that JRS was first and foremost a football stadium didn't help any. People who paid $30 for a club-level seat, just above the lower deck, reached their seats by walking through an enclosed, carpeted, air-conditioned concourse that felt more like a hotel lobby or an airport terminal than a sports arena. On that concourse, vendors hawked frozen yogurt, ice cream, mixed drinks, beer and splits of fine wine. To get to their seats, club–seat ticket holders pushed through swinging glass doors, at which point they were assaulted by a blast of hot, humid outside air. Ah, Florida in the summer. No wonder the Marlins played almost all their games at night. "Play in the day here and you'd have sweat squishing around in your shoes," Zimmer said.

Club-seat fans who didn't like the heat and humidity could sit in air-conditioned comfort on a stool in JR's in the stadium, a bar tucked behind the lower-deck, right-field stands. The stools looked out over the field, and waitresses brought patrons drinks, buffalo wings, chicken tenders and other cholesterol-laden bar food.

All this wasn't to say the park had no redeeming features. One of its biggest fans was Zimmer, whose 45 years in professional baseball gave his opinion some weight. "I think they've done a hell of a job," he said. "I was here last winter for a Dolphins playoff game, and I couldn't imagine how they'd make a ballpark out of it. But it looks great. And the players will tell you this is the best, truest infield in baseball." Maybe so Zim, but I couldn't wait to get out of there.

Despite the hideous ballpark, however, the Marlins were a forward-thinking organization, stamped out of the Dodgers' mold. The Rockies may have been 1993's box-office champs, but the Marlins envisioned their fans numbering in the hundreds of millions by the end of the decade. The Marlins were thinking big, and with good reason. Perched as they were on the rim of the Caribbean

Basin, the nation's southernmost big-league baseball team hoped to grab a market extending from Cuba south toward Tierra del Fuego.

"We want to be known not as America's team, but the team of the Americas," said Don Smiley, the Marlins vice president of sales and marketing. "We know that it takes time, and that we have to earn that distinction by going out there and gaining respect. But the local Hispanic fan reaction has been fantastic, and that gives us some confidence."

Strolling through the stands of Joe Robbie Stadium, I heard as many people speaking Spanish as English. What struck me was how the Spanish-speaking fans seemed evenly distributed throughout the ballpark, with as many sitting in the expensive box seats as up high in the grandstands. At other ballparks I visited, including Denver's, I saw relatively few blacks and Hispanics in the more expensive seats.

Support for the Marlins from Miami's huge ethnic community wasn't surprising, given baseball's prominent place in the cultures of some Latin American and Caribbean nations. But the Marlins had been aggressive in going after those fans, and with good reason. The Marlins knew that to succeed they'd have to appeal to people from Spanish-speaking countries. In 1990, according to the Census Bureau, Dade County's population was 49.2 percent Hispanic. Overall, 33 percent of south Florida's residents—and that was the Marlins' true market—were of Hispanic origin.

"Marketing to them is a must, there's no question about it," Smiley said. To reach Spanish-speaking fans, the Marlins hired two Hispanic firms: Zubi Advertising and a public relations firm. "Everything we do in English, we do in Spanish as well," said Adolfo Salgueiro, a bearded, red-haired Venezuelan who worked in the team's media relations department. A Spanish-language radio station broadcast all Marlins games, and the team received extensive coverage on the area's two Spanish TV stations, two big Spanish daily newspapers, and dozens of smaller, weekly Spanish papers. All Marlins games were beamed by radio to the Dominican Republic and Puerto Rico. By 1994, Smiley said, Venezuela and perhaps Colombia would get the games by radio as well.

Knowing the demographics of their Hispanic fans, the Marlins decided to woo not only local Latin populations, but their relatives in Colombia, Venezuela, the Dominican Republic, Panama, Costa Rica and Nicaragua, to name a few. In July, the Marlins hired Tony Perez, a great first baseman for the Cincinnati Reds in the 1970s, as their director of international relations. When he was introduced to the home fans before a Rockies game, he received a thunderous ovation. Perez's duties were to include organizing off-season caravans of players and team officials to various Latin American countries. "We have general sales agents working full time in seven countries—Costa Rica, Venezuela, Nicaragua, Panama, Colombia, Mexico and the Dominican Republic—as well as Puerto Rico," Smiley said. These agents were responsible for marketing the Marlins as another Florida tourist destination, like Disney World or the world-class shopping venues around Miami that always have lured wealthy Latins. "We want the Marlins to be another element of the tours packaged for Latin Americans coming to Florida," Smiley said.

Though one year formed an insufficient basis upon which to judge the success of the Marlins' efforts, team executives saw some encouraging signs. Salgueiro's primary responsibility was working with foreign sports reporters, and they always seemed to be in town. He said the Marlins had issued "many more than 100" credentials to print and broadcast reporters from Latin America from April through June. "Not only do they come to cover the Marlins, but it gives them a chance to interview a player from their country when he visits Miami," Salgueiro said.

Three Venezuelan TV crews were in town when Andres Galarraga of the Rockies took the Joe Robbie Stadium field in mid-July. Galarraga was on his way to becoming the National League batting champ, and even as far back as July, he was a big story in his native country. Miami's Latin flavor made it a fun place for Latin stars like Galarraga to visit. The Big Cat seemed to thrive on the attention he received from the Venezuelan press corps. He hung out with them at the team hotel, and as if to impress the folks back home, he hit a towering, 430-foot home run that got big play on Venezuelan TV. He also made a defensive play at first base—diving full out for an errant throw while somehow keeping his toe on the bag—that left even grizzled sportswriters slack-jawed.

"Believe me, I don't know how I do that play," Galarraga said following the game. "I try to do that in practice and I can't do it." But he acknowledged the Venezuelan media spurred him on, because he knew his whole country was watching the game.

"I gave three interviews today for my country, an hour each one," Galarraga told me after the game, as a cluster of Venezuelan scribes noted his every word. "It was enjoyable. I really like doing that for my people. I'm glad I could hit the home run for them."

Playing the Marlins also provided Galarraga with the chance to extract some vengeance for what he considered shabby treatment the previous winter from Marlins general manager Dave Dombrowski. "My first thought in the fall is that I am a free agent and I have an opportunity to sign with Miami. A lot of people from Venezuela can come see me play, plus I can be so close to my country. But Dombrowski, he say I can't play no more, that I'm all washed up. I try to play the same against everybody, but I think now maybe I play a little harder against the Marlins."

CHAPTER EIGHT

LIFE ON THE ROAD II: CHEERING FOR THE HELL OF IT

Until 1993, I'd seen major league baseball games in just a handful of parks—Comiskey Park and Wrigley Field in Chicago, Yankee and Shea stadiums in New York, Memorial Stadium in Baltimore and Fenway Park in Boston. I'd never longed to take one of those crazed, caffeine-driven trips around the country, hitting 28 ballparks in 28 days. But I had always loved exploring new ballparks, and it had always seemed a waste to visit a new city in the spring or summer without taking in a game. My trips with the Rockies were, for the most part, pretty business-like affairs. Sure, I got to explore ballparks and talk to fans, but I always had a notebook tucked into my pocket, and I never stopped thinking about what angle my stories could take. Here I was in the middle of a fan's dream—covering a team for a season—but I wasn't enjoying life as a fan. I couldn't cheer, I couldn't have a beer during the game, and I even missed entire innings while doing interviews.

So I made sure to work a few trips into my schedule where I could act, at least part of the time, like a fan. My first such trip was a pure lark—a long weekend's driving trip from Denver to St. Louis with two close friends to see the Rockies take on the Cardinals in a three-game set. The second was a solo journey 75 miles down Interstate 25 to reacquaint myself with the joys of minor league baseball at Sky Sox Stadium in Colorado Springs. And the third was an end-of-the-season trip, with the Rockies, to San Francisco and Atlanta for the team's last five games of the year. That last trip was, I suppose, more business than pleasure. But as luck would have it, the Rockies, 36 games out of first place, were in a position to determine who would win the National League Western Division. The Giants and Braves were fighting it out tooth and nail and the Rockies were looking forward to playing spoiler. I'd never been to a game with post-season implications, so I figured to be in for a treat. I may have been a member of the official traveling press corps on this last trip, but I was damned if I was going to watch from the press box and sit on my hands.

The trip to St. Louis came about after a long, lazy conversation over coffee with a couple of old college friends in the spring of 1993. Bryan Carr, a chef by trade, was leaving Colorado to move back home to St. Louis.

For Bryan, moving back to St. Louis meant reigniting his long love affair with the Cardinals. Bryan was the kind of baseball fan who could rattle off the batting average of every member of the 1967 or 1968 Cardinals without missing a beat. He could also argue eloquently the strategic implications of walking a weaker right–handed batter so a stronger lefty would have to hit against a south-paw bullpen stopper.

So when Bryan stopped in Denver on his way east on I-70 to St. Louis, he urged me to come visit in July, right before the all-star break, to see the Rockies play the Cardinals. "We'll whip your ass, but you'll have fun anyway," he promised. Doug Jewell, another college friend, was sitting there with us at my dining room table when Bryan extended the invitation. Doug, a chief deputy district attorney in Denver, spent his early years in Michigan and Illinois, but moved to Denver as a wee lad and was, for all practical purposes, a native.

At that point, the gears in my head started turning. Here was a natural story, I thought. Doug, representing all neophyte Colorado fans, journeys east into the heart of baseball tradition to meet Bryan, Sophisticate Fan. Two baseball cultures would meet, and I'd be there to chronicle it. Since St. Louis was the closest major league city to Denver, a story of this type that included some travelogue might interest my editors.

At the last moment, Dan Gardner, a Colorado Springs physical therapist and my ex-college roommate, decided to come along as well. Dan had grown up all over the country. His dad had been transferred several times, and he had spent parts of his childhood in Maryland, Delaware and Utah. But for some reason, he had been a devoted Mets fan since he was a boy. So, I reasoned, Dan could represent that other segment of mountain states baseball fans—the savvy transplants: people who knew baseball, grew up with the game, and were thrilled to death to have it moving into their neighborhood. Dan hadn't missed a beat in transferring his allegiance to the Rockies.

Our journey began on a perfect day for such an undertaking. It was a hot July morning, and the call of the road was as loud and insistent as the humming of cicadas. It was a Thursday; we had given ourselves 36 hours to make the drive to St. Louis for Friday night's game. Dan, in a Sky Sox T-shirt, his hair pulled back in a ponytail, let out a war whoop as we drove down the ramp onto I-70 for the start of our 1,726-mile odyssey.

After a lunch break in Goodland, Kansas, we hit the road again and discovered that the Rockies afternoon game in Mile High Stadium against the Florida Marlins was coming in loud and clear on the radio. We whooped and hollered along with the play-by-play as the road sucked us eastward at 75 miles per hour. Curtis Leskanic, an erratic young pitcher, was threatening to pitch the Rockies first-ever shutout. Invariably, at tense moments in the game, a siren would sound over whatever dippy little Kansas station we were tuned to, and an announcer with a pronounced twang would read a lengthy list of tornado warnings over the air in a slow drone. "Shut up and let us listen to the game!!" Dan screeched. Doug listened more quietly, sprawled out in the back seat, spitting Copenhagen juice into an empty beer bottle.

Leskanic took us as far as Hays, Kansas, which we reached in the top of the ninth. Darren Holmes came in to pitch the ninth, with the Rockies leading 3-0. Signs advertising the Ellis County Fair and Historic Fort Hayes dotted the landscape. The Marlins put a man on base. Over the radio, we could hear the fans at Mile High screaming for the shutout. Marlins outfielder Jeff Conine stepped up to the plate. The siren sounded and Tornado Man came on the air for the third time that hour. "A possible funnel cloud has been spotted approximately 20 miles east-northeast of Garden City," he read, stumbling over the words. "If you see a funnel cloud approaching, seek shelter. If you are outdoors and cannot seek shelter, lie flat in a ditch." We were a long way from Garden City, but I glanced up at the sky. Not a cloud in sight. Tornado Man signed off, just in time for us to hear Wayne Hagin announce, "And the final score from Mile High Stadium—Rockies 3, Marlins 2." Dan pummeled the radio. "Marlins 2? What the fuck happened?" After a few minutes, Hagin came back on and told us that Conine had lined a home run off Holmes, ruining the shutout. I reclined in the front passenger seat and took a nap.

By 3:00 p.m. the next day we were rolling up to Bryan's front door in Clayton, an upscale suburb west of St. Louis. Stepping out of our air-conditioned station wagon into St Louis' heat and humidity was like sinking into a bucket of warm spit.

Without wasting a minute, we headed for downtown St. Louis, about five miles to the east. We hadn't had a beer for at least an hour, so we stopped in at the Tap Room, St. Louis' only brew pub, an easy walk from Busch Stadium. As we sipped our pale ales, Bryan filled us in on a bit of local baseball lore. "You've probably noticed that there are a lot of Cardinals fans in Denver," he said, his soft voice bearing the distinct accent of his southern Missouri upbringing. "That's because until the Giants and Dodgers moved to California in 1958, St. Louis was the southernmost and westernmost major league city. People may not do what you guys did much anymore, but baseball fans used to come here regularly from as far west as Denver and as far south as New Orleans."

As we started in on our sandwiches and second pints, Bryan launched into a soliloquy on the 1993 Cardinals, who at that point in the season—the weekend before the all-star break—were making a serious run at the Phillies. "What can you say about Ozzie Smith? He's the consummate professional. He may not have the range he once had, or the bat, but then he'll do something like walk out to the mound and calm down a pitcher, or work a walk, or advance a runner, and you can just see his keen intelligence at work. And Gregg Jefferies. Man! What a year. He may have been a whiner and a baby where he played before, but he's had an MVP year for us. Just watch him hit. You'll see what I mean."

Bryan had learned the game from his father, who had the unique ability to follow a game's play-by-play on the radio while fast asleep. "He'd always have the game on, on the veranda. He'd turn the fan on himself and lie out there and fall sound asleep. I'd pass through and say "What's the score?" and he'd answer, "Four-two, Cards. Simmons just hit a homer.""

From his father, Bryan had inherited the ability, when talking about baseball, to bring people forward in their seats, to make them want to just drop everything and head straight out to the ballpark. So that's what we did.

In 1966, the old Busch Stadium, previously known as Sportsman's Park, closed and was replaced by a prototype of the symmetrical, artificial-turf stadiums that infected cities throughout the 1970s. I immediately noticed a lot to dislike about Busch Stadium, with its ugly green carpet and the logo of Anheuser Busch plastered on every available surface. Perhaps the most offensive manifestation of the beer-baseball marriage in St. Louis was a twisted variation on the seventh inning stretch. In most ballparks, the organist plays "Take Me Out to the Ballgame" and the crowd sings along. In St. Louis, the Diamondvision screen flashed a film of the Anheuser-Busch Clydesdale horses trotting out of a brewery gate. The organist played the Bud jingle, and the crowd clapped along, clearly loving every minute of it. Bryan looked sheepish; Dan, Doug and I booed robustly.

But Busch Stadium had its charms as well. To begin with, it was smack in the heart of downtown. The skyline and the awe-inspiring Gateway Arch loomed above the stadium, visible to people seated along the first base line. "It's easy to criticize the Busch family for building an ugly park and putting beer ads all over it," Bryan said. "But the stadium really saved downtown. And remember, there's not a penny of public money in Busch Stadium. The Busch family built the place with their own money, so I guess they've got the right to advertise to their heart's desire."

For Friday's game, Bryan had bought four $9.50 seats in the upper deck far down the left-field line. We could see perfectly, if with a bird's-eye view. Doug and Dan donned their Rockies caps. Bryan ran out to a concession stand and bought a $10 Cardinals hat. He shook it in Doug's face. "You'll be wearing this 'ere the week-end is through," he said. "Dream on, pal," Doug replied.

The beer (Bud and Busch, of course) flowed freely as the game progressed. Dan kept score and Doug peered over his shoulder, as the Cards inexorably built a 4-2 lead that they carried into the ninth inning. It was time for Lee Smith, the imposing closer, to put the Rockies out of their collective misery. Bryan was smirking. It looked hopeless. Smith retired hot-hitting Andres Galarraga. Fans started heading for the exits. Charlie Hayes sliced a double into the gap. Dan, the eternal optimist, leapt to his feet cheering. Doug and I exchanged glances and sipped our beers. Centerfielder Chris Jones, a free-swinging career minor leaguer, stepped to the plate. The ball rocketed off his bat, rising, rising toward the left-field wall. Dan, Doug and I jumped out of our seats. The ball landed well back in the bleachers. We slopped beer as we high-fived and jumped for joy. To hell with the press box, I thought. This is a lot more fun. Bryan slumped over and buried his head in his hands. "Oh, Lee, how could you?" he moaned.

So now the game was tied. Someone, I can't remember who,

flied out. Second-string catcher Danny Sheaffer stepped to the plate. BOOM! The moment he hit it, there was no question. The ball screamed to center field and hit some plantings above the wall. The crowd was stone silent, except for the three of us, dancing in the aisles and screaming ourselves hoarse as Sheaffer crossed the plate. "Sit down and shut the hell up," some woman behind us said. We ignored her. Smith got the final out and walked oh, so slowly off the mound, head hanging low. The crowd booed loudly. "I hate to hear that," Bryan said. "I don't care how much these guys make, there's no cause to boo them."

The Cardinals went down without a fight in the ninth, and the glum crowd shuffled out into the streets of downtown.

We were surrounded by morose St. Louis fans as we sat in a local bar following the game. They couldn't know it at the time, but that game marked the beginning of the Cardinals' sure and steady demise in the 1993 pennant race. Yes, the Cards won the next night, pounding the hapless Butch Henry 9-3, and sending him to the minor leagues. But the Rockies won again on Sunday, 4-1, and St. Louis sunk slowly into oblivion.

After Sunday's game, the four of us, along with Bryan's kid brother Dane, lingered in the stadium until all the other fans were gone. We sat in some box seats and watched the grounds crew pamper the infield. In the upper deck, a few kids chased each other through the expanse of empty red seats. Bryan pointed to a portico high up in the center field upper deck. "I remember seeing Willie McCovey hit a home run that must have traveled 500 feet. It disappeared through there." We followed the imaginary trajectory traced by Bryan's finger and shook our heads. We were seated in the shade, sipping lemonade out of huge plastic cups, and we didn't want to leave. Those 863 miles of road had sped by fast on the way out here, but they seemed daunting as we contemplated the return voyage.

We stopped by Bryan's place to grab our bags on the way out of town. He reached into a cupboard and produced three sleek, contraband Cuban cigars, a gift, no doubt, from some well–heeled club member. Then we said our goodbyes. As we drove west out of town, first Doug, then Dan and finally I, non-smokers all, lit our cigars. The car filled with blue smoke. It was wonderful. We were on the road, we'd seen three baseball games together, and now we were headed home.

While the Rockies took an extended trip to the East Coast I stayed home in Denver. At this point in the season, I'd been to 70 ballgames. Instead of relishing the interlude, I found myself experiencing pangs of withdrawal as the Rockies' absence stretched to two weeks. But there was baseball close at hand, I realized, just 75 miles south down Interstate 25 to Colorado Springs, where the Sky Sox, the Rockies Triple A affiliate, played. So, on an overcast day, grey clouds cutting the Front Range in half and a fine, misty rain blurring the windshield, I headed down the road to catch a night game between the Sky Sox and the Albuquerque Dukes.

Denver had been a Triple A town until 1993, and I had heard grumbling from a small contingent of fans who didn't enjoy the hype and hoopla that came with major league baseball. They had a point, I thought, as I drove toward the Springs. It used to be utterly relaxing to go to Zephyrs games. A crowd of 5,000 seemed huge. Everyone had three or four seats to sprawl across, and you were practically guaranteed a seat between third and first base. You could lean back in your seat and look at the vast, empty expanses of Mile High Stadium's upper decks. Way up in left field, about 10 rows back in the upper deck, two seats were painted orange amid the sea of blue. Back in the late 1980s Joey Meyer had blasted a home run 500-plus feet and hit one of the seats. It was a prodigious blast, duplicated in 1992 by John Jaha of the Zephyrs. No big leaguer came close to hitting one that far in 1993. On the day of the home opener, I glanced up toward the two orange seats and discovered they had been painted over blue. "Hey," I said indignantly to Rockies public relations director, Mike Swanson. "What happened to the Meyer and Jaha seats?"

Swanson sneered. "That's bush league. We're in the big leagues now," he said. Painting over those seats was one of the Rockies' few big PR blunders that first year. It was as if the organization decided it wanted no part of the city's distinguished minor league past.

I never once regretted the coming of big-league baseball to Denver, but I did occasionally wax nostalgic for the bush leagues. During Zephyrs games, the big video board didn't flash loud ads or show moronic blooper films. Food was virtually inedible, but at least it was cheap. You could drive up to the front gate one minute before game time, park right there for a couple of bucks, and buy a ticket without waiting in line. After several months of fighting traffic around Mile High Stadium, paying $10 for parking, up to $14 for tickets and a king's ransom for food and drink, only to see bad baseball, I thought people might enjoy knowing that they could still see bad baseball without all the peripheral aggravation.

Triple A baseball, while not up to the caliber of the big leagues, actually wasn't all that bad. In fact, the pitching and defensive weaknesses of minor league ballplayers made for some thrilling games. I still have taped to my refrigerator the ticket stub from a Zephyrs vs. Buffalo Bisons playoff game I attended with Doug Jewell on September 8, 1991. If memory serves, The Zephyrs went into the ninth inning of the game leading 9-0, and pitcher Greg Matthews was hurling a no-hitter. But the Bisons caught up to him in the ninth, and started rocketing the ball all over the yard. We could see the Zephyrs losing their collective composure as the Bisons rallied. Before long, the score was 9-8. There were two outs, and an inhumanly speedy guy named Greg Edge was on first, having singled as a pinch hitter. The next batter smashed a ball down the left field line. Mickey Brantley, the Z's left fielder, bobbled the ball for a moment, and Edge came flying around third, the coach frantically wind-milling his arm to send him home. Here came the throw from the left-field corner, a perfect strike to the third baseman, Charlie Montoyo. He wheeled and threw home just as Edge reached catcher Joe Kmak. There was a collision, a cloud of dust, and a moment of total silence as the umpire crouched over the play. Then he chopped his right arm down, thumb extended. "Yeerrrr ouuutttt!" we could hear him shout from our seats behind the on-deck circle. That ended the game. Edge jumped up covered with dirt and bumped the umpire with his chest. The Zephyrs were celebrating on the mound while the entire Bisons team surrounded the ump and chased him to the clubhouse like a swarm of hornets. I was completely hoarse. I'd never seen anything like it, and still haven't.

So I was looking forward to a solo evening at Sky Sox Stadium. I parked at the stadium gate for $2, bought a seat four rows off the field behind the home-team on-deck circle for $5.50, snagged a hot dog, a bag of peanuts and a beer for $8, and hunkered down in the mist to watch the game.

The full minor league picture was spread out before me. The 6,200-seat park felt cozy and intimate. Barren hills rose up just beyond the left field wall, and out past center, it seemed, you could see clear to Kansas. Soon, I speculated, the landscape would be covered by ticky-tacky housing developments as the sprawling city oozed ever eastward. I dropped my gaze into the park. Painted ads covered the outfield walls. A sign atop the right-field wall proclaimed Sky Sox Stadium "The world's highest pro ballpark—6,531 feet." The crowd was so small and so quiet that I could hear a rope clanging against an aluminum flagpole, and the thunk of a bat weight as rehabbing catcher, Joe Girardi, dropped it on the on-deck circle. I could hear the scratching sound of the Dukes pitcher digging a trough for his foot on the mound, and the cries of the infielders as they called for pop-ups.

There was none of the glitz and glamour of big-league baseball, it was true, but the old-fashioned schmaltz was laid on thick. In the middle of the third inning, a woman was hoisted onto the roof of the Sky Sox dugout for her big chance to win some really terrific prizes!! She tossed two huge, inflatable dice on the field. They bounced twice and then a gust of wind almost cartwheeled them into the outfield. Had she thrown snake-eyes, she would have won a party for 45 people at a local pizza restaurant. The crowd let out a collective groan when the dice came up 6 and 4. An inning later, Royal Caribbean Cruise Lines sponsored a boat race, a poor cousin to those annoying, electronic dot races on flashy big-league scoreboards. This was strictly low-budget, with three park employees running behind the outfield wall holding aloft three plastic boats glued to broomsticks. The crowd largely ignored it. I laughed so hard that several fans looked at me askance. Yet another promotion offered one lucky fan the chance to win $1,000 each time a Sky Sox player hit a home run off a drum mounted above the right field wall. On this particular night, a radio station allowed two fans to come onto the field after the game and grab as many compact discs as they could carry.

This was all classic minor league hokum, but none of it rivaled the old Zephyrs promotion, called "If the shoe fits." A randomly selected fan was brought onto the field between innings at each Zephyrs home game, and was allowed to choose a shoe out of a large crate. If the shoe fit the fan, he or she won a gift certificate from a local shoe store. They were pretty lenient with that promotion, because I never saw anyone fail to win.

So when I really thought about it, I guess there were as many peripheral distractions at minor league games as at any big-league game. But they were a hell of a lot more entertaining.

When I mapped out my season with the Rockies back in the early months of January 1993, I decided that a well-rounded chronicle of the inaugural year should include being present for the first and last games of the season. I had no way of knowing when I made plans to travel to San Francisco and Atlanta for the Rockies final five games that they would represent anything more than an anti-climactic end to a remarkable year. But they did. As luck would have it, the Rockies flew into the teeth of one of the most fierce pennant races in a decade, and they were in a position to determine the outcome.

There was an added poignancy to this pennant race, because 1993 was the last year that baseball would have just one tier of play-offs. True baseball purists never forgave the lords of baseball for going to a divisional set-up when the leagues expanded by two teams each in 1969. Up until then, there was the American League and the National League, and the first place team in each league met in the World Series. Starting in 1969, each league was split into two divisions, east and west, and the winner of each division played a best of five series to determine the league pennant winner, who would then go to the series. The playoffs went to a best of seven format in 1986. As a teenager influenced by my father's tastes in baseball, I was dismayed by the divisional set-up. But over the years I had gotten used to it, and more often than not found the playoffs to be more exciting than the series.

But now, beginning in 1994, owners greedy for the added TV revenues to be generated by an extra tier of playoffs, were going to divide each league into three divisions. A wild card team—the team with the best record that wasn't a division winner—would be added to the mix as well. So now there would be divisional playoffs before the league championship series. Baseball fans were uneasy about the looming changes, while team owners promised that this would keep more teams in contention and more fans engaged in the late-season action.

As a result of this coming upheaval, the pennant race in 1993 between the San Francisco Giants and Atlanta Braves was being billed by some as the last great pennant race. The Giants, revived by a new owner and the presence of $43-million Barry Bonds, had jumped out to a huge lead in the Western Division and appeared to be coasting to an easy finish. But then the Braves, on paper the best team in baseball, traded for slugging first baseman Fred McGriff in July, and began eating inexorably away at the Giants' 10½-game lead. In mid-September, the Braves caught the faltering Giants, then passed them and went ahead by four games. But just when it appeared that the Giants were dead, they were resurrected by great clutch-pitching performances. By the time the Rockies rolled into San Francisco, the Braves and Giants were in a dead heat.

I had stories to write, but I didn't want to watch these games from the press box. They figured to be exciting, and I wanted to be able to let out of a yell if the mood struck. So when I arrived at

Candlestick Park and found the press box overflowing with national baseball writers sent to cover this crucial two-game series, I was happy for the excuse to flee. "I guess I'll have to go watch from the stands," I said to a Colorado scribe, feigning displeasure. "From WHERE?" he asked, his voice tinged with disbelief.

It so happened that Colin Sacks, my closest friend from high school, lived in the Bay Area, and was an avid Giants fan. He'd been born in Berkeley and moved to Chicago at age 9. He never gave up his allegiance to the Giants, though he became a middling Sox fan and a denizen of the Wrigley Field bleachers in his college years. Colin, a child psychologist, was the type of fan who took baseball personally. When he was younger, a Giants loss was a personal affront, and at times he went into day-long sulks when they were doing badly. As he'd matured, he'd mellowed, but only somewhat. The first time I called to tell him I was coming to San Francisco, I got his answering machine. Instead of a regular message, he had taped radio announcer Hank Greenwald calling a Matt Williams home run. "There's a deep drive to left field! Gilkey's drifting back! He's at the track . . . he's at the wall . . . he's looking up!!! Home run, Matt Williams!!" And then the beep of the machine.

That was before the Giants started losing. After their fall from grace, he had recorded a depressed-sounding "This is Colin. Leave a message." He had almost decided to record a few bars of Mozart's *Requiem,* he said, but feared too few people would catch the drift.

Colin, a bachelor, had moved back to the Bay Area in 1991. I knew one of the primary reasons for his return had been the Giants, and I wondered how he had taken the team's near-departure for St. Petersburg, Florida the year before. The Giants had been sold to a group of Florida investors for $115 million in the summer of '92. All that stood in the way of the move was the approval of other big-league team owners. But that approval never came. Instead, owners forced Giants boss, Bob Lurie, to sell the team for $100 million to local bidders headed by Safeway supermarkets magnate, Peter Magowan.

Still, the memory of that near-loss chilled Colin. "It would have been immensely empty. I shudder at the thought of not being able to bring my kids to the games my dad brought me to." Colin's father died in the early 1980s, and going to Giants games never failed to kindle memories that warmed him even as the chill ocean wind cut through the cavernous stadium. "I really feel now for the people of Brooklyn and New York who had their teams move out here in the 1950s. I never thought about what that must have felt like until now," he said, puffing on a cigarette as the first game unfolded below us.

Denver was worlds away from that kind of chill. With a new franchise radiating health and a new ballpark under construction, there was nothing on the horizon to furrow the fans' collective brow. And yet, nothing leads to a downfall faster than overconfidence.

Colin never failed to bring his mitt to games. It was ancient—cracked and creased and stained, the rawhide laces frayed and thinned with age. An avid softball player who roamed the outfield with a fluid grace, Colin got a charge out of going to the ballpark early to shag batting practice home runs. He had an unerring eye and perfect timing, and rarely failed to catch a ball, even when surrounded by much taller and meatier competitors.

On Wednesday afternoon, September 29, Colin and thousands of other Giants fans arrived at Candlestick Park early for the last Giants home game of the year. Their team had beaten the Rockies convincingly the night before to remain tied for first, and a win this day would keep pressure on the Braves, who had been showing a few cracks in their armor. The Braves were playing that night, so a win would leave the Giants, for a few hours at least, alone in first place. I met Colin out in the new left-field bleachers Magowan had installed that year. These fans got to sit behind Barry Bonds, their icy hero. Unlike Rockies outfielders who had forged a bond with the Rockpile maniacs in Denver, Bonds ignored his worshippers completely. They didn't seem to mind; it made them think he had his head in the game.

Now, 90 minutes before game time, hundreds of brawny men were lumbering around after batting practice home runs hit by

Rockies players Charlie Hayes and Andres Galarraga. Colin stood there biding his time, until Jerald Clark hit one high and deep. It was coming close, but looked to be over our heads. Before I knew it, Colin was gone, two rows back and several seats over, and then he was back with the ball in his glove.

That, however, would be the high point of Colin's day. The Rockies spoiled the Giants party, beating them 5-3. "I want to stick around after the game to see what kind of hand the fans give this team after the great year they've had," Colin said during the ninth inning. So we sat there after the last out was made. The Rockies ran out onto the field to congratulate one another, and the Giants began walking down the right field line to their clubhouse in small clusters. The fans got up and shuffled to the exits. There wasn't a cheer to be heard. "Huh. How disappointing," Colin said with a shrug. I glanced over at him. He was tight-lipped, his eyes obscured behind his aviator's shades. I thought I detected a little of the edgy sullenness of old. His team had let him down. How could they do that to him, after all the psychic energy he had poured into cheering them on?

We paused on the concourse in the upper deck, and looked out over San Francisco Bay as we said our goodbyes. It was time for me to follow the Rockies to Atlanta, to see if they could crash the Braves party as well.

I didn't have any friends in Atlanta who were rabid baseball fans, but I was willing to bet I'd be able to find some Rockies fans to spend some time with amid the Braves boosters. Rockies fans, after all, seemed to be everywhere. Not that it would be easy, given the fevered pitch Atlanta fans had reached for this final weekend. Braves fans were famous for their Tomahawk Chop, a repetitive hammering motion made with the forearm, hand unclasped and held rigid. While they chopped, the fans would sing in unison a pseudo-Indian war chant. I didn't think much of the chop. It seemed pretty insensitive, even if the politically correct Jane Fonda, as Mrs. Ted Turner, had started participating in the moronic ritual. But I'd always thought the chant sounded pretty intimidating when I heard it on television during the 1991 and 1992 playoffs and World Series. When I got to Atlanta, I was disappointed to learn there was nothing spontaneous about it. Braves fans were like fans anywhere else, docile and bovine until prompted by the video board or organ. The Tomahawk Chop never started until the organist played the first few chords of the war chant. Then everyone would dutifully join in. I wondered idly what fans would do if the video board flashed the message "spit on your neighbor." There'd probably have been a massive brawl. The chop was initiated each time the Braves showed any sign of rallying. I kept a tally during the final game Sunday, and counted 22 chops in the course of a nine-inning game. It got old very fast.

Indeed, I did find some Rockies fans in there, amid the Georgia women with tomahawk earrings and the men with tomahawks shaved into the hair at their temples. There were those Coloradans who serendipitously ended up in Atlanta on business during the final weekend of the 1993 baseball season. Enterprising fans like Karl Eggers of Arvada managed to find a couple of much sought-after tickets to two of the weekend's three games.

"Man, this is great! It's like playoff atmosphere," Eggers said early during Friday's game, which the Rockies lost, as they did all three games in the series. Eggers was in Atlanta for a huge insurance brokers'convention. As luck would have it, the convention was being held at the Marriott Marquis hotel downtown, the same hotel that hosted the Rockies. "I'm a season-ticket-holder and I never got an autograph until I got here," Eggers said. "Today I got a bunch just by hanging around the lobby."

I met Eggers as I strolled the concourses under the stands Friday evening. He was standing next to a beer stand, chatting with an elderly gentleman decked out head-to-foot in Rockies regalia. The man was George Baylor, the 66-year-old father of Rockies manager, Don Baylor. To Eggers, this was too good to be true. Baylor the elder, a retired Missouri & Pacific Railroad worker, represented another core of Rockies fans I found in Atlanta—people with close ties to the team. George had flown in the previous evening from his home in Austin, Texas to be with his son during the team's final games of the season. Prior to this, he had seen only the Rockies home opener April 9 and a couple of games in Houston.

"This whole year has just been blessed," Baylor said. As he spoke, he fingered a diamond-studded gold pendant bearing the Minnesota Twins insignia, that Don had given him after he played on the 1987 world championship team. "I saw Don play in three World Series, but watching him manage a team that is playing so well now tops even that." I reminded Baylor that I had sat with him for an inning during the Rockies home opener nearly six months before. "Well, that's right," he said, grinning and slapping me on the shoulder. He bought me a beer and commanded me to come on down to his seats behind the plate and meet the rest of the family.

He pointed out Don Jr., a senior at Georgetown University, who had flown in from Washington, D.C. for the weekend with a couple of friends. From nearby came Don's first cousin, Carolyn Baylor and her 5-year-old son, Michael, both Atlanta residents. Carolyn, 43, a tall woman with a beaming countenance looked ready to chew her fingernails to the quick. "You might say my loyalties are divided here," she said with a laugh. "There's blood money in this, because of Don. I'm letting Michael wear my Rockies hat. And as you can see I'm dressed all in black for the Rockies. But I always wear my tomahawk earrings." She pushed aside her hair and, sure enough, there they dangled.

Although they grew up several hundred miles apart, Carolyn and Don saw a lot of each other as youngsters. He was two years her senior. "Don taught me how to catch with a glove," she recalled. "I went on to play catcher on the women's team for Southern Bell. And we weren't half bad."As the Rockies struggled valiantly but in vain to conquer the vastly superior Braves, Carolyn thought back on her early years with Don. "Most of the Baylors are kind of short, so he always towered over everybody," she said. "He always had that overpowering 'I'm not gonna move' type of attitude. I knew he had the temperament to be a good manager of an expansion team. He's a combination of super nice and super authoritative."

Carolyn looked over at George, who was completely absorbed in the game now, and smiled. "He's a sweet man, and Don's mother was a wonderful woman. Lillian. She died in 1988. I really regret she didn't live to see all of this, and I know Don does too."

The third category of Rockies fans I found in Atlanta came across the Caribbean to see these final Rockies games. At least 20 Venezuelan television, radio and print reporters flocked to Fulton County Stadium to witness the coronation of countryman Andres Galarraga as National League batting champ, the first Venezuelan ever to garner that honor. Unlike sports reporters in the U.S., who at least pretended to be objective, the Venezuelans acted like charter members of the Galarraga fan club. They clustered around him during batting practice, clearly thrilled to be in his august presence. They peppered him with questions in rapid-fire Spanish, even as he stood in the batting cage trying to take some swings. Galarraga was an accommodating sort, and never shooed the Venezuelans away. He obligingly posed for pictures with them and answered every question, no matter how inane. The Venezuelans insisted they were giving their people what they wanted.

"The economic situation in our country is very difficult," said John Carillo, a broadcaster with Union Radio of Caracas, which was beaming the games live to Venezuela. "People are not very happy. The news of Galarraga has been like a fresh breeze blowing through the nation." Galarraga would certainly be invited to meet with the president when he returned home later in October. He could also look forward to a parade in his honor.

"For the past 30 days people have talked of nothing but Galarraga," said Ruben Mijares, another Union Radio correspondent. "And this from not just the people you'd expect, the fanatics. I mean everyone. Women in line at the bank, airline pilots, everyone."

Mijares paused. I could see his brain working. This Gringo speaks passable Spanish, he thought, so why not? He clicked on his tape recorder and said in rapid-fire Spanish, "Alan Gottlieb is a news reporter for *The Denver Post* who has followed the Rockies and Andres Galarraga, El Gato, all year. Tell us, Mr. Gottlieb, what do the people of Denver think of Andres Galarraga?"

I told them, and just like that, I was a media star throughout Venezuela.

CHAPTER NINE

THE FANS: NEOPHYTES, TRANSPLANTS, AND PINING LOVERS

It was a lot of fun being out on the road, but my real work was in Denver, where this unprecedented fan phenomenon was unfolding. Over the course of the year, I watched various fan cultures and sub-cultures developing in Denver. The largest grouping, without a doubt, consisted of baseball neophytes who came to the ballpark out of curiosity, to be part of the action. These fans, for the most part, while long on enthusiasm and loyalty, lacked the seasoning and savvy of more established fans. I randomly selected a guy in the third level of Mile High Stadium during the last week of the season, and decided to anoint him "Every Fan." He didn't let me down. John Goutell, a twenty-something yupster, readily admitted he wasn't much of a baseball fan, but here he was attending his third Rockies game of the year, on a brilliant weekday afternoon, in the company of a couple of friends.

"I probably wouldn't have come even once, except I work at the Castle Pines Country Club (one of the most exclusive in the Denver area), and people have been so unbelievably excited about it," Goutell said. "It's fun. It's something to do in a town that didn't have that much to do before, unless the Broncos were playing."

Lifelong aficionados who moved to Denver from baseball cities may have cringed when they heard native Denverites refer to the umpires as "refs" and managers as coaches. But for the most part, the knowledgeable fans were pretty tolerant of the ignorance that surrounded them, at least until the fledgling fans started doing the hated "wave." But hell, this inaugural season should have been regarded as one big tutorial for everyone, right?

If so, then Jim Merriott wanted in the worst way to be the professor. Merriott, a freelance outdoors writer and hunting and fishing guide, made his first try at denting Denver's collective baseball ignorance one evening in late July, when he taught a three-hour class entitled "Let's Play Baseball" in the Jefferson County Adult Education program in the suburban town of Wheat Ridge. I'd never heard of a class on how to be a baseball fan. It had to be a uniquely Denver, 1993 phenomenon, I thought, so I drove out there on a hot summer night, passing up a Rockies-Braves game to attend.

The 10 baseball novices who signed up for the class were almost pathetically eager to grab ahold of the tail of this baseball comet and go along for the ride. Trouble was, baseball to them was a garbled foreign tongue, or a culture so alien that its rituals seemed random and incomprehensible. Merriott proved to be a nice guy, brimming with enthusiasm, but unfortunately he succeeded only in confusing his poor, doting students even further. He bounced from topic to topic like a super ball in a 4x4 room. After awhile, most of his students stopped taking notes and just stared at him, slack-jawed.

The class at least started out in a promising fashion. Merriott had laid out boxes of Crackerjacks and bags of peanuts at the door. "Grab some and come on in!!" he thundered to every new face that appeared in the doorway. The students complied, then shuffled into a room festooned with old-time team pennants, and lined with balls and bats and posters autographed by the likes of Mickey Mantle and Hank Aaron. Most of the students had been to at least one Colorado Rockies game. But they admitted to being baffled by the lingo, the subtleties of baseball, and even the basic rules of the game.

For Barbara Gagliardo of Wheat Ridge, learning more about baseball was a form of homage to her parents. "I have loved baseball all my life, but I've never understood it that well," she said. "I grew up in Detroit, and my parents used to take me to games all the time, from the time I was a baby. I was held by Babe Ruth when I was very little. Somewhere, I have a picture of it."

Students undoubtedly left Merriott's class with at least as many questions about the game as they had coming in. But if nothing else, they learned that baseball is a game capable of making a grown-up act like an 8-year-old leaning over the dugout begging for an autograph. Merriott's ardor was endearing enough to be contagious, even if it was somewhat incoherent.

"Until you walk into the stadium and feel the hair rise on the back of your neck, you don't understand what baseball means," the bearded instructor said early in the class. The remark drew some baffled glances from the baseball neophytes. So he tried again. "The biggest thrill of my entire life was April 9, 1993—opening day— being able to take my boys to a major league baseball game in Denver." A few people nodded this time. That made some sense.

"My wife, my two boys and I were the first people—the VERY FIRST PEOPLE—into the South Stands on opening day. I had to be there. Had to. I was also at the first-ever game of the Kansas City Athletics in 1955. My dad took me to that game, and my whole life changed. As my dad would say, I went to hell in a handbasket."

A young couple seated in front of me stole a quick glance and then dropped their heads, suppressing giggles. Merriott, oblivious, forged on, pacing the room with a maroon fungo bat in his hand. "I knew there was a void in Denver, a big void, as soon as I moved here from Kansas City in 1976." Suddenly, he stopped, and changed the subject. "You know what it means to be a real, true fan? It means being willing to wear a Yankees hat into the bleachers at Fenway Park in Boston. That's got to be the worst feeling in the world. And you know what every true fan should do whenever possible? Get to the park when the gates open. Go see batting practice—BP as we fans call it. The best part of a game is watching batting practice, and it's a great time to get autographs as well. And when you get to the park early, the park will talk to you. I know that sounds silly, but each park has its own echoes.

"My favorite kind of game? Extra innings. Once when I was a teenager in K.C., I went to a twi-night doubleheader. The first game went 14 innings, the second 17 innings. So now it's 2:00 a.m. and my poor mom has the cops out looking for me."

Once his 45-minute, free-form sermon ended, Merriott got down to the business of teaching the basics. As he rambled on, he covered topics ranging from how to get a good parking spot ("Park on an outside aisle in a lot near I-25") to how to read a box score. More than an hour was devoted to learning how to keep score, an exercise that clearly intimidated Merriott's students, none of whom had ever attempted it.

They still seemed somewhat shaky on scorekeeping by the end of the class, but a few of Merriott's pupils had a chance to put their new knowledge to work four nights later at Mile High Stadium. Merriott had bought a block of $4 tickets to the sold-out night game on Friday, July 30 against the mighty San Francisco Giants, and sold them, at face value, to students at the end of class. The seats were located in the third level of the East Stands, high above left field in foul territory. After an early evening rain shower, the skies cleared, and it was a perfect night for baseball.

Genie deLouise, one of Merriott's students, had gone shopping and bought a purple shirt for the occasion. As the game unfolded before them (the Rockies were pasted 10-4 as Barry Bonds crushed two home runs), Genie and her husband Rudy agreed that the atmosphere inside the buzzing stadium was something special. "We used to come to Zephyrs games, but we never paid much attention," Rudy deLouise said. "This is a different world. It's overwhelming."

Genie, who in her younger days was Miss Genie on the local version of the Romper Room kid's television program, was enjoying her chance to be a student for once. Merriott settled his large frame into a seat beside her and watched as she tried to apply the classroom lesson—keeping score—to a live game. Merriott, for some reason, decided that just scoring every play wasn't good enough. He made Genie track every pitch. This forced her to focus her concentration on the game. "Scoring is not a science," Merriott reminded her. "The point is to have fun coming to the game."

But if part of the point was to soak up the ambiance, then Merriott the stern taskmaster was depriving Genie of that pleasure. Tracking each pitch was hard work. Her job was made more difficult by the Giants, who were circling the bases with abandon, but by midgame she was scoring like a pro. By the fifth inning, she was beaming as she studied the newly comprehensible squiggles on her scorecard. "This is fun," she said.

Her husband smiled. "Genie's gotten to be quite a fan," he said. "We were out here one night in the rain. I was ready to leave, but not her. She stayed in her seat and got all wet."

That revelation alone was enough to make her the teacher's pet.

If you wanted a real taste of Colorado baseball fans, you had to spend some time in the Rockpile. Over the course of almost eight months covering baseball, I watched games from a lot of different vantage points: from the press box, from luxury suites, and even inside scoreboards. But by far the most enjoyable times I had were the two games I spent sitting in Mile High Stadium's $1 seats. The Rockpile's denizens were a varied bunch, ranging from the unemployed and unemployable to tradesmen on a budget. There were also a fair number of hard-core baseball fans who thought the view was dandy, the atmosphere exhilarating, and the price right. This was where you sat if you wanted to make some serious noise and, no doubt about it, quaff a beer or 12. After all, with the ticket costing just a buck, some people had a pocket full of bills to spend on brews.

These were the cheapest seats in major league baseball. And with earplugs and aspirin, you could have a fine time sitting in the Rockpile to watch Colorado's new team. But the Rockpile was not for the squeamish, the meek or the timid. It was fortunate—and absolutely by design—that the Rockpile was located in three lower-deck sections of left-center field, as far from the ritzy seats as you could get. Rockpile fans liked to make noise—constant, serious, vulgar, plebeian noise. My first night in the Rockpile, during an 11-2 Rockies blowout of the Chicago Cubs on April 27, a bunch of heavyweights jumped up and down with such ferocity that they rattled loose a support girder under the Rockpile stands. The clang of it hitting the cement could be heard even over the unending cheers and chants.

The Rockpile floor was made of steel sheeting. When the fans get to jumping, which happened several times each inning, the whole section vibrated, creating a tsunami effect in beers sitting on the ground. In addition to the sound of thunder fans made by the stomping on the floor, the first thing I heard when I walked into the section was a chorus of voices singing (screeching may be a more accurate description) "Here we go Rockpile, here we go!!" THUMP, THUMP. "Here we go Rockpile, here we go!" THUMP, THUMP.

Because Mile High Stadium was so huge, the team could afford to offer a large block of cheap seats. The Rockpile held roughly 2,000 people. Tickets went on sale 2½ hours before each game. Invariably, the line was long and boisterous when the box office opened. It didn't take long for the word to spread: The Rockpile was a happening place.

The first person I met as I entered the cheap seats was Ruben Valdez. He rushed over to shake my hand as soon as I sat down, even before I pulled out my notebook and identified myself as a reporter in search of a story. He considered himself the section's official greeter and cheerleader. Everyone was welcome here. "Call me Chip, man," he said in a raspy voice. Valdez was a 33-year-old bundle of manic energy with longish hair and dark eyes that glowed with a fanatic's light. He liked to grab a seat on the aisle between sections 134 and 135, right down front. But he never spent more than 10 seconds at a time in his seat. He must have run half a marathon over the course of a nine-inning game, much of it up and down the steep aisle. Not surprisingly, Valdez didn't have an ounce of fat on him.

To his everlasting shame, Valdez had missed two of the team's first 10 home games. He didn't want to miss many more. But he worked for his family's concrete company, and he couldn't sneak away for those weekday afternoon games, not when his dad was the boss. Valdez had great plans to become the unofficial Rockpile mascot. When he wasn't at work or in the Rockpile in those early weeks, he was at home, sewing together a costume. "Yeah, it's gonna be great!" he said, his voice so hoarse it hurt to listen to him. "It'll be a pinstripe uniform top with number zero-zero on the back and purple fuzzy pants. Then I'm gonna take a hard hat and paint it black, put the Rockies logo on it and pound dents in it so it looks like Fred Flintstone's hat. I'm gonna call myself Chip. I want to be able to run up to the top of the aisle and roll down the stairs like a boulder." I had no doubt Valdez would try it, and probably wouldn't hurt himself. Even if he did, he'd come back for the next game, in a body cast if necessary. And he still would have led the cheers. Unfortunately, the Rockies put the kibosh on Valdez's plans. "Yeah, they asked me to lay low, 'cause things were so wild in here anyway," he said at season's end.

You had to see Valdez to believe him. From an hour before game time until the last out was recorded, he was on his feet, hollering with the tattered, bloody-sounding remains of his voice, stomping with both feet on the steel-sheet flooring, starting cheers ("Scrub the Cubs!" was big that first night), and, of course, sprinting up and down the aisle, high-fiving all his new-found friends. "I've been waiting my whole life for baseball to come to Denver," he rasped. "Now it's finally here. I'm here, all the way. Before this year is over, I want them to rename this place the Wild Pile."

Valdez plopped himself down in a seat next to mine. It was the second inning, and already he looked wrung out. "Man, I have a killer headache," he confided. "Last night, I didn't get one until the fourth inning." The he hopped to his feet and sprinted up 50 steps to the top of the aisle. "SCRUB THE CUBS!" he shouted, then bounded back down to the front row, taking three steps at a time.

Neck-and-neck with Valdez in the unofficial mascot sweep-stakes were the Irish brothers, three beefy guys with voices just as hoarse as Chip's. The oldest was George, 24, a furniture mover for Allied Van Lines. He'd been to all of the games until the last three of the first home stand, when a moving job dragged him off to Minnesota. "We live right nearby, at 17th and Grove, so we don't have much excuse for not coming," he said last week. "Shit, I shoulda quit so I wouldn'ta missed those games."

Under most circumstances, George would have seemed like a pretty rowdy guy. But compared with Valdez and the two younger Irish brothers, Chris, 22, and Wayne, 17, George looked tame and mellowed by age. Chris Irish, a student at Denver's Colorado Institute of Art, had made up "Rockpile Maniacs" T-shirts. They featured an airbrushed, purple mini-truck with the Rockies inter-locking "CR" logo painted on the sides. The artwork would have looked just right on black velvet. He was the dandy of the family—his hair was moussed and carefully coiffed.

Wayne Irish was the true maniac of the bunch. The Rockies souvenir helmet he wore for the first 10 games was smashed to bits one weekend night, after one too many head-slaps from his brothers and Valdez. Or perhaps it was because he kept taking the cheap plas-tic headpiece off and banging it on the seat in front of him. After the helmet shattered, Wayne wore the brown plastic undergirding on his head for part of a game, until a fellow fan with deeper pockets took pity on him and donated a new one to the cause.

Wayne wasn't real swift on the uptake, but he had a sweet, goofy grin and I couldn't help but like him. He was a high-school dropout without a job, so he was in the Rockpile every game. He lumbered from one end of the $1 sections to the other, waving a Rockies flag over his head. His baggy, patched denim shorts rode low on his hips, and a "street life" tattoo glistened in the sweat on his shoulder. His voice was shot. I didn't see how any of these guys were ever going to sound remotely normal again.

Did the players notice the maniacs? How could they not?

"It's to the point where I kind of look forward to going out there every inning, messing with them," said Rockies outfielder Daryl Boston, who played center field the first night I sat in the Rockpile. "They like to be part of the game, and it's fun to bring them into it. I always wave to 'em, say hi, acknowledge them. A lot of times, that's all they want." Boston had the Rockpile pegged perfectly. He whipped the fans into a frenzy by leading cheers, and turning around and signalling to the crowd after each out how many outs had been recorded that inning. "We love you, D-BO!" they shouted to him, and he'd turn around and beam.

Alex Cole, the other regular center fielder, was another Rockpile favorite. When he was released by the Rockies at the end of the season, he said his biggest regret about leaving Denver was having to say goodbye to the Rockpile.

One thing it might have surprised Boston and Cole to learn about the Irish brothers and Valdez was that they didn't drink beer, at least not in the stadium. All of that energy was fueled by adrenaline, not alcohol. "Hey, I walk here for free and pay a buck for my seat," Chris Irish explained. "Why am I going to spend $3.50 for a beer?"

The cheerleaders might have stayed sober, but plenty of others in the Rockpile didn't follow suit. As far as team officials and the police were concerned, the Rockpile was a necessary evil, and a place to watch over carefully. Alcohol consumption in the cheap seats was monitored on a daily basis, according to Bernie Mullin. If things ever really got out of hand, access to beer would have been curtailed. Throughout the season, the Rockpile led the stadium in beer consumption per customer, but the section was never cut off.

If the Rockpile maniacs wanted beer, however, they had to go find it. Unlike the box seats, where beer vendors strolled the aisles constantly, blocking the views of paying customers as they dispensed their wares, the Rockpile was off-limits to beer vendors. A catered beer party, the Rockies felt, would have courted disaster. But the short walk to a beer stand didn't seem to bother most folks.

"Spirited, that's how I'd describe the Rockpile," said Mullin. "We keep it flooded with ushers and guest relations workers and monitor it closely. It's a wonderfully spirited atmosphere, and that's just what you want. But if anyone steps over the line, we move in fast."

According to Denver Police Captain Mike O'Neill, 20 to 30 Rockpile drunks were ejected from the stadium in the first couple of weeks of the season. The pace remained pretty constant all year—an average of two or three drunks booted per game. "It's not a big problem at all, so far," O'Neill said in late April. "I just don't want to see it get the allure and reputation of the Bleacher Bums in Chicago. Then people feel like they've got to go in there and go crazy. Right now, it's just the occasional individual who gets out of hand and makes it tough for everyone, especially if they're there with family."

The cops tried to make sure that people ejected for drunkenness learned a hard lesson, one they wouldn't care to repeat. Unless they were with a "quasi-sober" companion, drunks were sent to Denver CARES, the city detox center, for the night. The ride over to the center, in a windowless drunk-mobile usually spattered with vomit, was enough to sober up most people fast. And the detox center was no picnic either. "A night in there and you'll never touch a drink again," O'Neill said with a laugh.

On my second night in the Rockpile, Michelle Ramirez, a young but steely Andy Frain usher, confiscated a quart of Tequila from a man who was already drunk beyond all redemption. "Bottles aren't allowed in the stadium, and you're going to have to leave," she said, touching his elbow. The man stood unsteadily and followed her down the aisle. Near the bottom, just as a couple of Ramirez's male co-workers were moving in to help, the man reached down and picked someone's beer up off the ground. He flung it flush into Ramirez's face. Valdez and the Irish boys were there in a flash, ready to help restrain the guy (or, no doubt, get in a few licks), if necessary. But they were kept at bay, as three very large ushers escorted the guy out of the stadium. I don't believe his feet touched the ground between the Rockpile and the stadium gates.

"Hey, the ushers in this section are good people," Valdez said.

"They're part of the scene." He threw an arm around Eugene Pigford, a mountainous Rockies guest relations worker in a purple blazer. Pigford grinned and patted Valdez's shoulder. "This is fun, a lot of fun. I wouldn't be anywhere else," Pigford said.

The Rockpile had its quiter side, as well. During day games, the place was full of kids, including school groups during the spring. Savvy teachers knew a cheap, fun, field trip when they saw one. One perfect April afternoon, as the Rockies battled the Cardinals, 52 sixth-graders from Angevine Middle School in suburban Lafayette bused down to catch the game. Their assignment was to keep score. They were to hand in their scorecards to be graded after the game. The boys had peeled off their shirts to display "Go Rockies!" in purple and black greasepaint written across their bony chests. The girls sat in sedate groups, keeping score and sipping cokes.

The Rockpile was also popular with older (relatively speaking) fans who wanted to attend a lot of games but operated on a limited budget. Joe Dempsey, a 37-year-old carpenter who missed just a handful of games all year, thought the Rockpile was a perfect way to spend most evenings. His wife Jane and son Stephen, 12, seemed to agree. They were with him more often than not. The Dempseys even celebrated their 16th wedding anniversary in the Rockpile.

Joe grew up in Brooklyn, a Mets fan. "I still have a piece of the Shea Stadium turf from the day the Amazin' Mets clinched the division in 1969," he said. Jane was a native Bostonian who used to live and die with the Red Sox. "This place is great," Jane said during the Rockies-Cardinals game. "Get kids into this early, keep them off the streets. I'd come every day except I have to stay home once in a while to do laundry, and I play on a softball team."

Other than that, the Dempseys figured they'd only miss Rockies games if the Grateful Dead scheduled a concert that conflicted with baseball. They'd both been Dead Heads for 20 years, and one of their best friends was a Dead soundman, which guaranteed them backstage passes.

Joe wasn't sure whether he preferred the Rockpile by day or night. "The day game crowds are a lot more polite and sedate," he said. "It's relaxing out here in the daytime, but I like that rowdiness too." But Dempsey had no aversion to the box seats. Reverse snobbery wasn't his thing.

"This is like church," Joe said, obviously not referring to the noise level or language being used around him. "Sitting in the pews is nice, but if you get a chance, by all means sit by the altar."

Over the course of the season I talked baseball with some people who had an interesting theory about one segment of Rockies fans—the quiet, lifelong baseball worshippers. Many of these fans, some observers felt, were transplants from baseball cities. Over the years, their longing for baseball grew so intense that they overcompensated in unusual ways. These were, by and large, mainstream people, well-educated, articulate and white collar. But when it came to baseball, they were stark, raving mad.

What is it about baseball that causes some people to get lost so completely inside the game? You never hear of anyone collecting football cards in the same way you do baseball cards. Baseball lends itself to long, drawn-out discussions on strategy and statistics the way no other sport does. The pace of the game has something to do with it, of course. Basketball is all flash and speed and athleticism; football relies on brute strength and military-like execution of complex maneuvers. Baseball looks deceptively easy. It's a game most men played as boys, and many of us still play softball as adults. And those of us who play or have played know there's nothing easy about doing it well.

But more than any of that, I think, baseball breeds the most devoted of fans because it is the game of our youth. Talk to any avid baseball aficionado and you'll find someone brimming with sweet baseball memories from his or her childhood. For many, baseball forged a strong bond with their fathers.

Any baseball city in North America has these deeply knowledgeable, obsessed fans. They act out their obsessions in funny ways. Some quietly collect memorabilia. Others build monuments. Yet others get so deeply involved in fantasy leagues—a sort of let's-pretend-game for grownups in which a group of guys (it's almost always all guys) build teams by selecting players from existing big-league teams and following their statistics throughout the season—that their summers are swallowed up in boxscores.

Some true fanatics had even more peculiar ways of displaying their loyalty to the game. At Comiskey Park, the biggest fan I ever saw was a fellow everyone knew as Andy the Clown. He got to be such a fixture that the team let him into the park for free. He wandered the stands in white clown suit with red polka-dots, a derby hat and big shoes. His red nose lit up, but only when he shook hands with a child or a pretty woman. He had the loudest voice I've heard, and a set of lungs to go with it. "Come OOOOOOOOONNNNNNNNNNNN, LOOOOOIEEEEEEE-EEEEEEEEEEEEEE!" he'd shout, and people would give him ovations. By 1993, Andy was pretty old, and the White Sox's heartless owners had banished his clown outfit from the new Comiskey Park. But he still attended most every game, wearing a sweatshirt emblazoned with "Andy the Clown." And people were always coming up to him and pumping his hand, telling him how much they'd loved him when they were little.

Big-league baseball was new to Denver, but the city already had its share of this type of fan. If you spent any time poking around in 1993, it was impossible not to stumble across them.

On a crisp fall evening the week the 1993 World Series ended, I paid a visit to Barrie Sullivan's home in central Denver. Sullivan, you may recall, was the lifelong Red Sox devotee I met in Tucson during spring training and then again at the first Rockies-Mets game in New York. He had shared with me his philosophical musings about baseball—he flatly stated the game was his religion. But to understand Barrie and his relationship to the game, I knew I had to see his collection of baseball memorabilia.

He let me into his spacious tudor home and down to the basement. When he clicked on the light I gasped. An entire 10x15-foot room was crammed floor to ceiling with baseball stuff. There were shelves of autographed balls in plastic bubbles, display cases holding old uniforms, shelves of books, cabinets full of binders containing complete sets of 40- and 50-year old baseball cards. There were dozens of autographed bats leaning up against the walls. In an adjoining room, Sullivan had fashioned a walk-in closet. Dozens of old baseball jerseys hung in plastic bags. His collection was heavy on Boston Red Sox memorabilia, but it went way beyond that.

Sullivan excused himself to help put his two young children to bed, and told me to browse freely. He clumped up the stairs, and I lost myself in a world of memories I'd never had. It's impossible to say how long I was alone down there—an hour, I'd guess—but I could have spent a week.

Sullivan ranked his collection among the top five percent in the country. He didn't like to place a monetary value on it, but his stuff must have been worth hundreds of thousands of dollars. I picked a spot in the room at random and started browsing. Here, in no particular order, is some of what I saw. Autographed photos of Ty Cobb and Babe Ruth. Bats signed by Carl Yazstremski, Ted Williams, Carlton Fisk, Don Baylor, Paul Molitor, Reggie Jackson. Bats that had been used by every Rockies player except Andres Galarraga ("I started too late on that one, and now it's going to be difficult to find and expensive.").

Complete Ted Williams and Dom DiMaggio uniforms from the 1940s. The original cleats worn by Paul Waner, who was inducted into the Hall of Fame in 1952. Hundreds of commemorative pins, including press pass pins dating back to World Series games in the teens. An autographed photo of Mel Ott. Hall of Fame induction pins. A gold glove (fielding trophy) from 1957 that belonged to Frank Malzone of the Boston Red Sox. Autographed lithographs of Charles Comiskey and Connie Mack.

Balls signed by (among many, many others) Mickey Mantle, an entire Yankees team of the late 20s or early 30s, including Babe Ruth and Lou Gehrig; individual balls signed by Ted Williams, Joe Morgan, Fergie Jenkins, Bill Buckner, Hank Sauer, Fay Vincent, Don Drysdale, Jackie Robinson, Billy Martin, Keith Hernandez,

Allie Reynolds, Charlie Grimm, the Red Sox pennant-winning teams of 1942, 1967, 1975 and 1986, Harvey Kuenn, and several bearing the signature of Ted Williams.

I was grinning as I walked slowly around the room. My God, here was a pitching rubber removed from the Milwaukee Brewers bullpen following Game 5 of the 1982 World Series in Milwaukee County Stadium. The Brewers beat the Cardinals that game by a score of 6-4, in case you were wondering. I strolled into the closet-room, fingered jerseys signed by Carl Yazstremski, Ted Williams, Stan Musial, Gaylord Perry, Wade Boggs, Don Baylor, Dwight Evans and Carney Lansford. There was all manner of stuff—caps, balls, boxes of cards—stacked in corners, because Sullivan didn't have room to display it all.

Perhaps the best of all was what I looked at last. In a glass case near the door, Sullivan had several items that had belonged to Ty Cobb, including his brass tobacco spittoon, a razor and leather strop, a folding knife, and a leather money pouch. Also in the case were a jigger and corkscrew that had belonged to Tris Speaker.

Sullivan came back downstairs eventually, and I asked him how he had gotten involved in collecting, and how he had begun taking it so seriously. "Getting serious was easy," he said. "It was a natural offshoot of getting started." In 1973, as he was preparing to move to Denver from Boston, Sullivan obeyed an order from his mother and cleaned his stuff out of her attic. There, he found old sets of baseball cards he had collected as a boy, and his autograph book stuffed with signatures.

"I saw a want-ad seeking autographs, and I sold the ones I had as a kid. But I kept those cards and brought them out here with me. Then, five years later, when I really started getting into this, I re-covered all the ones I had sold." Sullivan knew he was hooked when he started subscribing to several different collectors' maga-zines. "Back in the mid-70s, it was almost all cards. I used to buy cards by the boxload, make complete sets from the years I wanted, then sell or trade off the extras."

His next step was to start collecting World Series programs. By 1993, he had perhaps the closest thing to a complete collection to be found anywhere. Each year, two World Series programs are produced, one by each team to be used in their home park. Sullivan had all but five programs. He was missing both from 1903, the 1906 White Sox, the 1917 White Sox (the last year my boys won the series) and the 1918 Cubs. I asked him to show me the 1919 programs, the year of the Black Sox scandal, and sure enough, there they were, lovingly placed in a plastic slipcover.

"So what's the point of collecting all this admittedly wonderful stuff and having it around your house?" I asked Sullivan. He began his lengthy answer by pulling out a huge, bulging ledger book. "I got this from a dealer in Aspen, of all places," he said, opening it. A musty smell escaped. "Do you know what this is? It's the 1946 Red Sox ledger. It's the book kept by the general manager—by hand, I might add—listing the attendance and gate receipts for all games played that year. As you can see, he also glued the box score from each game in here. Now, I'm showing this to you because 1946 happens to be the year I saw my first game. It was June 5, 1946. I didn't remember the date when I got this book, but it was easy to find in here because I remembered the game ended in an 8-8 tie, called on account of darkness. I should have known then that someone was trying to warn me about my life as a Red Sox fan. Ever since then, I've been watching them almost, but not quite, get over the top. They won the pennant that year, by the way. Here, let's find the clincher. Yeah, here it is. They won it in Cleveland, 1-0, on an inside-the-park home run by Ted Williams."

Having all this stuff at hand, Sullivan said, was a way of reliving baseball's great moments, some of which he witnessed, but many of which occurred before his time. "There's a certain collector's mentality, just the satisfaction of having it," he said. "But what really drives me is my love of baseball. I mean, someone could hand me Johnny Unitas' football uniform and it wouldn't mean much to me. When I look at this baseball stuff, though, it's a passionate wow! every time. There's a happiness in having it; shoot, I get lost in it. I can get into pretending I was there."

If he had to choose his favorite items, what would they be?

Sullivan answered without missing a beat. Not the stuff with the highest price tag, and not the oldest museum pieces. What he cared for the most were the pieces to which he had a deep, personal connection. "I grew up in Boston in the 1940s, worshipping Ted Williams. So his uniforms that I have, those mean a lot. But the one single item I have that means the most is a personalized autograph I got from him when I was 11. It was February, 1950, and my dad took me to the baseball writers dinner at the Copley Plaza Hotel in downtown Boston. I had my autograph book with me because there were a lot of star players in attendance. But the one I really wanted was Williams. Well, he was walking from table to table talking to people, and he stopped at our table. I handed him the book and he said, "What's your name?" I told him and he wrote 'To Barry (sic), your pal, Ted Williams.' "

"Years later, as an adult, I had a few chances to meet Williams. I told him about that autograph, and he said, 'Let me guess, I wrote To Barry, your pal, Ted Williams.' Well, I was astounded. But he said that's how he always signed personalized autographs. He told me that when he was a kid, the only autograph he ever got was Babe Ruth's, and Ruth signed it 'your pal.' 'If that was good enough for the Babe, it was good enough for me,' is what Williams said."

As we were about to leave the basement, Sullivan took one last look at his collection. He sighed. "If I could bring anyone back from the dead for 10 minutes, it'd be my father and grandfather, just so they could see this." He clicked off the light and we went upstairs.

Without a doubt, one of the most engaging and eccentric characters I met in 1993 was an accountant named Bruce Hellerstein. He was born and raised in the Denver area, but he possessed the same obsessive love for baseball I observed in Sullivan and some of the other driven transplants. At first glance, he seemed like your regular suburban guy. Nice ranch house in the southeast 'burbs. A Rockies doormat on which to wipe your feet. Inside, the house was tastefully furnished. His wife, Lynn, and daughters Annie, 12, and Becky, 9, (wearing Rockies T-shirts, of course), doted on him. The scene was all very normal, until he showed me the backyard and . . . the baseball stadium. It was in miniature, granted, but it was a stadium nonetheless, and it took up about a third of the family's spacious yard. It was meticulously cared for, the small plots of grass mowed to an inch high, dirt infield raked to perfection.

This was a classic, old-time park, which Hellerstein had given the unlikely name of Pass the Torch Field. Its outfield sloped gently uphill as it neared the wall—just as Fenway Park in Boston and Crosley Field in Cincinnati had in the early part of the century. The wall itself was unusual as well. It started out low near the foul lines, but rose to Green Monster heights as it moved toward center field. The result looked something like a dark green, symmetrical Mount Evans, the 14,000-foot peak that dominates Denver's mountain backdrop.

There was no artificial turf in sight. In fact, Hellerstein was wearing a T-shirt that bore the message "Real Grass Only. Bad Hops, Not Bad Knees." He pulled no punches when discussing Astroturf. "I've waited my whole life for major league ball to come to Denver. But if Mile High Stadium or Coors Field had artificial turf, I'd never go to a game—ever. I'd even have boycotted opening day."

The stands, even the upper decks, of his Pass the Torch Field were practically on top of the action. Hellerstein was a firm believer in authentic, old-time ballparks, like the dearly departed, old Comiskey Park in Chicago and Detroit's Tiger Stadium. There was nothing wrong with steel support columns obstructing the view from a few dozen seats, he believed. The columns allowed the upper deck to be built more directly on top of the lower deck, instead of raked back as the upper decks are in newer ballparks. That's how his ballpark would be, truly old-fashioned.

Hellerstein, a former member of the Colorado Baseball Commission, was pretty well known around Denver, at least within baseball circles, for the elaborate ballpark museum he built in the early 1980s in the basement of his home. A homemade shingle hung outside his front door: "Home of B's Ballpark Museum." The museum

occupied the entire basement of his home. You entered it by pushing through a turnstile from the old Connie Mack Stadium in
Philadelphia. Once inside, you could relax in a seat from Wrigley
Field, vintage 1950. A huge facsimile of the Wrigley Field scoreboard took up one wall, and a mural the other. On the wall beside
the stairway leading to the basement, Hellerstein had hung a series
of gorgeous lithographs of old ballparks. They were aerial views,
with loving attention paid to detail. Staring at them, you could almost smell the spilled beer and hot dogs, and hear the trolleys rattling by.

I asked Hellerstein if he had grown up rooting for any particular
team. "I've always pulled for ballparks, not teams," he replied. "One
of the biggest thrills of my life came in high school, when I traveled
to Chicago and saw games in Comiskey Park and Wrigley Field. It
was neat getting to see Ernie Banks and Luis Aparicio play, but the
real joy for me was seeing the parks."

Hellerstein had talked his way into a seat on the advisory panel
for the design of Coors Field. He didn't have much hope that his
ideas, admittedly extreme, would be considered seriously by the ar-
chitects or the team. He lamented that the city was going to blow
its chance to build a classic ballpark. Instead, Denver was going to
get a Coors Field closely modeled on Baltimore's Camden Yards,
the stadium opened in 1992 to almost universal acclaim. Hellerstein
hated it. "The thing that's going to make Coors Field a good place
is it's location (in a district of old brick warehouses just northwest of
downtown). It's not going to be Wrigley or Comiskey by any
stretch of the imagination. It's what I call state-of-the-art old-fashioned. Camden Yards is definitely not a classic ballpark. It's too
cutesy. It's configuration is basically artificial.

"They've programmed all these eccentricities into it. A ballpark
can't be classic unless its defined by surroundings. Wrigley Field is
all crammed into one square block, for example, and it's a real,
organic part of that neighborhood. Do you know what's a natural
ballpark that verges on the classic? Mile High Stadium. It's got that
big bulging outfield and the short left-field wall, because it has to

deal with the constraints of those movable east stands and the fact that football is played there."

Pass the Torch Field came into being because Hellerstein needed to express concretely some of his ideas about how a true Denver ballpark should be designed. Building the model ballpark was fun for Hellerstein, but that didn't mean he took it lightly. He hired a landscape architect, laid special bluegrass sod, and carefully replicated many features of old Bears Stadium, where he watched ballgames as a boy. He incorporated some touches of his own as well. In keeping with the Rockies color scheme, Hellerstein planted small purple flowers along the base of the wall. In a real park, he said, ivy and purple flowers could climb the outfield walls, creating a Wrigley Field effect, but in technicolor.

Hellerstein went inside and brought out a box of Hartland Figurines of players from the late 1950s and early 1960s. They were a little too big to fit the scale of Pass the Torch Field, but Hellerstein enjoyed playing with them. He spread them around on the emerald-green grass. "Let's see, Nellie Fox at second base, Aparicio at short, Warren Spahn on the mound, Eddie Matthews at third, Campanella catching. Let's put Willie Mays out in center, and this old timer here (it was Babe Ruth) at the plate."

Pass the Torch Field was a clunky name, but to Hellerstein it embraced Denver baseball history instead of turning away from it, as the Rockies had done. The name acknowledged the end of the minor league era and the advent of Denver's time in the big-league spotlight. As a symbol of that torch passing, Hellerstein's ballyard included a cut-out of the old Denver Bears mascot, bolted to the top of the outfield wall. In one paw the bear carried a Colorado Rockies banner. "They had a bear like this one, only much bigger, of course, in left-center field above all the billboards," Hellerstein said. "The bear carried a sign that said 'Hit me for $50,' and if a player hit the bear, he got the money."

"You know, having the Rockies here is a lifelong dream come true, but what hit me most on opening day was reliving some great moments in old Bears Stadium, reliving my childhood. I really miss some of that minor league stuff. I just got back from a trip to the deep south. I went to see some old ballparks and some minor league ball. God, there are some great old minor league ballparks out there."

Lynn Hellerstein laughed when I asked her what it was like being married to a man possessed. "Well, we were married a year or two before I knew about this. If I'd only known before . . ." she laughed again. I asked Hellerstein his age. "Six," Lynn replied without missing a beat. "Six going on 44." "Which was Hank Aaron's number, by the way," Hellerstein added.

The two girls didn't seem to mind that Pass the Torch Field has appropriated a chunk of the backyard. They carefully stepped around the 12 square feet of newly sodded yard, avoiding the miniature pitcher's mound and tiny bases. When the family terrier, Toto, scampered across the infield, knocking Nellie Fox face-first onto the infield dirt, they shooed him away.

It was a kiln-hot July day, and it was pleasant to sit in the shade on Hellerstein's back porch and look over the miniature Pass the Torch Field. Three chipped wooden seats from Tiger Stadium in Detroit were bolted to the cement directly behind home plate.

Why Tiger Stadium? "It's my favorite ballpark, believe it or not," Hellerstein said. "There's something magical about it. The most special thing about a ballpark is the acoustics. In Tiger Stadium, when you close your eyes, there's so much of the game you can hear. That's intimate, and that's what we'll miss when Coors Field opens."

Barry Fiore grew up on the North Side of Chicago, the son and grandson of restaurant owners. To say he was raised a fanatical devotee of the Cubs would be a gross understatement. Fiore hasn't collected mounds of memorabilia or built baseball monuments in his home, but he wins hands-down the competition for most baseball-crazed fan in Colorado. I base this admittedly arbitrary distinction on a spiral notebook Fiore kept on the shelf in the office behind his sports bar and restaurant in the far south suburbs. He once had 14 of the notebooks, one for each Cubs season from 1957-1970. He stopped filling them in 1970, the year his son Todd was born. He still had four of the notebooks as keepsakes, a testament to the power baseball held over some people.

"Yeah, I kept pretty detailed stats on the Cubs over 14 years," he said one spring day. What an understatement. What he'd done was all the more remarkable because it predated the era of home computers. "I cut out all the *Sporting News* articles, followed the *Chicago Sun-Times* and did a game-by-game account for 14 seasons. I wrote down the standings every week, but I kept track of every hitter and pitcher on a daily basis, calculating out the batting averages and earned run averages by hand. I wrote down for every game what every individual player did in that game. I kept track of pitcher's batting averages, pinch hitting, team fielding, all game-by-game and composite. Total runs by inning, record in one-run games, night games, extra inning games. Games when they rallied to win after the sixth inning. Games where they led and lost after the sixth inning. Record by day of the week. Attendance by team they were playing, home and away. You know, I can't begin to count the number of hours I spent on this stuff. My wife once said to me, 'Jeez, if you had spent all that time and energy on something more profitable, you'd be a billionaire by now.' I just enjoyed doing it."

In 1969, the Cubs choked away the division title, losing a big lead to the Mets in the final weeks of the season. As a 13-year-old White Sox fan (which by definition means Cubs hater) it was one of the most sadistically satisfying summers of my life. But Cubs fans remember 1969 the way the South remembers Antietam. "I was so despondent about 1969," Barry said, still unable to laugh about it in 1993. "Even after the Mets clinched I kept thinking something would change. Then, in the last couple of days of the season, I stopped keeping the stats. I was just too heartbroken. I was so despondent that I took all my notebooks, representing thousands of hours of work, and threw them out in the garbage. My mother, bless her, saved four of them. I keep one here in the office. Here, have a look."

I took the priceless document in my hand. The cardboard was worn fuzzy, as soft and supple as velvet. I looked at the handwriting on the cover. Cubs Stats—1969.

CHAPTER TEN

PLAYERS: SLIDING OFF THE MOUNTAINTOP

Although I never became friends with any of the Rockies players, I spent a lot of time in close proximity to them. My life had little in common with theirs. It was an interesting mental exercise to imagine what it must feel like to be a big-league baseball player. You're born with a physical gift that, thanks to the crazy times you happen to have been born into, ends up making you millions of dollars before you turn 30. You've never done anything to reduce human suffering or increase knowledge, but millions look upon you as a hero. It's not hard to get used to a life like that.

But then, one day, it's suddenly all over. Your physical skills erode and you're no longer able to play the game at the stratospheric level required of major leaguers. What do you do then? What's it like to adjust to being just a regular guy?

By the end of the Rockies first season, three players who started the year with the team had retired. One of them, Mark Knudson, went semi-voluntarily. The other two, Bryn Smith and Dale Murphy, left because the team told them they could no longer produce. These three guys, I thought, should have an interesting perspective on the ballplayers' life, and on life after baseball. So at the end of the season I checked in to see what had become of them after they fell off the sports pages. I also wanted them to think back on what being a pro athlete had meant to them. As soon as they left the team, they ceased to exist for most baseball fans. But they were still living their lives and trying to figure out what to do next.

I had talked at length to Bryn Smith during spring training, because I had hoped to profile the 37-year-old veteran pitcher throughout the course of the season. He thought that sounded fine, and expressed willingness to make himself available whenever I felt like talking to him. We had our first session in the Rockies dugout in Tucson. Smith, who had just had arthroscopic knee surgery to repair torn cartilage, sat rolling a bat between his palms, and talked in the drawn-out cadences of a Southern Californian.

Despite his knee injury, Smith wasn't thinking that the end was near. Quite the contrary. He pushed himself hard in rehabilitation, and he was ready to pitch the Rockies home opener April 9, a day he later described as the highlight of his baseball career. Smith signed with the Rockies as free agent after an elbow injury curtailed his 1992 season with the St. Louis Cardinals. The beard he'd worn for years was shaved to comply with the Rockies' strict grooming policy.

Although retirement was the last thing on his mind that lovely desert spring day, I asked Smith as we sat there what he thought he might do when his career ended. "Once it's over, I'd really like to coach. At the big–league level would be an ideal situation. But the possibility of going back to my home town (Santa Maria, California), and doing something with the local high school, where I went to school, that's pretty appealing, too. If an opportunity were to come in the professional ranks I'd have to seriously think about that. I rode a lot of buses for a lot of time in the minor leagues and I really don't know if I'd care to go back to that. But I might miss it so much, I'll decide to do it. Because I don't know anything else. I don't have any degrees, don't have a passion of going to work or establishing a business. All I know is baseball, so maybe baseball is where it's at.

"I haven't really thought about going back to school. I'm thinking about raising my kids (a boy, Cody, who was 10 at the time and an infant girl, Cady), and enjoying some time, just time. It's been 20 years. It sounds nice to go home to the local fair and the rodeo and the things I remember growing up."

Among the group of boisterous young men that populated the Rockies clubhouse, Smith had a unique perspective born of relatively broad experience. At 37, he was five years older than any of his teammates. His face carried a few more lines and his body a few more scars. Most players had taped their baseball cards or press clippings over their lockers. Smith displayed photos of his two children. While some guys pumped iron or rode the exercise bike, Smith was known to puff on a cigarette or two in his off-hours. More than many of his teammates, perhaps, Smith had a life outside baseball. After he finished his day's work in spring training, he drove back to his mobile home parked well away from the center of town. He just wanted to kick back and take things slow.

He was born in Marietta, Georgia, and moved at age one to Santa Maria, three hours north of Los Angeles. Smith had an older half-brother, but he left home when Bryn was nine. "After he left, I was pretty much on my own for a long time, which was a pretty rough road. You know, there were a lot of ways to go, and some weren't all good. But baseball, thank God, saved me."

His first baseball team was in the Pee-Wee League. "I was seven. You were supposed to be eight, but they snuck me on the Columbia Records team." Smith played right field and second base that first season. His second year, he started pitching. "I remember a clipping from the local paper, when I walked 13 people and struck out 12. I think that was my pitching debut. Things got a little better after that." But baseball was his secondary sport. Golf was his love. "I was playing 36 holes a day every summer, and at 12 and 13 I was winning some junior tournaments and thinking about trying to play golf professionally." Then he got to high school. "A few people started razzing me about the game of golf, you know, saying it was a sissy's game. So I had a choice of baseball or golf, and I had to switch to baseball, just so people would get off my back."

Smith decided he wanted to be a professional ballplayer the first time he set foot in a big-league park. At 15, he went to a baseball camp near Los Angeles. His mother came to visit and took him to a game at Dodgers Stadium. An old friend of hers was a big-league umpire, and he got the Smiths some field-level seats. "I remember telling my mom, 'This is something I'd really like to do.'"

He never thought he had a shot at it. But he was invited to a tryout by the Baltimore Orioles a year out of a high school, and the club offered him $1,000 to sign. He did. Smith, married by then, struggled for six years on a minor leaguer's salary. "I didn't know what else to do, and somehow we were surviving, getting by. But things kinda got stalemated for a while."

He was traded to the Montreal Expos system in 1977. There he got to know Bob Gebhard, who became the Rockies first general manager, and Larry Bearnarth, the Rockies pitching coach. At one point, after a disastrous stint with the Denver Bears in 1978, Smith was demoted a step to Double A baseball. Feeling discouraged about his prospects of ever making it to the majors, he went to Gebhard and told him he was thinking of quitting.

If Smith was expecting sympathy from Gebhard, an affable but business-like baseball executive, then he was about to learn his first lesson about baseball as a business. "He told me, 'You know, Smitty, baseball is gonna be here whether you quit or not, so I'm not gonna tell you yes or no. If that's what you want to do, then do it.' So I thought about it a little more, and didn't do it."

He was added to the Expos' major league roster in September 1981. He still remembers that first day. "I was in awe. It's hard to describe. It's like you've reached your goal, and you're there but you're really not. It took a while for it really to set in that I'm at the major league level."

He came into the Rockies camp with 11 big-league seasons under his belt. The awe was long gone, but not his appreciation for a great way of life. Still, Smith didn't have to think long when I asked him to describe the best and worst things about a baseball career. "When you ask that question, people obviously focus on the money a lot. But I honestly think that every baseball player will play the game regardless of what the money situation is. Baseball has given me everything. It's given me some fame, it's given me a very comfortable way to live, a lot of fun. But most important, it's getting to that mountaintop. It feels good to stand on top of that mountain."

But life in the big-time had its down side. "You've really made a sacrifice, in terms of family. That hurts some. Also, the way people change their attitudes toward you because of who you are and not what you are. I would rather have people know me for me, rather than judge me by how much I make or what I do. You learn to take the verbal abuse from fans. You're never going to please everybody, no matter what you do and how well you do it. At first you hear people. But you just have to remind yourself that they really don't know. They just don't know what's going on. They've had a bad day at work and you're just the guy they're going to take it out on. And you can take so much, more than you might think. You have to. Because once you acknowledge the fact that the obnoxious fans are there and they've said something, then all of a sudden your attention is somewhere else, and that's kinda what they want to do to you. You learn what to say and how to shut 'em up and after a while it kinda quiets down.

"As far as your life off the field as a ballplayer, sometimes you have to buy whatever privacy you want, which I don't think is fair, but that's part of the job. If you don't want to be bothered, then you buy enough space to where you're comfortable and you fence everybody else out. And when you go out, people sometimes are uncomfortable, or they think that you owe them something. Again, they don't know, and I think if you're nice enough towards them to where you make yourself understood in a polite way, things work out OK. I like people and I want them to like me. So I treat them the way they treat me. If it's fair, if it's open, if it's on the same level, then we're going to get along. If not, I can just close you out, see you later, I don't want anything to do with you."

Smith's year started in glorious fashion. He pitched eight shutout innings in the Rockies home opener. But from there, it was all downhill. He was released on June 2, after compiling a horrendous 8.49 earned-run average and a 2-4 record in 11 games. As is usually the case when players are cut, Smith became a non-person immediately in the Denver media. It wasn't a deliberate snub. It was just a fact of life that players came and went and the important ones were the 25 in uniform on any particular day. The last thing people in Denver read about Bryn Smith was that he was hoping to hear from another team. The opening day hero, the great veteran hope of the shaky young pitching staff, was history.

I reached Smith at his Santa Maria home in early October. "It was almost a relief when things finally happened and I got released," he told me over the phone. "I mean, it was pretty obvious to me that I had been on the edge for a while. After it happened, suddenly I didn't have to worry anymore about how my arm felt, my knee felt."

Smith hung around Denver for awhile waiting to see if another team would call. He and his wife packed boxes that, ironically, had just arrived from St. Louis the day he was released. But if the Rockies, with far and away the worst pitching staff in the majors, didn't want him, who would? It became increasingly obvious, as the days passed, that no one was going to call. "Then we took a nice leisurely drive back home, going through Yellowstone, just relaxing and hanging out and enjoying being together. It was nice to get home. Since getting back I haven't been doing a whole lot of anything major, just enjoying some quality time after all those years of traveling for baseball. It's almost like a vacation. I'm just trying to take care of the family, play some golf, do some fishing."

I asked Smith how much he missed baseball. "I miss playing," he said with no hesitation. "I miss the camaraderie with my teammates, the atmosphere in the clubhouse. I miss the competitiveness of getting out there on the field. But I'll tell you, I do *not* miss the hustle and bustle, the grind of traveling, the mental preparation, the day-in, day-out of it."

Having said that, however, Smith confessed that he considered his summer vacation just an extended off-season. "I haven't picked up a baseball since that last time in Denver, but I think I'll start throwing again in November, see how it feels. I'd like to go to spring training with someone, actually, see if I can make the squad. I'd really like it to be the Rockies. If that doesn't work out, I'd like to get into coaching or the instructional end of things, maybe working under Larry Bearnarth. I can't imagine a year without spring training. I have no idea what that would be like."

Even the most grizzled sportswriters had a soft spot for Mark Knudson. He was a big, broad-shouldered, right-handed pitcher, born and raised in suburban Northglen. He had good years with the Milwaukee Brewers in 1989 and 1990, winning 18 games over those two seasons. But his career had foundered and he'd spent the 1991 season pitching for the Denver Zephyrs, the Brewers Triple A farm club, and the 1992 season with the Las Vegas Stars, the San Diego Triple A team. He signed with the Rockies as a free agent on October 29, 1992, went to spring training and pitched well, almost well enough to make the club. He had promised himself he'd retire if he was sent to the minors before the season began, but Bob Gebhard said they'd give him a shot at the majors early in the year if he'd just hang in there. So Knudson went down to Colorado Springs and pitched for the Sky Sox. He got the call to join the big club on May 5. But his stint with the Rockies lasted just 12 days. On May 6, he was brought on in relief against the mighty Atlanta Braves. Finally, the moment he'd been waiting for. He was pitching in front of his home-town fans in a big-league uniform.

It was a disastrous outing. He allowed eight runs in one inning of work, including three home runs. He pitched in three games after that, but things didn't improve enough to reverse that awful first impression he'd made. When he was told in San Diego that he was being shipped back down, Knudson had allowed 14 earned runs in just over five innings of work. He knew then that the jig was up. He made good on his promise to himself and his wife Allison, and retired.

"When my chance came, it was short-lived, and I don't really know why," Knudson said during an interview in his livingroom in early June, three weeks after he quit baseball. "I don't think anyone ever thinks they got enough of a chance. Five innings isn't a lot. I know my first outing was horrid, but it was just one game. There are a lot of guys on the team who've had a bad game. After that, I think I threw the ball a little better. I know this was a business decision. It was not directed at me the person. I'm disappointed, I don't agree with what they did, but I understand why they did it. I still root for the Rockies. They're the team I'm going to root for the rest of my life."

Knudson started rooting for the Rockies long before the team existed. He had grown up fantasizing about playing for a big-league team in Denver. He rode the emotional roller coaster as a fan in the 1970s when Denver almost landed the Oakland As. And when the expansion derby heated up in 1990, the Colorado Baseball Commission recruited Knudson to help get out the vote for the stadium tax.

"In 1990, I came home for the all-star break. I no more hung up my coat when I was on the phone with someone from the baseball commission. And they shuttled me around for three days, what seemed like non-stop. I barely saw my family, I barely had a chance to watch the all-star game. I went everywhere, from Longmont to Littleton, to bars, little-league fields. I believed in it and everything, but God, I was exhausted when I got on the plane to go back to Milwaukee later that week."

When he thought back on it, Knudson realized he may have been just a little too eager to sign with the Rockies over the winter of 1992. "I might have made some mistakes along the road, being a little too anxious to sign with them. It's kinda like you're in a dance club and someone is pestering you to dance with them. You tend to shy away from them. Whereas if you're the one doing the pursuing, you appreciate them a little more. The Rockies wanted me, no question, but they took me for granted a little bit because I was so anxious to sign."

The end came for Mark Knudson in a San Diego hotel room May 18, halfway through a two-week road-trip. Gebhard and manager Don Baylor took the 32-year-old pitcher aside and told him he was being demoted. "I know Don (Baylor) had a hard time doing that with me. We've been friends for the last few years. Don was real sheepish about it. He didn't do much of the talking. So the last thing I told him before I left was 'Look, smile. It's going to be all right.'"

But it wasn't an easy moment for Knudson either. "It was a jolt at the time, but it wasn't like I hadn't been thinking about it for a while. I thought about this last August, when I didn't get called up by San Diego, and I sat there the whole month of August making a road trip from Las Vegas to Edmonton to Calgary to Phoenix, with lots of puddle-jumper stops in between. That was just a bear, and I remember sitting on a flight and thinking, I don't want to do this anymore. This is no longer fun. It's fun being a major leaguer. The minors are no fun. I don't want to be a minor leaguer anymore. I can make a living some other way."

An imposing 6-foot-5 and 200 pounds, Knudson spent four of his nearly 12 years in professional baseball in the big leagues. Although he verged on stardom with the Brewers in 1989 and 1990, he struggled the rest of his career to prove himself good enough to pitch in the majors. When I asked Knudson to recap his career for me, he settled back on the couch, with a view out over a suburban golf course, and talked without pause for 45 minutes. Clearly, he enjoyed reminiscing about the ups and downs of his years in the game. What was striking about his story was how capriciously fate had dealt with him. A few breaks here and there could have made him a star instead of a journeyman.

"My first taste of the big leagues came in 1984, when I went to spring training with the Houston Astros. I'd been drafted by them in the third round in 1982, after graduating from Colorado State University. At spring training, I got to be around guys like Nolan

Ryan and Phil Garner. They taught me a lot. They gave me a lot of confidence, gave me the sense that I could really do this. They told me there was really no reason I couldn't play major league baseball. That made me turn it up a couple of notches."

In 1985, Knudson was placed on the Astros' big-league roster for spring training, and was called up to the big club in July. That's when he caught his first bad break. "I was only up for two starts because I got hurt. Actually, I was probably hurt when I got there. I had a sore arm when I got there and pitched really poorly, and got knocked all over the place. I ended up going on the disabled list for a while, and then back to the minors." In 1986, Knudson again started the season in the minors, but was called up in June. "I did OK. My record wasn't real good (1-5), but I pitched competitively and I knew I could pitch in the major leagues. That was the year the Astros won the division. I got to pitch with Mike Scott, who won the Cy Young Award, Nolan Ryan, Bob Knepper. Then I was traded to the Brewers in the stretch drive for a veteran player, Danny Darwin. That was really frustrating, because I felt I was right on the verge and I was on a first-place team. So I wound up sitting in my hotel room in Milwaukee watching the highlights of Mike Scott throwing a no-hitter against San Francisco to clinch the division title. That whole experience was tough, to have to start over from scratch."

Once again, Knudson started the season in the minors in 1987. I asked him if that was difficult. "Yes and no. It's a letdown, but it's a reality check too. You realize you're playing with the best players in the world, and if you're not quite up to snuff, there are just so many jobs to go around. Actually, when you're young, being sent down makes you hungry. It makes you push yourself a little bit more, maybe sometimes push yourself a little too much." Knudson was called up to the Brewers before the all-star break, and compiled a 4-4 record. But the Brewers made a lot of personnel changes, and Knudson found himself back in Denver with the Zephyrs at the start of 1988. He pitched for the Zephyrs until September, when the Brewers called him up again. He didn't fall into the minors again until 1991.

That was the year he was hit with his biggest dose of misfortune. He'd had those two winning years with Milwaukee, and suddenly, because of injuries to other pitchers, he got the chance of a lifetime—to pitch on opening day 1991 in Texas, against none other than Nolan Ryan. Knudson went five innings and got the victory. But less than 24 hours later he came down with a mysterious viral illness that's never been conclusively diagnosed. "It was somewhere between a flu and mono. They didn't really have a name for it. I got tested for everything. I'm sure they tested me for AIDS and everything else, but they couldn't come up with anything. I was (bedridden) for about eight days. I went home from Texas and I lost 12 pounds in 10 days. I just lay there. I couldn't do anything. I was pretty much a wreck."

The team needed Knudson—he was their number one starter—and he didn't want to miss the chance of a lifetime. So he rushed back into action, only to discover that the illness had left him too weak to pitch at anything approaching a big-league level. After a couple of weeks, the team conducted muscle tests and discovered that "I was just ridiculously weak. My left (non-pitching) arm was 100 times stronger than my right arm. I had no resistance power in any of the muscles in my right shoulder."

He was put on the disabled list and never had consistent success in the majors again. In 1992, he signed with San Diego, but spent a long, lonely season in Las Vegas and never made the big-league club. He became a free agent at the end of the 1992 season and went after the Rockies.

The timing of his retirement couldn't have been better as far as his wife Allison was concerned. On May 24, six days after Knudson left the Rockies, she gave birth to triplets—one boy and two girls. They were two months premature, but all three were healthy. "With the triplets, it's great having him around all the time," Allison said, sliding her husband of 3½ years a sly, sweet smile. "Under any other circumstances, I don't know how I'd feel about it. I was pretty used to him being away all the time." Three weeks into retirement, Knudson was frantically busy, shuttling back and forth to the hospital in Denver to see the triplets, who were kept in the nursery for five weeks. All the activity provided a welcome distraction. "If it had to happen, the timing was pretty good," Knudson said. "It's not like I had time to come home, sit around and mope about it. I had some major things happening in my life that helped take up the slack."

Still, he'd found the time to contemplate a future beyond baseball. He had a journalism degree from Colorado State University and hoped to put his education to use as a sports columnist or radio broadcaster. Carl Scheer, a former basketball executive who now acted as a sports agent, was working with Knudson. And Knudson didn't feel like he could afford to loll around enjoying his leisure. Despite a couple of years earning well into six figures with the Brewers, he was feeling some financial pressure to get to work soon. The bright, spacious home he bought in 1992 absorbed a lot of the family savings, and the prospect of raising triplets would be enough to make anyone's wallet bleed.

"Certainly I don't have the luxury of sitting around for a few months. I've got to get to work as soon as I can. I know most of the media outlets, until you reach the pinnacle, don't pay that well, so we're going to have to tighten our belts a little. But our expenses will be a lot less now that we'll be traveling around less."

I checked in with Knudson again in late September. I'd seen him once during the summer, wearing a crew-neck Rockies sweater and shaking hands in the clubhouse, showing off photos of the triplets, who were growing like weeds. He'd been hired part time by the Rockies Youth Foundation. "I'm doing a lot of clinics at elementary schools, coaching high schools and stuff. Promoting the team, talking to the kids, and teaching. It's a good way for me to stay in touch with the community, and that's something that always has been really important to me. I'm working for them maybe three days a week. It's not taking up a whole bunch of time, but it's fun to get out and see kids and try to promote baseball."

Knudson also was hard at work trying to break into broadcasting. He was doing a weekly, hour-long call-in baseball talk show on a UHF-TV station, and casting about for other opportunities.

"Certainly it's a little frustrating because I need to get back to work. But at the same time I have to be a little patient," he said.

Now that he'd been out of baseball a few months, did he find himself missing it, or regretting his decision to retire? "You know, sometimes I do feel pangs, but when I'm able to sit back and look at the overall picture I really don't regret it, because certainly I don't miss the minor leagues, not even a little bit. I know I could still be playing if I wanted to bounce around in the minor leagues and get my shots here and there at the big leagues. But I didn't want to do that, and I have absolutely no regrets about the decision. It was the right decision."

I asked him if he felt a new sense of distance when he visited the clubhouse he'd once been a part of, if only briefly. "No, not with the players. Everyone has been great to me. They want to see pictures of the triplets, we talk, go out and play golf and stuff. The guys have been great, just like I never left. And I really appreciate that. They've helped me out in a couple of situations. I have a charity that I'm very deeply involved with—Children's Outreach Project for handicapped preschool children. I'm on the board of directors and in a constant fundraising situation. So I make use of my connections anytime I can. Like this weekend, I'm borrowing Darren Holmes and Chris Jones for a couple of hours to sign autographs to raise money for the school. The guys are great to me."

Knudson hadn't gone to a Rockies game since his retirement. But in late September, he ventured out to a game against the Dodgers. "Allison and I went, and watched some of the game. And there were moments . . . moments where I missed it. But also I was able to look at it from an analytical standpoint. Since I hope to get into broadcasting, I tried to look at it in what was for me a new way. I was not critiquing the pitchers from a competitive standpoint, but I was watching and thinking about what I would say in a broadcast. It was a new and different way to watch a baseball game, but I kind of liked it."

When the Rockies signed slugging outfielder Dale Murphy as a free agent two days before the team's opening game in New York, the move was hailed in sports pages as a gamble with very little risk involved. True, Murphy was clearly over the hill, his 15 all-star years with the Atlanta Braves but a distant memory. He'd played with the Philadelphia Phillies for the past three seasons, and his productivity had dwindled each year. But he looked like a perfect fit for an expansion team that needed some veteran leadership and the power his right-handed bat could provide. After all, Murphy had 398 career home runs. Wouldn't it be something if he hit number 400 in Mile High Stadium? And of course, it couldn't hurt to have a legend on the team, a sure-fire hall-of-famer who was a world-class nice guy to boot.

In all his years of stardom, Murphy had never let success go to his head. Everyone who knew him said he'd remained the same easy-going, accommodating, aw-shucks-modest kind of guy throughout his career. Unfortunately, his playing days didn't have a storybook ending. Anyone who watched him play in a Rockies uniform could see he had nothing left. Not only did he fail to hit a home run—ending his career just two short of that magical 400—he failed to do much of anything before the team forced him to retire in Houston on May 27. He batted 42 times, hitting just .143, with 15 strikeouts, five double plays and just one extra-base hit, a double.

But Murphy went out with class, as with everything he did. The team held a retirement ceremony for him on May 31, which felt a little forced since he had no career to speak of in Denver. But when I saw Murphy in the Rockies clubhouse in Atlanta during the final weekend of the season, he couldn't stop talking about the send-off the team had given him.

"I just can't say enough about the way I was treated in Denver," said Murphy, his arms veined and sculpted with lean muscle even after four months of enforced idleness. "That retirement ceremony, it . . ." Not the world's most articulate guy, Murphy had to struggle for words to describe it. "It was just such a nice thing for me and Nancy, just a highlight of my career. We couldn't get over how nice that was."

But the end had been bittersweet, he admitted. "Yeah, I never thought it would end that way, but hey, that's how it goes. Things didn't work out in Denver and I was kinda depressed about it for awhile. You know, getting 400 home runs was on my mind so much, it might have . . . but hey, it didn't work out. I had my chances to hit them. Seemed like every day while I was playing this year I was asked about 400 home runs. All I can say is I played enough years to get two more home runs somewhere along the way. Oh well."

Like Knudson, Murphy went home to a house full of children and had plenty to keep him busy. He lived on a farm 45 miles south of Atlanta, and loved working outside and playing with his seven boys, who ranged in age from 13 to 2. An eighth child, a girl, was due in the late fall of 1993.

"It's been fun being home for the summer. I spent what seemed like the whole summer at little league games. It was great getting to see the boys play. Now it's fall, so I'm spending a lot of time at soccer games."

But Murphy felt as though there was a hole in his life. He heaved a sigh, then grinned. "I'll always miss the game, especially when I come down here and see the guys. But there's a lot of things I don't miss, to be honest. Being away from home, traveling all the time. I was ready to come home. What's surprised me though is how much I've missed baseball. I probably miss it a little more than I thought I would. But I promise you one thing: I'm not going to make any comebacks."

CHAPTER ELEVEN

HAPPY ENDINGS

The attendance numbers just kept piling up for the Rockies at a pace that defied explanation. By the end of the season, the team's owners could only shake their heads, laugh and count their money. Four million, four-hundred eighty-three thousand, three-hundred fifty. Rockies media relations director, Mike Swanson, had a lot of fun with that number—the Rockies' inaugural season home paid attendance—on the day of the team's last home game. The Rockies had already shattered every imaginable major-league attendance record over the course of the season. Reporters had grown numb to the new records that kept falling, so Swanson tried to come up with unique ways of putting the Rockies' phenomenal drawing power into perspective.

"Attention, media," Swanson said over the press box public address system during that final home game September 26. "Today's attendance: 70,069, for a season total of 4,483,350, establishing a new major-league record. Today marks the tenth sellout of the year and the ninth time the crowd has exceeded 70,000. The paid attendance has gone over 60,000 27 times, and exceeded 50,000 63 times. The

Rockies' attendance (as of) today surpassed the population of our 31st state, Minnesota, which comes in at 4.48 million. On the year, the Rockies attendance also went over the population of 24 countries."

It didn't seem to matter how well or badly the Rockies played, people just kept coming to Mile High Stadium. It was a party, a happening, a love-in, a chance to hang out with friends and wear purple clothes. Everyone who came to the park, it seemed, was wearing a Rockies cap, or T-shirt, or jacket. The games were of secondary importance. Bernie Mullin had guessed right way back in March: Mile High Stadium was the place to be in Denver during the summer of 1993.

Baseball has always been a statistics-mad game, and some of the more arcane numbers are an exercise in absurdity. How many times during a post-season telecast does some announcer exclaim something like this: "Well, Al, that establishes a new World Series record for most batters hit by a pitch in the fourth inning by a left-handed long reliever!" But some of the statistics and numbers have real meaning. Consider the records the Rockies shattered in 1993:

All-time major league single-season attendance. Had it not been for two rain-outs, the Rockies would easily have surpassed 4.5 million. It's a record that may never fall. No team had ever hit 4 million before 1991. That year, the Toronto Blue Jays, playing in the spanking-new Skydome, a tourist attraction in and of itself, came in just over 4 million, a feat the Jays repeated in their world championship years of 1992 and 1993. The Rockies' attendance also obliterated the National League record of 3,608,881, set by the Los Angeles Dodgers in 1982.

Fastest to 4 million. It took the Rockies 71 home dates to reach the magic number. The Blue Jays didn't crack 4 million until the final home game in both 1991 and 1992. They did it in the second-to-last game of 1993.

Fastest to 3 million. 53 dates. The previous record was held by the Blue Jays, who took 61 dates in 1992.

Fastest to 2 million. 36 dates. The Blue Jays did it in 41 dates in 1992.

Fastest to 1 million. 17 dates. The Blue Jays hit a million in 21 dates in 1992.

Largest opening day crowd. The 80,227 who overflowed Mile High Stadium April 9 (with the help of temporary bleachers erected for just that purpose), eclipsed the Dodgers record set April 18, 1958, the first big-league game played in Los Angeles.

Largest 4-game series crowd. A late July series against the St. Louis Cardinals drew 251,521, barely beating the Rockies own 251,486 set in a series against Atlanta in May. Before 1993, the biggest-ever 4-game series drew 218,948 for a Dodgers-Giants set in L.A. The Rockies held the 3-game series record as well, until the last day of the 1993 season, when the Cleveland Indians topped it. The Indians drew over 70,000 per game over a three-game weekend for the last-ever games at the enormous old Municipal Stadium, affectionately known as "The Mistake by the Lake."

National League night game. The Rockies vs. Giants game July 31 drew 72,208. The crowd got to see the Giants edge the Rockies 4-3.

But who were these people? The Denver metro-area's population didn't top two million, according to demographers' estimates, until the first week of October 1993. Are we to believe that every man, woman and child in the area attended two games in 1993? Or did the Rockies draw from a far broader area?

Thanks to those lap-top computer studies Bernie Mullin commissioned back in the spring, the Rockies had some answers by October. They knew, for example, that for any given game, 27 percent of the people in Mile High Stadium had driven over 50 miles each way to attend the game. They came from places like Colorado Springs, Grand Junction, Pueblo, Canon City, Cheyenne, and Casper; and from more distant venues including Grand Island and North Platte, Nebraska, Goodland, Kansas, Salt Lake City, Albuquerque, and Santa Fe. The Rockies could legitimately lay claim to being a regional franchise. More than anyone expected, the vast western open spaces and the western mindset—"Aw, heck, it's only 200 miles; let's just get in the car and go"—worked to the Rockies' benefit.

That 27 percent didn't even include the out-of-state tourists who had flown in for a Colorado vacation and decided to take in a Rockies game or two. John McHale, who became the keeper of the demographics after Mullin's departure, also said that 25 percent of people on weekends and 20 percent on weekdays came to Rockies games from out of state. The crowds were young—over half were under 44 years old—and many attended more than three but fewer than 10 games.

In the end, it was almost frightening how well things turned out for the Colorado Rockies. Although they lost their last three games of the season to the Braves in Atlanta, the Rockies won 10 of 13 games during their final homestand, leaving Denver fans with some sweet autumn memories. By losing "only" 95 games, the Rockies achieved Bob Gebhard's pre-season goal of losing fewer than 100.

But while the successes on the field were modest, the Rockies were a smash hit financially. In late October, team officials told the city council they had generated $43.3 million in revenues in 1993. Before the season began, the Rockies had estimated they'd rake in $17.1 million. In May, with attendance figures soaring, the team revised its estimate upward, but only to $37 million. The $43.3 million came from ticket sales and the team's share of concession money. That was enough money to go out and buy some first-rate free agents, if the Rockies chose to go in that direction. The city government benefitted as well, reaping $5.4 million through a baseball seat tax and parking revenues at Mile High Stadium.

Having the Rockies in town was an economic boon for Denver as well, though no one had any precise estimates as to how much money the team generated for bars, restaurants and hotels, or how much sales-tax revenues the team brought in.

"What John McHale has been saying, and I don't disagree, is that when we estimated 2 million fans, we were looking at something on the order of $100 million in economic impact," said Ford Frick, a consultant who did some work for the Rockies throughout the season. "If that was accurate, then at 4.5 million, they probably had an impact of closer to $250 million."

But, Frick cautioned, these types of numbers are "squirrely"—unreliable and easily manipulated. "It's kind of a useless number, really. Most of that $250 million would have been here anyway, in one form or another. We estimated that 40 percent or more of it was entertainment money; a choice between going to movies or bowling or to the Rockies.

"There are a number of issues as to what constitutes an impact. What we really don't know is, how many people came from out of town and spent the night away from home in association with the Rockies? The Rockies blew it. They did these surveys of their fans and they never asked that question. So we don't know whether the 27 percent of fans who drove more than 50 miles each way to see the game then drove home again that night, or whether they got a hotel room and stayed in Denver. That would make a big difference. Based on their license-plate surveys, I'd estimate that 15 percent of the tickets were sold to people who came from far enough that somehow they must have stayed the night. Of course, we don't know whether they were here already, or if they were, did they stay longer to catch a Rockies game?"

In any event, Frick said, the Rockies proved to be a powerful economic generator, belying one of his favorite truisms about the sport. "Baseball, I have always argued, is not a great economic generator. It is largely local entertainment. The Rockies made me say that in softer tones. I think they were quite an economic generator, and I think there is a lot of anecdotal evidence that they retained people in this area, that tourists passing through spent a night so they could go to a game. I think they really had an impact. Unfortunately, I don't know any way, given the questions they didn't ask, to quantify that."

The Rockies were also a big hit on the baseball merchandising front, another sports-related industry that had taken off in recent years. In July of 1993, the Rockies passed the White Sox and became the most popular team in the nation among fans purchasing caps, shirts, and an ever-expanding variety of team-related novelties.

Back when I was growing up, displaying team loyalty was simple and cheap. You could go to a sporting goods store or a ballpark and for a few bucks buy a cap or T-shirt bearing the logo of your favorite team. The caps had elastic backs that stretched to accommodate all sizes, and were made of felt and cardboard. The T-shirts were basic and inexpensive. But an outfit known as Major League Baseball Properties (MLBP) has made sure that those days are long gone. In a world of commerce where everything seems to be based on snob appeal, even baseball novelties have become expensive, high-end products.

For a quick lesson in the mega-business of baseball merchandising, I hooked up with Mark Ehrhart, the Rockies director of merchandising, and took a stroll through the Rockies Dugout store in downtown Denver. The selection of Rockies caps alone boggled my mind. The stuff for sale was undoubtedly of high quality, but the prices were outrageous. There was, for example, a fitted pro-model, 100-percent wool cap, with the purple and silver interlocking "CR" logo. It sold for $22, and was just one of approximately 25 styles of Rockies caps available in the store.

If caps didn't interest you, then there were 20 different T-shirt designs to browse through, and an equal number of golf/polo shirts, a dozen or more sweaters, shorts, jackets, sweat shirts and sweat pants.

Shoppers who were feeling flush could treat themselves to the most expensive item in the store—a $1,250 Jeff Hamilton jacket with all the Rockies colors and the team logo tooled in leather as soft as butter.

That was just the clothing. Shoppers could also procure Rockies bubble gum, hot mitts, dish towels, aprons, pens, pencils, paperweights, cameras, troll dolls, glassware, ceramics, lapel and hat pins, golf bags ($199 a pop), key chains, earrings and notepads. And that list barely scratches the surface.

"At any given time, we have between 550 and 600 different items for sale in here bearing the Rockies logo," Ehrhart said. That sounded excessive, but it only represented about 20 percent of what was produced by licensees. Different, lower-quality Rockies merchandise was sold at convenience stores, supermarkets, department stores, sporting goods stores and just about every mom and pop store west of the Mississippi.

This abundance of Rockies merchandise was produced by more than 350 licensees of Major League Baseball Properties, the merchandising arm of the big leagues that was formed in 1987. Before that, teams marketed and licensed their own merchandise. Some were better at it than others.

By 1993, every team, from the lowly Cleveland Indians to the lofty Atlanta Braves, sold a dazzling array of merchandise. According to Tom Miller, national accounts supervisor for MLBP, retail sales of licensed baseball products topped $2.4 billion in 1992, compared to $1 billion in 1989. Neither Miller nor Ehrhart would reveal how much the Rockies and Major League Baseball made on sales of Rockies paraphernalia. Just because the Rockies sold more novelties than any other team didn't mean they earned more money off their goods than the others. In the world of baseball merchandising, a rising tide lifted all ships. Licensees paid a royalty to MLBP based on their wholesale prices. Royalty money was pooled and divided evenly among the 28 big-league teams.

Why did Rockies stuff sell so well? "The Rockies combine a couple of things that are important not only with the licensing community but also the fashion industry," said Miller of MLBP. "The metallic silver (is) a great fashion color, as is purple with the accents of black. When licensees have the opportunity to use those three colors on a product, the results are rather striking."

As the final homestand wound down, the Rockies basked in their successes and looked toward the future with both optimism and apprehension. How could they top 1993? Everyone agreed that would be a tall order. The team brass was estimating privately that the Rockies would draw an attendance of between 3.5 and 3.75 million in 1994, a come-down from the inaugural season, but still more than respectable, and highly profitable. They figured to jump right back to 4 million in 1995, when the 50,000-capacity Coors Field opened. As Bob Howsam discovered way back in 1948 with Bears Stadium, a new ballpark draws fans. With 50,000 seats, Coors Field figured to be a sell-out most nights in 1995. Beyond that, as John McHale was fond of saying, "we've got to get better."

The weather prognosticators warned of slashing winds, low scuttering clouds and rain or snow for the afternoon of September 26, 1993, the day of the last Colorado Rockies home game of the year. In all likelihood, the weather wasn't going to matter much in terms of attendance. Through this season of 4,483,350 fans, people had displayed a willingness, an eagerness even, to attend games in all types of weather. But certainly it didn't hurt any when the day dawned gloriously clear, one of those crisp, sun-kissed early autumn Colorado days.

The Rockies' suddenly robust on-field performance didn't hurt any either. Following a dismal spell, ending August 6, in which they lost 13 straight games, the Rockies turned on the afterburners and finished the season as the best expansion team in National League history.

So players were extra loose and jovial on the 26th as they prepared to play one last game in front of 70,069 screaming fans. They had nothing to lose—they already knew they weren't going to lose 100 games. But they were bound and determined to have some fun in front of the home crowd this last day. Something about their attitude infected the crowd, and the day took on a giddy, carnival atmosphere. September 26 felt uncannily like April 9.

Outfielder Daryl Boston strode toward the batting cage 90 minutes before game time and glanced up at the rapidly filling stands. "Damn," Boston said, a smile cracking his stern countenance. "Opening day all over again." He proceeded to step into the batting cage, and in a booming voice, shout, "Time to take it DOWNTOWN!" He swung mightily at every pitch, moaning "OOOOHHHHHHH!" at top volume as he followed through.

Fans leaning over the dugout begging for autographs heard Boston's comedy act and laughed. His teammates were doubled over.

Others decided to get into the act as well. "Hey, A.O.!" outfielder Eric Young shouted to hitting coach Amos Otis as he stepped into the batting cage for his practice hacks. "Looks like 80,000! That means I'm going deep (hitting a home run)!" Young, a slight, speedy singles hitter, had electrified Colorado by hitting that improbable home run as the first-ever Rockies batter at Mile High on opening day, with over 80,000 frenzied fans on hand. It was the only home run he had hit all year. But now, he was telling everyone he saw, "I'm going deep today, just wait and see. I feel pretty good, pretty good."

Sure enough, at 2:41 p.m., in the fourth inning, Young fulfilled his own prophecy by lofting one over the left-field wall. The crowd went berserk. As if that weren't dramatic enough, and to put a finishing touch on his Mile High season, Young blasted another home run to deep left-center field 44 minutes later. The crowd shook the stadium, especially when Young emerged from the dugout, arms aloft, to take his second bow of the day.

"That first one, man, I was sure it was foul," Young said after the game, a 12-7 Rockies' win over the Cincinnati Reds. He was sitting in his underwear in the clubhouse, surrounded by dozens of reporters. "But that second one, as soon as I hit it, I knew it was gone."

As a town with more than its share of baseball neophytes, Denver may not have appreciated the uniqueness of the bond that had developed between Rockies players and their fans. In other cities, there were always crowd favorites, and there were good guys who went out of their way to sign autographs and acknowledge the fans. But in Denver, the affection without question ran both ways. I never heard a player complain about the crowd, other than to wonder why the fans weren't more critical when the team was playing so poorly in late April and through May.

What better place to gauge fan sentiment during this final home game than out among my old friends in the Rockpile? I headed out there in the second inning, after noticing from clear across the stadium that the fans in the $1 seats were making far more noise than anyone else. Number-one-fan, Ruben "Chip" Valdez, in fact, should be credited with inventing the trademark cheer that reverberated through the stadium all season. Valdez, whose manic energy never diminished, would stand up, gesticulate wildly, then shout, "One, two, three!!" And hundreds of Rockpile denizens would shout "GO!" in unison. Seconds later, the rejoinder "ROCKIES!" would echo back from across the stadium. Valdez would get his chant going again, and the west stands would answer. Pretty soon, 70,000 people would be chanting "GO!" "ROCKIES!" The effect was dramatic. People out walking two miles away could hear the cheer if the wind was calm.

Indeed, the team's hardest-core fans were in fine fettle this final day, cheering their heroes and receiving waves and bows in return. All of the regulars were there, including Joe Dempsey (71 games), Valdez (74 games), and Wayne and George Irish, who had no idea of how many games they'd seen.

"I hated to miss the games I missed," Dempsey said. "Next year? Maybe this many again, But I hope I'll see more." Dempsey proudly had his son Stephen, 13, show me a brand-new bat Eric Young had given him before the game. "E.Y.'s great, but so are a lot of these guys. Stephen's got some of E.Y.'s batting gloves, a wristband from Mariano Duncan (of the Philadelphia Phillies,) Curtis Leskanic's gloves, and over 50 balls guys have tossed him. This has been really great for Stephen. He has attention deficit disorder, and this has given him something to focus in on. He is so into baseball now. I tried to bring him to all the games with me. I think he made it to all but two."

I asked Dempsey what the highlight of the year had been in the Rockpile. "Oh, man that's hard to say," he said. "I guess maybe Alex Cole recording that announcement (on the scoreboard) thanking the Rockpile for our support. Or maybe the way he ran out to center field in the first inning today and pointed to us right here in the front row."

As if on cue, Andres Galarraga punctuated Dempsey's musings with a two-run home run deep into the south stands. The cheers were deafening. And when he emerged from the dugout for a well-earned curtain call, the Rockpile all but lifted into orbit.

I'd heard from fans all season about their devotion to the players, but I decided to spend some time in those final days asking the players what they had to say to the fans. I asked them to address my tape recorder as if they were talking directly to the fans. All the players I approached were eager to say something. They hadn't the time nor the inclination to reach out to all their fans in person, but they wanted people to know they had been noticed and appreciated. I could only imagine the kinds of answers a similar exercise would have yielded in New York, or even Miami.

Andres Galarraga: "Thank you for all the support you have given to me to push me to do better and better, every day."

Dante Bichette: "Thank you for a dream come true and probably the most memorable year of my career."

Eric Young: "Throughout my career as an athlete and playing in front of crowds, I've never experienced excitement and enthusiasm like what we've gotten all year from the fans here in Denver. I don't think anyone could ever top that in my mind. I just hope the enthusiasm continues every year, for the team and for me individually, if I'm here. If I'm not here, I will always look forward to coming to Denver to play. I think I love the city so much that I'm going to stay here, and that's because of the fans."

Freddie Benavides: "You're the greatest fans in all of baseball. Period. Early in the year it was like, 'whoa, that's a lot of people out there.' But now we look up in the stands, see 40-50,000 people, it's like, 'where is everybody?' We got spoiled with it. It kept us going, knowing you were behind us."

Darren Holmes: "You're awesome fans. I appreciate your hanging in there with me and not giving up on me."

Jerald Clark: "Thanks, you've been tremendous. You have been the only steady thing all year. We've been up and down, but you've been the most consistent part of this game here. Believe me, coming from San Diego, when you play in a stadium where there are fans and you play in a stadium without fans, there is a difference. A big difference."

Joe Girardi: "If only we could get all you people on the road with us . . . I think we could win the World Series next year."

When that final game ended with a 12-7 Rockies' win, the fans didn't want to go home. They stood and cheered at the top of their lungs for what seemed like an hour. Following the game, the team gave away five new cars to randomly selected fans, in a schmaltzy but somehow moving ceremony. Five fans had been selected at each of the 12 final home dates to participate in the car giveaway lottery. As soon as the whipped Reds had left the diamond, the 60 contestants were brought onto the field and lined up along the two baselines. An usher walked over to home plate with 60 slips of paper in a box. First, Bob Gebhard fished out a name and gave away a car, then Joe Girardi, followed by Andres Galarraga, whose thick Spanish accent rendered the winner's name unintelligible, and finally Jerry McMorris. Players stood in clusters near the dugout, laughing and applauding as the stunned winners were led to their new Chryslers and Plymouths.

As the winners motored off the field and the 55 less-fortunate souls headed back into the stands, Baylor said a final goodbye, standing at a microphone in front of home plate. "The Rocky Mountain region is the envy of major league baseball," he said to a huge roar. From a distance, his eyes looked teary. Later, he elaborated on his thoughts. "It was truly amazing to be involved in something that probably will never happen again in major league baseball. I don't even know how to say it, really. All year, the fans were unbelievable. Just unbelievable." He looked emotionally spent.

Finally, as a final gesture to the fans, the team took a victory lap around the warning track from first base out to right field, and then around to left. The cheers for Dante Bichette from the south stands behind right field, where he had played all year, were deafening. He lagged behind the rest of the team, absorbing the adulation, a dopey grin on his face. Fans leaned over the railing high above him and flailed their arms, unable to reach Bichette but trying nonetheless to touch him.

The roar increased as the players passed the rowdy Rockpile.

From the field, I could see my buddies right up front. Joe Dempsey was hollering and jumping up and down. Ruben Valdez was leading cheers. Wayne Irish, in a clown outfit and green wig, looked disturbingly like a young John Wayne Gacy as he screamed himself hoarse yet again. The biggest Rockpile ovations were reserved for outfielders Boston, Cole, and especially Young.

Finally, Young, the hero of the day, could contain himself no longer. He sprinted over to the left field wall and reached through the wire mesh fence to shake hands with a fan he recognized. People were screaming louder now, and thrusting their hands through the fence. Young trotted along, slapping high fives with everyone. His grin was huge and his eyes were glimmering with tears. He gave high fives all the way along the left field track and then down the left field foul line to the clubhouse entrance half-way back to third base. Then he gave a final, exaggerated wave to the entire stadium, and the crowd roared at him. He walked toward the clubhouse, spikes clattering on the cement floor of the entry-way, his grin undiminished. You could just tell Young was still going to be grinning hours, maybe even days later. After all, he had a lot of memories of 1993 to savor.

It had been quite a day, and quite a season.

AFTERWORD

SHIFTING ALLEGIANCES

Watching Eric Young walk off the field with tears in his eyes put a lump in my throat, I must confess. The final sentence in the final chapter of Denver's first big-league season was almost too perfect. It had been hard, as I walked around the warning track behind the players, not to cheer them—and their fans—myself.

Sometimes, being a journalist can be almost dehumanizing. We wade into the joys and sorrows of everyday life, chronicle people's reactions to overwhelming events, and force ourselves to remain detached. After a while, it becomes second nature.

There were other times in 1993 when I wanted to cheer for the Rockies. This happened with greater frequency late in the season, when that rag-tag assembly of cast-offs suddenly jelled into a real team and started winning with some consistency. But I clamped the lid on my feelings and sat there in the press box, making snide and cynical comments along with the best of them.

By October, though, after seven months spent covering the Rockies for *The Denver Post,* I felt the need, as a lifelong baseball fan, to visit Chicago, my native city, and do some real, heartfelt cheering.

I'd been a fan of the Chicago White Sox for 37 years, so I figured the gods of journalism would forgive me if I used media credentials to get into Comiskey Park and scream my lungs out for my boyhood heroes who, for the second time in my sentient life, had made it into the playoffs. Little did I suspect that I'd leave Chicago for Denver two days later feeling like Benedict Arnold.

I'd been writing a series of articles entitled "Behind The Seams" all season for the *Post,* and this, I thought, would be a natural way to conclude it. I could describe for Denver fans, who no doubt would have to wait many years for a winner to occupy Coors Field, what it felt like to root for your home team in a championship series after years of dashed hopes and futile longing.

But, sad to say, I found my self-assigned task impossible to perform.

I arrived at the hulking, three-year-old Comiskey Park on Tuesday, October 5, three hours before the start of the first American League playoff game between the Sox and the Toronto Blue Jays. Walking up to the press gate, I was so excited I was almost hyperventilating. Finally, I'd get to see the red, white, and blue bunting that always festoons stadiums come playoff time, hanging from the railings of Comiskey Park. There would be my team, lining up along the first base line during pre-game introductions. And here I was, witnessing it.

But then I walked into that soulless stadium, and my heart fell into my shoes. From that first moment, it was impossible to muster the enthusiasm and sense of anticipation I had expected.

The reason was clear. I hated the new Comiskey Park; hated it so much I found myself grinding my teeth. As I entered the press gate, I cast a longing glance across 35th Street to where the venerable old park stood until the greed of Sox-owners Jerry Reinsdorf and Eddie Einhorn reduced it to rubble in 1991. I'd spent hundreds of enjoyable hours bathed in my father's cigar smoke watching ball games in the creaky old park. I'd drunk some of my first beers there, thanks to vendors who, back in the early 1970s, didn't bother to ask for identification from their customers. Nothing could ever replace that encrusted old shrine in my heart.

What sits there now is a parking lot and a series of pedestrian ramps leading into the sterile concourses of the new Comiskey. As soon as you enter the new stadium (how dare they call it a park?), your senses are bombarded by a blizzard of brightly-lit advertisements for Winston cigarettes, Union 76 petroleum products, Coca-Cola and countless others.

Music at ear-splitting volume is pumped endlessly over massive speakers into the stadium. Before the game, the music is a free-form selection of contemporary tunes, liberally sprinkled with full-volume commercials. Once the game starts, the music accompanies a stream of video presentations on what must be the biggest screen in any big-league ballpark, save the mega-mall Skydome in Toronto.

The videos that week invariably highlighted the glorious triumphs of the 1993 White Sox. This is all well and good, until you consider the context. While all those home runs and strikeouts and diving catches from months gone by were being flashed on the big board, the Blue Jays were beating the tar out of the White Sox down there on the field.

My father, at 75 a veteran of seven decades of White Sox baseball, had a succinct reaction to the multi-media onslaught as we sat in the right field stands in a stiff breeze and balmy temperatures on the afternoon of Wednesday, October 6. "This," he said, "is really obnoxious."

Equally obnoxious is the blatantly class-conscious design of the stadium. Messrs. Reinsdorf and Einhorn, eager above all to please their well-heeled customers, built an enormous, two-tiered system of skyboxes. This forced the upper deck into the stratosphere. If you can afford a skybox, Comiskey probably is a great place to watch a game. If not, you have to tolerate a distant view of the field and all that deafening noise. It's all enough to make a socialist out of Rush Limbaugh.

The noise and videos seemed to numb the fans, who sat in a stupor, making very little noise and watching the flashy scoreboard instead of the game. True, the White Sox played miserably and lost both games I attended, but that had little to do with my bitterness.

How could I root for a team that played in such an awful environment? Why should I subject my senses to such abuse? The whole experience was enough to shake my sense of allegiance to the White Sox. I felt disloyal to my hometown, to my family, even, but I couldn't help myself. My Comiskey Park experience left me emotionally flat after all those months of objectivity, and seeking my identity as a fan.

Everything snapped into focus in November. The Rockies made a concerted bid to sign Ellis Burks, a talented, 29-year-old outfielder who had played the 1993 season with the White Sox. He had been a major contributor to the team's division-winning success. The White Sox wanted him back, but the Rockies offered Burks, who has a chronically bad back, a longer contract and more money. So he chose the Rockies, and financial security, over a chance to go to the World Series sooner.

My sister Martha, a die-hard White Sox fan who lives in Chicago, was despondent at the loss of Burks, as was my brother David, a recent transplant to Denver. I expected to find myself commiserating with them. Much to my surprise, though, when I first saw the *Denver Post* headline, "Burks Chooses Rockies," I had to stifle the urge to gloat.

No doubt about it, something happened to me over the course of the 1993 season. Gradually, insidiously, my reflexive allegiance to the team of my youth shifted to a new team; a team that plays in the shadow of the Rockies, in the city I now call home.

INDEX

INDEX